*Fenians and
Anglo-American Relations
during Reconstruction*

Fenians and Anglo-American Relations during Reconstruction

By BRIAN JENKINS

Cornell University Press

ITHACA AND LONDON

Standard Book Number 8014-0500-9

Library of Congress Catalog Card Number 79-81595

PRINTED IN THE UNITED STATES OF AMERICA
BY KINGSPORT PRESS, INC.

For my parents, my sister,
my sons, and Sian

Acknowledgments

I wish to express my gratitude to Professor Maldwyn Allen Jones of the University of Manchester, not only for suggesting this topic, but also for his subsequent advice. For their uniform kindness and assistance I thank the staffs of all the libraries I visited and particularly Miss Catharine Hayes, Associate Head of the Department of Special Collections at the University of Rochester Library. To Father William MacVean of Emmanuel College, Saskatoon, who read and criticized the manuscript, I cannot do justice in a brief acknowledgment. Indeed, in some measure, this book is a MacVean project, for his wife, Margaret, typed much of the final draft, discreetly corrected errors of punctuation, and is compiling the index. Of course, I would be remiss if I failed to thank my wife, Sian. She possesses every virtue for which the wives of scholars have been memorialized, and participated in both the research and the writing of this book. Thus, like all who have helped me, she should receive credit for whatever merit it has but is not responsible for its deficiencies. I wish to thank the Earl of Clarendon for permission to quote from the Clarendon deposit at the Bodleian Library and the National Library of Ireland for permission to quote from the Larcom Papers. Quotations from the Adams Papers are from the microfilm edition, by permission of the Massachusetts Historical Society. Finally, I wish to acknowledge permission from the Manuscript Division of The New York Public Library (Astor, Lenox and Tilden Foundations), the University of Rochester Library, the Library of Congress, and the British Museum to use manuscripts in their possession.

BRIAN JENKINS

University of Saskatchewan, Saskatoon
January 1969

Contents

*Fenians and
Anglo-American Relations
during Reconstruction*

1

Introduction: The Cause and the Contestants

To describe the modern history of Ireland as unhappy might justifiably be considered another example of English understatement. For when Henry VIII, anxious to prove to the Irish that among other things the Bishop of Rome was not their monarch, summoned a parliament to meet in Dublin in June, 1541, to confirm his new title of "King of this land of Ireland as united, annexed, and knit for ever to the Imperial crown of the realm of England," he played his role in a tragedy which saw successive generations of that island's inhabitants doomed to a life of misery. Misery was the inevitable result of the efforts of Henry and his royal successors—and of Parliament when it acquired direct powers of government—to assert their authority over a people equally determined to reject that authority and to maintain a separate national identity.

Failing to advance his imperial ambition through a policy of conciliation, Henry resorted to military repression, but this proved at best a palliative. The army could maintain order but only in those areas where it was garrisoned, and England did not possess the military strength to garrison the entire island. Yet as soon as troops were withdrawn, disaffection quickly revived. It was apparent that a more permanent instrument of control was needed, and one that suggested itself was the settlement of loyal Englishmen in Ireland. Between 1565 and 1575 a group of private promoters, in whom hopes of profit and reasons of state were fused in that peculiarly Elizabethan manner, undertook the first systematic experiments in the planting of Englishmen overseas. Although these early ventures failed, they were not without significance. They were important, as A. L. Rowse has said, "not only in what they foreshadowed for Ireland—the substitution of English society for Celtic in that island—but, what is vastly more important for the world, in pointing the way to the English colonization of America." [1] Led by Humphrey Gilbert and his half-brother Walter Raleigh, the same group of West Country men who attempted to promote the settlement of Ireland was impelled by the same motives of profit and national interest to cross the Atlantic.

Almost from their inception, then, the problems of the Anglo-Irish relationship embraced America. Initially, Ireland provided the English with a pre-American experience in the techniques and hazards of overseas settlement. Certainly Gilbert's "experience in Ireland broadened his conception of the purposes of colonisation: the transplanting and reproduction of English society in American soil, territorial wealth and power for its promoters." [2] It also conditioned both promoters and settlers for their encounter with the American Indian. The Irish were a savage and barbarous race, little if any better than beasts, or so many Englishmen believed. Their dwellings were "rather swine sties than houses," and "the chiefest cause" of the Irishman's "so beastly manner of life and savage condition" was his custom of "lying and living

[1] *The Expansion of Elizabethan England* (New York, 1955), p. 136.
[2] *Ibid.*, p. 207.

together with his beast in one house, in one room, in one bed."[3] Yet even without this evidence of primitive domesticity the English would have found it difficult to accept as civilized a nation in which murder, rape, robbery, and theft were punished only by fine, not death.[4] Then, when they reached America, the English were confronted by more "savage" natives, whom they were soon disposed to equate with the Irish. At first this association may have prejudiced colonial enterprises in the New World, for the natives of Ireland proved difficult to subdue, but ultimately it merely encouraged the English to adopt a similarly repressive policy with respect to the Indians. Indeed it has been argued that "the doctrine that the only good Indian is a dead Indian first took shape . . . in the doctrine that the only good wild Irishman is a dead wild Irishman."[5]

The experience in Ireland notwithstanding, these early attempts by the English to plant North America failed. This was hardly surprising, for the successful founding of communities three thousand miles from the home country was beyond the means of individual promoters. Gilbert's ambition cost him his life and his half-brother lost much of his wealth; yet even in this moment of defeat another link was forged between America and Ireland. Discouraged by his failures in Virginia, Raleigh turned once again to Ireland and with him he brought the potato, a humble plant but one that played an important part in populating America in the nineteenth century.

Two hundred years after the initial English drive to settle North America, the American and Irish settlements were united in a common cause, a desire for emancipation from

[3] *Ibid.*, p. 105.　　[4] *Ibid.*, p. 109.
[5] Howard Mumford Jones, *O Strange New World* (London, 1965), p. 167.

their political subservience to the British Parliament. Quick to appreciate that the Irish "were strong in favour of the American case," [6] Benjamin Franklin visited the island in 1771, associated with the patriots, and as a result, served as "one channel through which Americans were made aware of Irish constitutional doctrines as well as Irish political sympathies." [7] However, Irish entanglement in the constitutional crisis with the American colonies extended beyond the mutual realization of a common bond of interest and sympathy. For American Whigs the contemporary plight of Ireland was an excellent source of propaganda; it served as a rallying call against the insidious dangers of Imperial legislation. Weighed down by taxation, rack rents, and commercial restrictions, this unhappy land was cited by the more radical colonial agitators as a clear warning of what was to come to America. Having destroyed the vitals of Ireland, the English parasites would transfer to America. "In this way the fear that British America would be turned into another Ireland was employed to strengthen the determination of Americans to resist parliamentary taxation in its very beginning." [8]

As this crisis of the First Empire deteriorated into rebellion, the English began to experience their first serious doubts about the role America would play in their relations with Ireland. For many of them the decision of the Continental Congress to prohibit the transportation of flaxseed to the island raised questions fraught with sinister implications. Was this a deliberate effort to cripple the native linen industry? Did the Americans see in the wake of further economic distress in a country already sorely overburdened with trade

[6] Verner Winslow Crane, *Benjamin Franklin: Englishman and American* (Baltimore, 1936), p. 126.   [7] *Ibid.*, p. 127.

[8] John C. Miller, *Origins of the American Revolution* (Boston, 1943), p. 292.

restrictions the shadows of sedition and rebellion? In short, would the Continental Congress rest until the "Irish had risen up to dethrone the King, kill Lord North and blow up Parliament"? [9] The answer was plain enough, or so it seemed in 1778, when the Irish not only boycotted English goods and undertook armed demonstrations but occasionally practiced what had at times since 1763 been the foremost American colonial sport—tarring and feathering. To sensitive Englishmen the Irish were giving every indication of playing off "the American hand of cards, up from deuces to aces." [10] Beginning in 1778, this sense of alarm brought a measure of economic and commercial relief to Ireland and, with the triumph of the American cause, political concessions in the form of parliamentary independence; but the political and religious base of Grattan's Parliament proved too narrow and the revolutionary examples of the United States and France too attractive for Wolfe Tone and his associates in the Society of United Irishmen. To them insurrection seemed to be the only hope for Ireland, but they were unable to duplicate the American success, and not the least of their difficulties was the proximity of England. The distance separating Dublin from the nearest British port, Holyhead, is fifty-seven miles, but the gulf separating the Americans in 1776 from the full weight of British authority was fifty-seven times greater. The Irish were doomed to struggle for the next century and a half. During this period the United States and its citizens exercised considerable influence. America, both by precept and example, provided inspiration; indeed its own Irish population was a continual source of moral, fiscal, and physical support for revolutionary activities. The natural sympathy most Americans had for those seeking to emulate their achievements, at least in

[9] *Ibid.*, p. 459.
[10] John C. Miller, *Triumph of Freedom* (Boston, 1948), p. 413.

the sense of establishing Republican institutions, when bolstered by the growing political influence of Irish-Americans, foreshadowed diplomatic tension with Britain. The attraction of the United States for Irish political refugees was obvious. Its revolutionary past, the common bond of sympathy and ambition, and its English-speaking civilization made it a natural haven. To the United States, then, several of the luminaries of the Society of United Irishmen fled after the 1798 uprising, and half a century later another unsuccessful rebellion was followed by a similar migration of frustrated revolutionaries. Yet the political impulse to Irish emigration should not be exaggerated, even during the 1790's.[11] The United States was always a place of economic asylum for the depressed and deprived. As early as 1790 the Hibernian Society of Philadelphia for the Relief of Emigrants from Ireland was in operation, and it had merely been an "outgrowth of the Hibernian Club and Friendly Sons of St. Patrick of that city." [12] Important as such assistance was, greater encouragement to Irish immigration came from the reports and letters that flooded back home portraying the United States as a land of social equality and of opportunity for men of experience and ability, and as a nation with a superabundance of food and wealth.[13] In short, it was all that Ireland was not. Nor was this popular impression in any way challenged by the generous gifts of food and clothes that arrived from America during the "Great Starvation." [14] Not surprisingly, therefore, when confronted with the alternatives of famine or flight to a land

[11] Maldwyn Allen Jones, *American Immigration* (Chicago, 1960), p. 74.

[12] Carl Wittke, *The Irish in America* (Baton Rouge, La., 1956), p. 21.

[13] Arnold Schrier, *Ireland and the American Emigration, 1850–1900* (Minneapolis, 1958), p. 148.

[14] Wittke, *Irish in America*, p. 25.

of abundance, those who could raise the passage money chose the latter. "In 1847 emigration to the United States exceeded 105,000 as compared with 44,821 in 1845; and reached nearly 113,000 in 1848."[15] By 1860 there were more than 1,600,000 Irish in the United States, and while nearly two-thirds of these were to be found in New York, Pennsylvania, New Jersey, and the New England States, large numbers were domiciled in practically every city in the country.[16]

The increasingly heavy concentration of Irish in a few states and the larger cities, where they quickly involved themselves in the "machines" of urban democracy, did not escape the attention of nativists. By mid-century they had already ceased to regard as amusing "the current joke concerning the schoolboy who was called upon to parse America. 'America,' he stated, ' 'tis a very common noun, singular number, masculine gender, critical case, and governed by the Irish.' "[17] Against the Irish immigrants, nativists quickly trundled out their all too familiar baggage train. The Irish were unruly, always fighting with one another or, what was even worse, with native Americans. As fashionable as the schoolboy jest was the equally adolescent pun: "While St. Patrick was the name of an order, St. Patrick's day is more associated with the name of disorder since the coming of the Irish."[18] Not only were they condemned for their lawlessness, they were also saddled with the responsibility for the low standards of municipal administration. To their increasing involvement in politics the nativists attributed, in direct ratio, the political corruption of American cities, and to their thirst, the perpetually open doors of city grog shops.[19] Last, but by no means least, the religion of the Irish was another reason for nativist hys-

---

[15] *Ibid.*, p. 7.   [16] M. A. Jones, *American Immigration*, p. 118.
[17] Ray Allen Billington, *The Protestant Crusade, 1800–1860* (Chicago, 1964), pp. 326–327.   [18] *Ibid.*, p. 196.   [19] *Ibid.*, p. 195.

teria. The influx of hordes of Roman Catholics, they charged, jeopardized the very foundations of the Protestant civilization of the United States and was in all probability part of some gigantic Papal conspiracy. The martyr's death of Elijah P. Lovejoy, the abolitionist, has tended to obscure the fact that he was convinced that slavery was yet another aspect of the Catholic policy of subversion.[20]

These fears, which found national political expression in the Know-Nothing movement, may have been irrational reflections of prejudice, but for that reason they were not easily dispelled. Indeed, immigrants did little to deflect the appeal of nativism when they exhibited a willingness, or so it appeared, to place the interests of their countries of origin before those of their country of adoption. As a result, they often threatened to drag the United States into international disputes in which it had no apparent interest, and this seemed particularly true of the Irish-Americans. Their organizations and activities threatened to embroil the United States in diplomatic crises with Great Britain, and the irritation this could engender among American natives was freely expressed by the *New York Tribune* later in the nineteenth century. "The Irish influence in questions of an international character," it observed, "is directly hostile to the United States, and it is one of the most serious dangers against which we have to provide. . . . If Irishmen can establish their independence, all right; let them do it; but they shall not use this Republic as a convenience. . . . The plain truth is that, where the supposed or real interests of Ireland are concerned, a large and noisy faction of the naturalized Irish in the United States are disloyal if not

[20] Louis Filler, *The Crusade against Slavery, 1830–1860* (New York, 1960), p. 76.

treacherous to the adopted country to which they have sworn fidelity." [21]

The dichotomy of Irish-American allegiance, of which natives as well as nativists complained, was evident almost from the day the first Irish immigrants landed in the United States. During the Federalist period the alleged pro-British sympathies of the governing party, and its aristocratic predilections, made it anathema to the new immigrants. Consequently, they gave their domestic political allegiance to the opposing Democratic-Republicans and seized every opportunity to express their contempt for the Federalists, their hatred of the British, and their continuing concern for their native land. In those eastern cities where they already constituted a politically significant minority, the Irish were quickly in the streets once the terms of Jay's Treaty were revealed. They vehemently denounced the settlement with England and ceremonially burned a copy of it outside the residence of the British Minister to the United States. [22] While it was possible to dress this kind of behavior in American patriotism—many natives considered the Treaty antithetical to the best interests of the United States—Irish interests were revealed with the organization of the American Society of United Irishmen. Its announced purpose was to further the revolutionary ambition of the Irish Society, and while it did not rescue that movement from utter failure in 1798, it did succeed in provoking an alarmed British Minister to lodge a formal protest with the American government. [23] On the other hand, the American

[21] December 18, 1883; quoted in David M. Pletcher, *The Awkward Years: American Foreign Relations under Garfield and Arthur* (Columbia, Mo., 1962), pp. 245–246.

[22] M. A. Jones, *American Immigration*, p. 85.

[23] Billington, *Protestant Crusade*, p. 23.

Minister in Britain was alarmed when he heard the disturbing rumor that the British government planned to reward Americans for their Irish sympathies by transporting to the United States the political prisoners seized during the insurrection. Good Federalist that he was, Rufus King lost no time informing the British of his government's disinclination to admit such obvious undesirables.[24] Much to his dismay and that of several of his fellow Federalist luminaries, many of these revolutionaries had already fled to the United States. This merely strengthened the determination of the Federalists to ensure that their country did not become a refuge for "hordes of wild Irishmen, nor the turbulent and disorderly of all parts of the world, to come here with a view to disturb our tranquillity after having succeeded in the overthrow of their own Governments." [25]

The threat posed by the Irish immigrants to good order in the United States, which for the Federalists was best illustrated by their anxiety to rush from the waist of transatlantic vessels into the arms of the Democratic-Republicans, left many of the members of the governing party impatiently awaiting an opportunity to strike at them. The first came with the hysteria that greeted the publication in 1798 of Talleyrand's contemptuous demand for a bribe before even considering negotiations to end French depredations upon American commerce. Now such ingrates as the Irish could be denounced as agents of revolutionary France. William Cobbett, an Englsh immigrant, described in a column of his *Porcupine's Gazette* a conspiracy of the French and that "restless tribe, the emigrated United Irishmen," to overthrow the gov-

[24] James Morton Smith, *Freedom's Fetters: The Alien and Sedition Laws and American Civil Liberties* (Ithaca, 1956), p. 25.
[25] *Ibid.*, p. 24.

ernment of the United States.[26] In this congenial climate the
Naturalization, Alien, and Sedition Acts passed Congress, almost tripling the period of residence before the granting of
citizenship and facilitating the expulsion of aliens and the
silencing of critics of the government. If the Sedition Act,
unlike the other measures, was not directed primarily against
immigrants, it is interesting that the first person prosecuted
under it was the nation's most notorious Hibernian, Matthew
(the Spitting) Lyon of Vermont. But the Irish- and
French-Americans had their revenge soon enough. Their
votes may well have made up the margin of the Democratic-
Republican victory in the elections in the pivotal state of New
York in 1799, and thus the margin of Thomas Jefferson's
victory in the presidential election the following year.
Twelve years later, however, the Irish had an opportunity to
strike a serious blow against the English. Then, when England
and the United States were already at war, the Irish, by their
very presence, helped further to exacerbate Anglo-American
relations—a by no means inconsiderable achievement.

Until the Fenian crisis later in the century, the British held
to the doctrine of inalienable allegiance, and in times of national crisis they were disposed to enforce it strictly. Many of
those born on British territory could testify to this after being
impressed into the British navy during the French wars, and
none more so than Irish emigrants, hundreds of whom were
removed from vessels carrying them to the United States
between 1810 and 1812.[27] Although their peculiar misfortunes
did not involve the government of the United States, the latter
certainly was involved when the British invoked the same
principle during the War of 1812 to segregate the Irish-Amer-

[26] *Ibid.*, p. 25.   [27] M. A. Jones, *American Immigration*, p. 90.

icans from other prisoners in preparation for their transportation to England for trial on a charge of treason. Of course the
government of the United States retaliated, for these men
were naturalized American citizens, and the ensuing controversy quickly became so embittered that ultimately even the
traditional practice of exchanging prisoners was stopped.[28]

If this naturalization problem was unforeseen even by the
Irish, it was the result of their determination to make a positive contribution to the war effort of their adopted country. It
was left to the dissident Hartford Federalists to investigate
their motives and conclude that their enthusiastic participation
was a product of anglophobia rather than American
patriotism.[29] Irish-Americans themselves lent some credence to
this interpretation, for at least one of their organs, the New
York *Shamrock*, had published on the eve of the war an
inflammatory letter calling upon them "to exult at the possibility of doing England an essential injury." [30] If they failed to
realize this ambition, the Irish-Americans did not permit failure to dampen their ardor for Irish causes. The passionate
nature of their interest in the affairs of their native land was
evident from the various associations of friends of Ireland that
provided pecuniary and moral support for the cause of Catholic Emancipation during the 1820's. Twenty years later they
were just as active organizing associations to rally support for
Daniel O'Connell's movement to secure the repeal of the Act
of Union with England, which had abruptly terminated Irish
parliamentary independence.[31]

While these activities fell within the bounds of interna-

[28] Glenn Tucker, *Poltroons and Patriots: A Popular Account of the War of 1812* (New York, 1954), I, 193–194.
[29] Billington, *Protestant Crusade*, p. 162.
[30] Wittke, *Irish in America*, p. 162.
[31] Billington, *Protestant Crusade*, p. 328.

tional propriety, the implications of Irish and Irish-American interest in the Anglo-American dispute over the boundary of Oregon was more sinister. One historian of America's Manifest Destiny has quoted at length from the *Dublin Freeman* to illustrate Irish sympathy with American expansionism, but that sympathy was not disinterested.

We must regard the annexation of Texas as a step that at once opens to the Americans the horizons of California. Such prospects must, for obvious reasons, confer upon the Oregon question great additional importance in the eyes of the Americans, and we can well believe, with our New York correspondent, that people will now reject with disdain the boundary which in early negotiations they themselves proposed as a compromise of their claims: the 49th degree of latitude.[32]

To encourage the United States to hold to its demand for all Oregon, albeit covertly, was to foment an Anglo-American rupture. Even the mild Lord Aberdeen, the British Foreign Secretary, would have had difficulty accepting and then justifying to Parliament any settlement above the 49th parallel. The article in the *Dublin Freeman*, then, was a very careful expression of a dangerous Irish nationalist belief that an independent Ireland would be one of the happier consequences of a war between the United States and Great Britain. Nor was this sentiment confined to Ireland; it was shared by Irish-American nationalists, who openly agitated for war with England in 1846 on the grounds that this "would bring freedom to Ireland and territory to the United States." [33] No doubt it was this unity of American and Irish interests which helped to inspire the bellicose oratory of Congressman Kennedy of

[32] Frederick Merk, *Manifest Destiny and Mission in American History: A Reinterpretation* (New York, 1963), pp. 83–84.
[33] Billington, *Protestant Crusade*, p. 328.

Indiana when, with a prophecy no less sanguinary than it was sanguine, he was reported to have informed his listeners:

The march of your people is onward, and it is westward; that is their destiny. They are going onward to the Pacific and if in the path which leads the British lion shall lay him down, shall we on that account be craven in our duty and our destiny? No, never. The American eagle shall stick his claws into the nose of the lion, and make his blood spout like a whale. This, too, is inevitable destiny.[34]

The frustration such nationalists undoubtedly experienced when the Oregon boundary was settled peacefully was quickly relieved. Hope springs eternal, and 1848 was a year of revolution. Encouraged by the example of Europe, where much of the established order had been put to at least temporary flight, and with economic and social distress widespread in Ireland, Young Irelanders were tempted into rebellion in August, 1848. Imbued with the romantic nationalism of the period, they turned to the Gaelic traditions of their past for inspiration and made national independence their goal.[35]

The ambitions of Young Ireland struck a responsive chord in an expansive Young America. Irish Republican Clubs were quickly organized, particulaly in New York, to rally support for the cause, but they did not confine their activities or attention to the United States and Ireland. Irish-Americans turned expectantly to British North America and its substantial Irish population, and by May of 1848 the Governor-General, Lord Elgin, was privately expressing concern at the possibility of Irish-American "fanatics on behalf of Republicanism and repeal . . . egging on their compatriots here to

---

[34] John Charles Dent, *The Last Forty Years: Canada since the Union of 1841* (Toronto, 1881), II, 60.

[35] Edmund Curtis, *A History of Ireland* (London, 1950), p. 366.

rebellion." [36] Nor had the danger of the "Yankee Irish" launching marauding raids against the British colonies escaped him. From Crampton, the British chargé d'affaires in Washington, he learned that while the Irish-American organizations were not at that time sufficient to "admit serious aggressions in Canada," this might soon change. The chargé d'affaires looked "forward with apprehension to the winter when the Irish have little work and the disbanded miscreants who are now returning in hordes from Mexico with appetites whetted for all deeds of rapine and blood will be ready for any congenial job." [37]

Further cause for concern to the British authorities, in addition to the danger of Irish-Americans inciting elements of the domestic population of British North America to rebellion or the prospect of raids by demobilized veterans of the Mexican campaigns, was the possibility of Irish and American ambitions fusing. The Mexican War had illustrated the growing appetite of Young America, and for sensitive Englishmen it did not appear entirely improbable that having made a meal of Mexico the United States might seek to gorge itself upon British North America. The presidential election campaign in 1848 did little to extinguish such fears. In their anxiety to attract the Irish-American vote, unscrupulous politicians pandered to this expansionist sentiment. [38] Consequently, as an understandably somewhat jaundiced observer of the American political scene, Elgin took the precaution of preparing for the immediate eviction of any Irish-American vanguard of Manifest Destiny. That an invasion of "Yankee Irish" failed to materialize the generously attributed to the loyalty of the French- and Irish-Canadians. Nonetheless, the affair had

[36] Sir Arthur G. Doughty, ed., *Elgin-Grey Papers, 1846–1852* (Ottawa, 1937), I, 149, Elgin to Grey, May 4, 1848.
[37] *Ibid.*, p. 223, August 16.   [38] *Ibid.*, p. 369, June 11, 1849.

suggested the extent to which immediate domestic political considerations might dictate the course of America's international relations. In a letter to the British Colonial Secretary, Elgin observed:

A very slight acquaintance with American politics enables one to affirm with tolerable confidence that if the reckless and powerful faction who were advocating in the States annexation of Canada as a species of retaliation for British misdeeds in Ireland had received much encouragement from this side of the border it would neither have been within the power of the United States Government nor in its will pending the canvass for the Presidential election to have restrained them.[39]

Yet Irish-American support for the nationalist cause in Ireland was not confined to whatever indirect assistance might have resulted from diversionary disturbances in British North America. The more ardent spirits planned to participate personally in the overthrow of British rule. Thus one of Elgin's informants in the United States forwarded the alarming news, which he claimed to have obtained from a leading member of the New York Irish Republican Union, that the "Yankee Irish" were busy exporting the materials of war to Ireland. In fact, recently demobilized veterans of the Mexican War were already on their way to the island, he added, to train an army of liberation which would be led by an American general when it took to the battlefield.[40]

This information did little to reassure a British government whose concern over the evident signs of disaffection in Ireland was sufficient to lead it to suspend the writ of habeas corpus there.[41] Orders were quickly issued to the Irish constabulary instructing them to seize, search, and, if necessary,

[39] *Ibid.*, p. 264, November 30, 1848.   [40] *Ibid.*, p. 209, July 18, 1849.
[41] *Ibid.*, p. 202, Grey to Elgin, July 21, 1848.

arrest all returning emigrants and Americans who excited suspicion. Behind this decision, however, there loomed the shadow of the dormant Anglo-American dispute over naturalization. Once detained, Irish-Americans were bound to appeal to the representatives of their adopted country for protection and assistance, but in English law, and hence in the eyes of the British government, such men were still British subjects. In short, the orders issued to the Irish police in August made a confrontation over the naturalization problem highly probable. Within two months the American Secretary of State, James Buchanan, was instructing the American Minister in London, George Bancroft, to uphold the American position that "British native born subjects, after they have been naturalized under our laws, are to all intents and purposes as much American citizens and entitled to the same degree of protection as though they had been born in the United States." [42]

Bancroft had moved to ensure the protection of all American citizens long before Buchanan's note was written. On September 12 he had asked the British government not only to provide him with copies of the orders they had sent to the Irish police but also to release the two Americans detained under them. In his reply, rejecting both requests, Lord Palmerston, the Foreign Secretary, gave expression to his government's mounting irritation over the activities of Irish clubs and associations in the United States. It was only their awareness of the constitutional problems which undoubtedly prevented the President from effectively repressing such groups, Palmerston remarked, that had restrained Her Majesty's government from pressing their American counterpart "with representations against a state of things which, under other circumstances, would scarcely have been compatible with the

[42] John Basset Moore, ed., *The Works of James Buchanan* (New York, 1908–1911), VIII, 231, Buchanan to Bancroft, October 28.

continuance of friendly relations between the two governments." [43] Undaunted by this response, Bancroft continued to agitate for the release of both men, even though one was naturalized, for he naturally refused to concede the British claim of inalienable allegiance. Nonetheless, when the British government demonstrated its willingness to avoid a controversy on this subject by releasing both men on the condition that they leave Ireland immediately, the American Minister was disinclined to press the issue of naturalization as a matter of principle.

Back in Washington, however, President Polk and his Cabinet decided that they could ill afford such pragmatism. With the House of Representatives breathing down their necks—on December 11 it passed a resolution calling for all information concerning the arrest of American citizens in Ireland—this did not appear to be the moment at which to embark upon a policy of laissez faire. Consequently on December 18, 1848, Buchanan wrote to Bancroft urging him to lodge a formal protest over the "invidious distinction" the British had drawn between native and naturalized Americans. "Both for public and private reasons," he concluded, "I would advise that you allude pointedly to this in your protesting note." [44] However, with the prisoners long since released and the offensive orders long since inoperative, Bancroft remained unconvinced of the necessity or expediency of forwarding an official protest. As a result, he continued to ignore directives from the State Department until further resistance was impossible. The Polk Cabinet, spurred on by the threat of the issue being raised in the form of a Congressional resolution, unanimously agreed in

[43] Florence E. Gibson, *The Attitudes of the New York Irish toward State and National Affairs, 1848–1892* (New York, 1951), p. 46.

[44] Moore, *Works of James Buchanan*, XI, 481.

February, 1849, that they should "place on record in the most solemn form the protest of the United States, so that the order of August last may not hereafter be drawn in question as a precedent, in which we acquiesced, to justify a similar exercise of power." [45] When he forwarded this news to Bancroft, Buchanan made it plain how unwise and impractical it would be for the Minister to attempt to obstruct the delivery of a protest. "The orders are a great outrage," he wrote, "and I have no doubt many persons in the United States are watching you with anxiety for your protest. I shall send you formal instructions upon the subject by the next steamer; but, if judicious, you might anticipate them." [46] Soon afterward Bancroft wrote to Palmerston formally remonstrating against any distinction being at any time drawn between native and naturalized American citizens. [47]

Although 1848 was yet another year of failure for Irish nationalists—the Young Ireland movement ended dismally with a forlorn attempt at an uprising in Tipperary—there remained a glimmer of hope for those possessed of truly extraordinary powers of vision. Under certain conditions the continuing attachment of Irish-Americans to Ireland might provoke an Anglo-American crisis. Certainly if a period of postwar adjustment coincided with an intense political campaign in the United States, then Irish-American nationalists might well grasp this opportunity to launch an invasion of British North America. How the British government would respond to marauding raids was open to conjecture, but more

[45] M. M. Quaife, ed., *Diary of James K. Polk during His Presidency, 1845–1849* (Chicago, 1910) IV, 332–333, February 13, 1849.

[46] Moore, *Works of James Buchanan*, XI, 484, Buchanan to Bancroft, February 5, 1849.

[47] A. Cockburn, *Nationality–Or the Law Relating to Subjects and Aliens with a View to Future Legislation* (London, 1869), p. 82.

amiable relations between the two countries seemed an unlikely result. Nor could the British be expected to react
phlegmatically if Irish-American revolutionaries continued to
disembark in Ireland, conscious as they were of the extent of
native disaffection. "The late events," Earl Grey, the Colonial
Secretary, wrote to Elgin in the wake of the 1848 troubles,
"While they have already proved that without External aid
the Irish can do nothing have shown no less clearly that there
exists general, I might say universal disaffection to this Country in the population at large which in the event of a foreign
war would render our position in the South of Ireland full of
danger." [48] Of course the Irish-American nationalists were
quick to appreciate the advantages they might gain from any
hostilities in which Britain was involved, and during the Crimean War they attempted, unsuccessfully, to interest the
Russians in their cause. Yet the war that many of them saw as
Ireland's ultimate salvation was Anglo-American. An independent Irish nation, an ever increasing group of nationalists
argued, would rise like the phoenix from the ashes. Imbued
with this faith, they were fully prepared to provoke hostilities.

Yet even as they turned toward war for their ally, the
Irish-Americans were still prepared to seek their goal by more
limited yet direct action. Thus when their offer to raise a
rebellion in return for support was rejected by the unimagina-
tive Russians, they went ahead alone. The Massachusetts Irish
Emigrant Aid Society broadened the scope of its activities
from the promotion of Irish settlement to the promotion of
Irish independence. It served as a commissary for the expeditionary force of Irish-Americans that was intended to serve as

[48] Doughty, *Elgin-Grey Papers*, I, 211, Grey to Elgin, August 10,
1848.

the nucleus of an army of liberation. While reports of a prospective invasion were casually dismissed by the American authorities as a practical joke,[49] the British were inclined to treat them with less levity.

Crampton, now elevated to the rank of Minister, broached the subject of an invasion to the American Secretary of State, Marcy, and the British Foreign Secretary, Lord Clarendon, raised it with Buchanan, now American Minister to Great Britain, on several occasions. Yet these recurrent expressions of concern may not have been entirely governed by the activities of the Massachusetts Irish. It may be significant that this problem and that of Russian privateers allegedly being fitted out in New York were discussed during those meetings between Clarendon and Buchanan at which Crampton's conduct in the United States was also debated. With the American government showing every intention of being intolerant of his alleged violation of American neutrality in the Crimean War by recruiting men for the British armies in the United States, Clarendon may well have been searching for an available diplomatic counter. If this was the case, it seemed possible that the Irish-Americans would lend him valuable support when three hundred of them landed in Ireland during the autumn of 1855, and during an interview with Buchanan, the Foreign Secretary vigorously expressed the opinion that these people were returning "to their country piecemeal to create disturbances." [50] This invasion did not presage rebellion, however, nor did it save Crampton from the indignity of being asked to leave the United States. Meanwhile the Massachusetts Irish Emigrant Aid Society sank into well-deserved diplomatic obscurity.

Although they had failed again—failed insofar as they had

[49] Moore, *Works of James Buchanan*, IX, 429, Buchanan to Marcy, October 30, 1855. [50] *Ibid*.

been unable to take advantage of British involvement in the Crimea—the Irish-American nationalists had grounds for continued optimism. There was no obvious slackening of support for the cause; on the contrary, there was every reason to believe that it would continue to grow in the United States. The extent of native disaffection in Ireland had persuaded some Englishmen that a policy of state-aided emigration was desirable, for it promised to relieve the condition of the country by removing in some way other than by starvation those who would otherwise need to be fed, and promised also to ease the position of the British by removing possible malcontents. However, instead of emigrating to British North America at state expense and under the restraint of military discipline, as Earl Grey proposed,[51] the Irish made their own way across the Atlantic. Denied public assistance, those who could raise the passage money crossed in the hundreds of thousands. In the year 1852 alone some 220,000 left Ireland to establish an Irish nation in America, and their destination was the Republic rather than the Colonies. For most of these emigrants, as for many of the Irish-Americans born and raised in the United States, Ireland always offered a sentimental appeal. It became, in the words of one Irish historian, "either a passionate memory or an ancestral poetry."[52] Unhappily this romantic vision was marred by British subjection, with the inevitable result that the great body of Irish immigrants to the United States and their descendants were animated not only by nostalgia but also by a savage hatred of England. Here, then, was a host of recruits for Irish-American nationalist organizations. And while their arrival provided additional grist for the nativist mills, prejudice merely intensified their

[51] Doughty, *Elgin-Grey Papers*, I, 211, Grey to Elgin, August 10, 1848.   [52] Curtis, *History of Ireland*, p. 370.

nationalism. For "so long as the Irish were unaccepted" in large areas of their adopted land, "they looked back across the ocean."[53]

In the seven years following the Great Starvation of 1847 more than 1,300,000 Irish made the crossing to the United States. The very magnitude of this migration had far-reaching implications for Anglo-American relations. The vast increase in the number of Irish-Americans—by 1855 they constituted a third of the electorate of New York City—promised to bring an ever increasing deference to their political wishes and ambitions. Demonstrating uncharacteristic fatalism at this turn of events, the London *Times* was later moved to comment:

The happy institution of universal suffrage, the foundation on which American institutions repose, has given the ignorant and prejudiced Irishman a power which he could never possess under any other circumstances. The Irish vote has become a matter of consequence, and American newspapers and American politicians have not been slow to pander to the weaknesses and delusions of those who dispose of it.[54]

Of those who sought to dispose of the Irish vote, the Fenians were the most significant.

The Fenian Brotherhood was yet another in the long line of Irish-American nationalist organizations. "No Irishman could have invented such a scheme," the *Times* sardonically observed. "No Yankee would ever have believed in it; but put American exaggeration and Irish credulity together, and you get Fenianism."[55] This society sought Irish independence

---

[53] Oscar Handlin, *Boston's Immigrants: A Study in Acculturation* (Cambridge, Mass., 1959), pp. 205–206.
[54] October 3, 1865.   [55] *Ibid.*, October 30.

both directly and indirectly. It attempted to incite rebellion in Ireland and when this failed, resorted to a campaign of terror in England. Also, it sought to provoke an Anglo-American rupture by reviving the naturalization controversy and by attacking the British North American colonies during a period when relations between England and the United States had already been seriously impaired by other problems, and at a time when the domestic politics of the United States had been thrown into confusion.

Political refugees such as John O'Mahoney, who had fled to Paris in the wake of the 1848 fiasco and then crossed the Atlantic six years later, assumed the initiative in forming the Brotherhood. But the continuity of the Irish nationalist movement was as evident in the name and policy of this new organization as it was from the personal history of the leadership. The goal was national liberation. The name Fenian was O'Mahoney's corruption of the Gaelic for the Irish militia of the distant pre-English past; thus it expressed his romantic nationalism and the militant Irish-American conviction that Ireland could be liberated through the sacrifices of a new generation of warriors. Yet, even the determined efforts of Irish-American Fenians might prove futile, as O'Mahoney and other prominent nationalists exiled in New York appreciated, unless they could be assured a solid base of support within Ireland. Therefore the exiles dispatched an emissary to Dublin in 1857 to seek and sound out James Stephens, who, although a fellow Young Ireland refugee, had returned to Ireland in 1856. He was quite willing to form a native organization but he exacted a high price. He demanded and received not only a promise of unfettered power over the Irish wing of the liberation movement, which he called the Irish Revolutionary Brotherhood, but continuous financial support from the supposedly inexhaustible treasury of Irish-America.[56] While an estimated half-million dollars had been raised by 1866,[57] precious little reached Ireland during 1857. That year was one of financial panic and economic recession in the United States; consequently money was a rare commodity for most Americans, including the Irish. Nonetheless, when it failed to cross the ocean in the expected quantities, Stephens went to the United States in 1858 to investigate the situation, and during this visit O'Mahoney was appointed head of the American wing of the movement, which he named the Fenian Brotherhood soon afterward.

O'Mahoney's principal task was to raise the regiments of Fenians. He was certainly assisted and encouraged by the fact that Irish-Americans had often retained and expressed their group consciousness in the past through the formation of Irish militia units. Now he and his colleagues provided them with an additional incentive to acquire something more than a passing familiarity with weapons. However, his plans to adapt the American militia system to the recruitment of Fenians were upset by the Civil War, which swept thousands of potential recruits into the ranks of the contending armies. Yet there was a measure of comfort in the knowledge that one reason for the alacrity with which Irish-Americans enlisted in the armies of the United States was the widespread belief that Britain was opposed to the Union cause; thus their participation was an indication of their passionate anglophobia.

---

[56] For the origins of the Fenian Movement, see C. L. King, "The Fenian Movement," *University of Colorado Studies*, VI (April, 1909), 187–213; J. Rutherford, *Secret History of the Fenian Conspiracy* (London, 1887); and William D'Arcy, *The Fenian Movement in the United States, 1858–1886* (Washington, D.C., 1947).

[57] Schrier, *Ireland and the American Emigration*, p. 125.

Meanwhile, to Fenian zealots, the war offered a valuable military education and an opportunity to win the gratitude of the American government. A sympathetic government in Washington would of course be an invaluable ally against Britain, and the harassed Lincoln administration did nothing to dash such hopes. On the contrary, by its tolerance of Fenian activities it encouraged them. Throughout the war Fenian organizers openly and freely created their own military formations within those of the United States, publicly announcing as they did so that their ultimate purpose was to wage war on the British. Even emissaries from Ireland, including Stephens, were provided with passes enabling them to travel through the ranks of the various armies addressing Irish-Americans and calling upon them for assistance in another national cause once the American conflict was over.[58] It was an indication of their success that members of the Armies of the Cumberland, the Potomac, and the Tennessee were given leave in 1863 to attend the first Fenian Convention, held in Chicago, where they and the other delegates drafted a constitution and began to erect the paraphernalia of an Irish government in exile.[59]

Prior to the Chicago convention, the Brotherhood's growth had been somewhat haphazard and its government an autocracy. Appointed head of the American wing of the Irish Revolutionary Brotherhood during a meeting at Tammany Hall in the fall of 1858, and subsequently designated "supreme organizer and Director," [60] and sole channel of communication between the Irish and American branches, O'Mahoney not only had extensive powers, but he was not held accountable to anybody for his exercise of them. Exces-

[58] Rutherford, *Secret History*, p. 241.
[59] Gibson, *The Attitudes of the New York Irish*, p. 186.
[60] D'Arcy, *Fenian Movement*, p. 12.

sive though it was, this centralization of power created few problems as long as the Fenian Brotherhood was confined to New York City, but gradually branches, or "Circles," were established in other cities in the Eastern states and also in Midwestern and even Far Western communities. Over each Circle, which might be composed of any number of men, since there were no specific requirements of size, there presided a Centre. Local Centres were elected by the members of the local Circles, but the senior officer in the state, the State Centre, was appointed by O'Mahoney, who changed his title to that of Head Centre when he renamed his organization the Fenian Brotherhood in 1859.

The modest pace of recruitment during the Brotherhood's infancy was to some extent attributable to the fact that it could not afford to employ full-time organizers. As a result, knowledge of the new movement spread slowly. Correspondence with prominent Irish-Americans in other cities was one way O'Mahoney could promote Fenianism; another was to dispatch the occasional agent on an organizational tour. John O'Leary, an envoy from Stephens, was sent out on just such a tour by O'Mahoney in 1859. No doubt the Fenians also derived some benefit from the existence of an Irish-American press. Wherever there were enough "Yankee Irish" to support a newspaper, one and sometimes several were established. While they were not by any means all Fenian organs, at least in the sense of being official mouthpieces for the Brotherhood, presumably they did sustain that cause, if only indirectly, insofar as they aroused Irish-American nationalism. Thus the official Fenian journal, the *Phoenix*, a weekly O'Mahoney founded in New York in June of 1859, was supplemented at one time or another by the *Irish Republic*, published in Washington and New York, the New York *Citizen*, the *Honest Truth* (dubbed the *Damned Lie* by the *Citizen*), the New

York *Irish News* and the *Irish-American*, the Boston *Pilot*, and a number of others, all constantly reminding their subscribers of the iniquities of British rule in Ireland. Not all of them were as rabid as Mooney's *California Express* of San Francisco, which was "notorious for its incendiary articles," [61] but all of them did stir Irish-American passions. For the more belligerent anglophobes, enlistment in the Fenian Brotherhood held out the prospect of participation in the overthrow of British rule.

The number of Circles multiplied during the Civil War, for the massing of thousands of Irish-Americans into military units encouraged the growth of a self-awareness of their national origins which in turn eased the task of the Fenian organizers. The need to reduce the Brotherhood to a more "liberal" and coherent administrative form therefore grew proportionately. By September, 1863, O'Mahoney was being pressed by several members to call a general convention, and one ultimately gathered in Chicago on November 3. In attendance were eighty-two delegates representing Circles in twelve states, the District of Columbia, and the Armies of the Cumberland, the Potomac, and the Tennessee.

It was generally agreed that the principal purpose of this first national convention was to draft a constitution that would place the Brotherhood on a basis "more in accordance with the habits and customs of the United States," or to be more specific, place the position of Head Centre upon a more democratic footing. It was O'Mahoney himself who proposed that this office should be elective and held for a fixed period. It was his suggestion also that the executive and financial departments of the organization be separated and a Central Treasurer be elected by the convention. In addition to receiving all funds and disbursing them, the Treasurer would forward

[61] *Ibid.*, p. 28.

monies to the Central Executive of the Irish Revolutionary Brotherhood (Stephens) and the Head Centre, and both officers would be accountable in future to an annual Fenian convention for their supplies. In fact, the Head Centre would be responsible to the convention, and to no other party, for all his official acts. To advise him and assist him to perform his duties, however, a central council, or cabinet, of five, nominated by him but elected by the convention, was created. With the passage of these reforms O'Mahoney resigned from his post, to be renominated and elected unanimously under the provisions of the new constitution.[62]

Quite obviously the Fenians had evolved a much more satisfactory system of government at Chicago, certainly one more in keeping with their American environment. For if it was understandable and perhaps necessary that Stephens be vested with autocratic powers in Ireland, and it had been the character of his office which had originally shaped that of his American equivalent, it was never probable that Irish-Americans would long tolerate a similar exercise of authority by O'Mahoney. Although the Fenian Brotherhood was still dominated by the Head Centre after the Chicago convention, he was nevertheless an elected officer and had been made responsible for all his actions to the representatives of the entire membership. Yet there were some who remained dissatisfied with what they considered the excessive centralization of power, particularly when O'Mahoney frustrated their plans to wage war upon the British immediately, and it was this group that successfully revised the Fenian constitution at Philadelphia in October, 1865, erecting a governmental structure that in form was almost an exact replica of that of the United States.

The Brotherhood had been scheduled to hold its second

[62] *Ibid.*, p. 37.

national convention in November of 1864, but it was postponed until January of the following year so that a report on
the progress and activities of the Irish Revolutionary Brotherhood could be prepared and presented. The size of the gathering at Cincinnati in January—348 delegates representing 273
Circles in 21 states and 4 territories—emphasized the growth
in membership since 1863. As the number of Fenians increased, so did the funds in the Fenian treasury. Each new
member paid a dollar initiation fee, and every Fenian paid
weekly dues of ten cents. This fairly constant source of revenue was supplemented by a number of others. Mass meetings were organized whenever an anniversary or some "act of
British injustice" suggested that it would be well attended,
and collections for the cause were taken up. Drawing upon
the traditions of the "American Democracy" and capitalizing
upon the gregarious nature of their fellow Irish-Americans,
the Fenians also organized picnics; indeed these became an
integral part of Fenian life. Relaxed and refreshed, entertained
by that act of which few Irish ever tired—verbal yanks and
tugs upon the Lion's tail—those in attendance were asked to
contribute to the Irish independence fund. To those who
were willing to gamble or could be persuaded that an Irish
Republic was just over the horizon, the Brotherhood sold
bonds. Issued in various denominations (ten, twenty, fifty,
one hundred, and five hundred dollars) they were "redeema-
ble six months after the acknowledgement of the Independence of the Irish Nation with interest from the date hereof
inclusive at six per cent per annum payable on presentation of
this bond at the Treasury of the Irish Republic." [63] By such
means as these Fenian revenues were increased, and in 1865
they amounted to $228,000. Such wealth provided the Broth-
erhood with the means of further expansion. Certainly, after

[63] *Ibid.*, p. 113 n.

the Cincinnati convention there was a more systematic approach to recruitment. Paid organizers had been sent out in increasing numbers since the Chicago meeting, but now central organizers were appointed. Each of these men was allocated an area, perhaps one, two, or even three states, and within this territory he promoted the formation of Circles. The success of this campaign was soon evident. By mid-April, 1865, sixty-seven new Circles had been established and in little more than a month sixty-seven more.

The decision to send out these new agents had been taken by the central council against O'Mahoney's advice, a rejection of the Head Centre's opinion which in this instance was illustrative of the more general breach that had opened up between O'Mahoney and his cabinet. At Cincinnati he had been re-elected, but the size of the central council had been increased from five to ten members, and to these positions the convention had elected "men of action." Convinced that the Head Centre was the "drag chain" on Irish independence,[64] they decided to rewrite the constitution and for this purpose summoned the representatives of the rank and file to Philadelphia.

More than six hundred delegates assembled in Fenian Hall on October 16 to endorse a revised constitution which abolished the central council and the title of Head Centre. Now the government of the Fenian Brotherhood was to be in the hands of a Senate, a House of Delegates, and a President, listed in descending order of importance. The Senate was composed of fifteen members who owed their rank to a complicated system of selection and election. Thus the constitution provided that "they shall be nominated by a committee of two from each state and district, elected by the delegates of each state and district in Congress assembled; and such nomi-

[64] *Ibid.*, p. 81.

nees shall be elected by a two-thirds vote of the said Congress." Once elected, the Fenian Senate was to select one of its members to serve as its President and the Vice-President of the Brotherhood. Whenever a President was incapable of performing his duties or removed by death or impeachment, the Vice-President was to succeed him. In addition to their control of the second office in the Fenian government, the senators were vested as a body with extensive fiscal powers. All "propositions for raising revenue and fixing salaries of officers and employees" now originated with the Senate, and no appropriation of money was valid without its consent. Finally, the Senate shared the legislative power with the House of Delegates chosen by the Brotherhood in proportion to the number and size of the Circles. Each Circle was "entitled to one Delegate for every hundred members, more or less, but not less than ten, and one additional Delegate for a fractional part of one hundred members exceeding fifty of such Circle." [65]

Executive power was vested in a President elected annually by the General Congress of Senate and Delegates. He was to be advised by a cabinet, which he appointed with the consent of the Senate, and its members were to include the Treasurer, an agent of the Irish Republic, a bond agent, a corresponding secretary, and a Secretary of War. Thus O'Mahoney emerged from the Philadelphia convention shorn of much of his power. This was a situation he could not long endure, however, and within two months his refusal to abide by all the restraints imposed upon him split the Brotherhood. The Senate continued to dominate one wing while O'Mahoney, reinvoking the Chicago constitution, commanded the other.

If they were unable to agree upon the organization of the

[65] *Ibid.*, p. 80.

Brotherhood, or the best means of realizing their ambition, the Fenians were united on that ambition: an independent Ireland. The seriousness of their intent was suggested by the Senate's renting of the Moffat mansion, near Union Square in New York, for eighteen months at a cost of $18,000. This became Fenian headquarters, and from its windows the Fenian flag, the Harp and Sunburst, soon fluttered.[66] Even more ominous than the renting of this expensive and no doubt imposing edifice, emphasizing as it did the Brotherhood's determination and wealth, were the Fenians' military preparations. O'Mahoney appointed Major Thomas W. Sweeny of the United States Army, a professional soldier and veteran of many campaigns, as the Fenian Secretary of War, and under his direction the military branch was organized. Charles C. Tevis, a graduate of West Point, was appointed adjutant-general and a Board, composed of three Fenian veterans of the Civil War, was established to examine candidates for commissions. The assistant inspectors-general provided the next link in this military chain, one being appointed for each state containing Circles. All were experienced soldiers whose tasks were to organize the military branch of their states and forward the documents of applicants for commissions. Finally, a number of subordinate departments were established. Thus with their Secretary of War, adjutant-general, inspectors-general, and quartermasters, their ordnance, subsistence, medical, and pay departments, the Fenians tackled the problems of military organization not only with seriousness but also with professional care and knowledge.[67]

The British grew concerned about Fenian activities long before the latter assumed such alarming proportions. The formation of the Brotherhood in 1858 caused them some uneasi-

---

[66] *Ibid.*, p. 81.   [67] *Ibid.*, pp. 101–102.

ness, but they were soon comforted by what they interpreted as evidence of native American hostility to the organization. They found further cause of satisfaction in the outbreak of the American Civil War. This abruptly ended any immediate danger of a massive exportation of men and munitions to Ireland, but as the war progressed, the records of the British Minister in Washington and the consuls in the larger northern cities began to swell with increasingly hysterical reports of Fenian activity. Edward M. Archibald, consul in New York, was well placed to be inundated with information forwarded by a willing if mercenary band of informants. From them he received and reported the alarming news that the Fenians planned to seize all the British ships in American ports and murder those members of the English population of Ireland who were thought to be opposed to their cause.[68] The persistent extravagance of such reports, incredible though they were, compelled the British to organize a more systematic and reliable network of agents and informers, infiltrators, and apostates, with the result that they were invariably better informed of Fenian intentions than the vast majority of the Brotherhood.

Whatever the source of the information, however, for the British there was no escaping the rising tempo of Fenian activity as the Civil War drew to a conclusion, and it was a problem the authorities in Canada and the Foreign Office had to confront. As early as 1864, Archibald had reported rumors (which he did not think could prudently be ignored) of Fenian preparations for a raid on one of the British North American colonies.[69] Against this background, the deployment of troops along the Canadian border, ostensibly to pre-

[68] Archibald to Russell, January 9, 1865, Foreign Office (FO), ser. 5, vol. 1334, Public Record Office, London.
[69] Archibald to Burnley, October 12, 1864, *ibid.*

vent a repetition of the St. Albans affair when Confederate raiders had used British territory as both a base and a refuge, also served as a precaution against possible raids in the other direction by Fenians. Meanwhile the Foreign Office began to show interest in the Brotherhood, and in December, 1864, Earl Russell, the Foreign Secretary, instructed British consuls in the United States to report to him all the information they could obtain on Fenianism.[70] From Archibald he learned of the formation of Fenian groups in Cleveland and Louisville, and from the consul in New Orleans news of similar activities there. Such expansion was by no means unpredictable. Ohio had a sizable Irish population, and in the larger cities of the ante bellum South the Irish had often been employed on work that was considered too dangerous for expensive Negro slaves.[71] In New Orleans alone there were an estimated twenty-five thousand Irish,[72] some of whom were undoubtedly anxious to support the Irish crusade for freedom.

If this expansion of Fenianism was in a sense quite natural, the active participation of a high-ranking member of the "reconstructed" government of Louisiana in the founding ceremonies in New Orleans provided Russell, or so he thought, with an opportunity to seize the diplomatic initiative. Fastening eagerly upon this information and the report that an officer of the Army of the Potomac had been given leave for the express purpose of attending the Fenian convention in Cincinnati in January, 1865, the Foreign Secretary lodged a formal protest with the government of the United States. Yet in February of 1865, the Fenians scarcely warranted the notoriety that an official diplomatic correspondence necessarily

[70] Russell to Kortwright (British consul at Philadelphia), December 23, *ibid.*

[71] Clement Eaton, *The Growth of Southern Civilization, 1790–1860* (New York, 1961), p. 64. [72] Wittke, *Irish in America*, p. 30.

bestowed upon them; indeed, the British government was well aware of the futility of protesting activities of this nature. Palmerston, now Prime Minister, had held back under provocative circumstances in 1848 because he realized that the Americans would reply with chapter and verse of their constitution, while Russell conceded in his protest note the limitations this document placed upon American governmental action. Thus when he observed that the British government "trusts that the attendance of civil and military officers . . . will be disapproved by the Government, and will not in future be permitted,"[73] he must have known that there was little chance of this actually happening. What then was his purpose? No doubt he and his colleagues were concerned by the danger of Fenian interference in disaffected Ireland. Palmerston, at least, thought it necessary to urge the Queen to send the Prince of Wales to Dublin to encourage the loyal elements of the island's population,[74] but the British government's diplomatic interest in the Brotherhood was probably a little less straightforward.

In February, 1865, the Confederacy was evidently in its death throes, but that offered little comfort to the British government. The Civil War had been accompanied by an unfortunate deterioration in Anglo-American relations which left the Americans with a list of grievances, real and imaginary, extending from the British Proclamation of Neutrality to the St. Albans raid. Once the war was over, it was not unreasonable to assume that the American government would raise these issues and press them with a vigor and persistence it had been unable or had considered inexpedient to exhibit earlier. Rather than sit back and wait for the inevitable chal-

[73] Russell to Burnley, February 25, 1865, FO, 5/1334.
[74] G. E. Buckle, ed., *Letters of Queen Victoria*, 2d ser. (London, 1926), I, 250–251, Palmerston to Queen Victoria, February 17, 1865.

lenge, Russell, operating no doubt on the familiar premise that attack is the best form of defense, attempted to dictate both the time and the weapons of the duel. In short, the heart of his note was a highly unfavorable comparison of the American government's toleration of Fenian activities and the "sincere" efforts of the British government to control those of Confederate agents in British territory. With heavy sarcasm the Foreign Secretary observed:

The accounts given in the Public papers of what passed in public meetings held in the United States . . . must surely have attracted the attention of the Government of the United States, and Her Majesty's Government might reasonably have expected that while the Government of the United States so loudly protest against the proceedings of the Confederate agents in this country; which are conducted with the utmost secrecy, and imputed blame to the British Government for not having put a stop to practices of which they had no previous knowledge and for not exerting powers beyond the law, the Government of the United States should at least have signified their disapprobation of such hostile declarations against the peace and security of the Queen's Dominions.[75]

It was evident, as the American Minister to Britain reported to the Secretary of State later in the year, that "the fact that this movement was stimulated from the United States seems to be eagerly seized in order to raise an offset to proceedings on this side during the late war." [76] This British strategy soon proved to be a dismal failure.

William H. Seward, the Secretary of State, was too "wise" a "macaw" to be drawn into the kind of correspondence Russell was seeking to open. With respect to the conduct of

[75] Russell to Burnley, February 25, 1865, FO, 5/1334.
[76] Adams to Seward, October 5, 1865, Charles Francis Adams Papers, Massachusetts Historical Society, Boston.

civil and military officials and his government's laissez-faire attitude toward Fenianism, he invoked the Constitution, as was only to be expected. Not content with this, however, for he could be as acidulous in his tone as anyone, he grasped the opportunity Russell's protest had created to express the prevailing American bitterness against Britain. He suggested, with a sarcastic allusion to the depredations of British-built Confederate commerce raiders and the St. Albans affair, that no grounds would ever arise for interference with the Fenians "unless renewed and systematic aggressions from British ports and provinces shall defeat all attempts to maintain and preserve peace with Great Britain." Finally, and most significantly, he carefully refused to be drawn into any comparative discussion of Fenianism and American grievances against Britain. Having expressed his intention to ignore the suggestion in Russell's note that toleration of Fenianism reflected American hostility toward Britain, he concluded:

I pass over in the same manner the allusion which you have made to the many well founded complaints which this Government had heretofore presented on aggressions committed by British subjects against the peace and sovereignty of the United States. This Government could not consent to weaken these complaints by entering, although even more directly invited, into an argument of recrimination.[77]

Obviously, Seward was going to press the American case at a time of his own choosing and had no intention of permitting the British to entangle Fenianism with the problems that had arisen during the war. Frustrated, the British were compelled to search for a new policy on Fenianism. The sharpness of the

[77] Seward to Burnley, March 20, 1865, Department of State, General Records, *Notes to Foreign Legations: Great Britain*, National Archives Microfilm Publications, vol. 99, reel 42 (NA/M99/42).

exchange between Russell and Seward suggested that additional diplomatic sorties, at least public ones, would achieve little except a further exacerbation of Anglo-American relations. This, in turn, might lead to the rupture that Irish nationalists would welcome as the harbinger of independence. Therefore, if the dangerously hostile Americans were to be mollified, and the Fenians controlled and their disruptive potential nullified, a new approach to this problem was needed.

2

The Policy of Sir Frederick Bruce

American hostility toward Britain was an indisputable fact in 1865. Many Unionists had been dismayed and antagonized by the attitude of much of the English press during the Civil War. The principal offender was the London *Times*, which for four years "taught the people of England to believe that the rebel Confederacy was a permanent and indestructible political fabric."[1] Indeed, as a result of the activities of a rabidly pro-Southern correspondent, Francis Lawley, it became a vehicle for Confederate propaganda. This was the root of the Northern complaint. To have believed in the Confederacy's ability to survive was in itself no more than a misdemeanor, but for many Americans the *Times* was guilty of the high crime of persistent misrepresentation, which could only have sprung "from a wicked animus."[2] The same animus had also guided the conduct of the British government, or so Unionists believed. British recognition of the belligerent rights of the rebels, they complained, had been extended with indecent haste. During the *Trent* affair the British Ministers

---

[1] *New York Times*, March 17, 1865.   [2] *Ibid.*, March 28.

had attempted to incite war fever against the United States, and when this failed, some of them had periodically denounced the efforts to subdue the Confederacy as a lust for empire which could only result in a "useless effusion of blood." Finally, the British government had neglected to take timely and effectual measures to prevent the building and fitting-out in England of destructive Confederate commerce raiders, such as the *Alabama*. All in all, this interpretation of the events drew from the *New York Times* the understandably acerbic comment: "The language and conduct of the British Ministry were expressly adapted to aid and comfort a rebellion which was striking at our national life." [3]

In Britain, knowledge of the depth of American bitterness pinched many an exposed nerve in 1865 and left the British, who by tradition and of necessity faced Europe, looking apprehensively over their shoulder. Their uneasiness was reflected in parliamentary and newspaper debates on the defenselessness of Canada and the probability of war with the United States once the Civil War was over. [4] This concern was shared by the Palmerston Cabinet, the majority of whom rejected on this ground Gladstone's proposals to cut government costs by not undertaking the construction of fortifications at Quebec and by paring five thousand men from the ranks of the Navy. Describing his colleague as "troublesome and wrong headed" again, Palmerston informed the Queen that the rest of her ministers were alive

to the very hostile spirit towards England which pervades all classes in the Federal States; and looking to the probability that, whenever the Civil War in America shall be ended, the Northern States will make demands upon England which cannot be complied with, and will either make war against England or make

[3] *Ibid.*, May 20.   [4] *Ibid.*, April 20.

inroads into your Majesty's North American possessions which would lead to war; and it is felt by the majority of the Cabinet that the best security against a conflict with the United States will be found in an adequate defensive force.[5]

Victoria herself was equally pessimistic; commenting upon the situation in her journal on February 12, she wrote, "Talked of America and the danger, which seems approaching, of our having a war with her, as soon as she makes peace," and "of the impossibility of our being able to hold Canada, but we must struggle for it."[6]

If the conduct of the British during the war was painted uniformly black in the victorious North, that of their inveterate enemy, Irish-America, was more checkered. Thus the moderate Irish support for the Confederacy and Irish leadership of the New York draft riots had been offset by massive participation in the Union armies. More than 140,000 Irish-Americans fought to preserve the Union, and the Irish Brigade boasted "an extensive and gallant record having shared in the glory of every engagement fought by the Army of the Potomac."[7] Decimated on the bloody slopes of Fredericksburg, it had still provided troops to help repulse Pickett's equally glorious and equally futile charge at Gettysburg. Here, then, was a record of service and sacrifice sufficient to ensure that in the aftermath of the war the British would not derive any aid and comfort from native American dislike of Irish-American nationalism. In 1865 it was as difficult to question the attachment of the vast majority of "Yankee Irish" to

[5] Buckle, ed., *Letters of Queen Victoria*, I, 248–249, Palmerston to Queen Victoria, January 20, 1865.

[6] *Ibid.*, p. 250, Queen's Journal, February 12, 1865.

[7] *New York Times*, January 20, 1865; Wittke, *Irish in America*, pp. 135–149; Gibson, *The Attitudes of the New York Irish*, pp. 111–173.

their adopted country as it was to doubt that they and native Americans would be bound by a common hatred of Britain. For Americans, Fenian assaults upon British territory appeared appropriate retribution for some of the wartime incidents. Thus, during a Fenian invasion scare in Canada, the *New York Tribune* gave vent to a popular sentiment when it gloated: "Our Canadian neighbours have an opportunity of appreciating the conditions of America a year or two ago, when they permitted bands of Rebel robbers to ride across the border and sack American towns." [8] Unpleasant as they considered this attitude to be, far more alarming for the British was the specter raised by the *New York Times*. "Weak as this Fenian movement is," it commented, "we say to-day, unhesitantly, that it needs from America but the same support which the Southern rebellion received from England to give it force that would rock the British kingdom to its foundations." [9] While such threats were never intended to be taken seriously, the humor was lost upon the uneasy British.

As early as January 9, 1865, Edward Archibald, in a dispatch to Lord Russell, had suggested some of the likely consequences of a blending of Fenianism and the anglophobia that was general throughout the Union States. Indeed he warned the Foreign Secretary that "any proceedings which the Fenians may adopt for drilling men—raising money and procuring arms, with a view to [action] . . . in Canada and Ireland, will, there is too much reason to fear, be allowed to take place with an indifference on the part of the local authorities and with the undisguised approbation of a large portion of the American people." [10] More important, however, was the attitude of the federal government, something Archibald found difficult to gauge at this time. But within a few weeks the London *Times* had published a report from an American correspondent which drew the attention of the newspaper's readers to Fenian boasts that among their sympathizers and financial supporters was William H. Seward. This item of news did not escape the attention of several Members of Parliament. The report prompted a question in the House, in answer to which the Foreign Office drew up a memorandum detailing the Secretary of State's past association with the Irish cause. Nevertheless, the British succumbed too readily to cynicism when they attributed this relationship solely to Seward's political ambition.[11]

He had visited Ireland briefly during a hectic trip to Europe in 1833 and had been struck by the miserable plight of the nation. The more obvious marks of the suppression of Irish nationality, such as the conversion of the Parliament into a bank, "its spacious halls now filled with money changers," [12] made a lasting impression on him. Thus it was as a personal sympathizer as well as a politician that Seward appeared as a guest speaker during St. Patrick's Day celebrations in the United States and at meetings to agitate for the repeal of the Act of Union which had united Ireland and England under one parliament in 1800. There seems little reason to challenge his sincerity when he pleaded guilty to the charge of being a repealer. "I ask for Ireland a parliament, a free parliament—a parliament which shall be her own parliament. I ask for her people free and equal suffrage in the choice of representatives in that parliament." [13] Nor was Seward surprised or unduly alarmed when their experience with liberty in the United States strengthened the sympathy of Irish-Americans for their

[11] Foreign Office memorandum, April 7, *ibid.*
[12] George E. Baker, ed., *The Works of William H. Seward* (New York, 1853–1884) III, 221.   [13] *Ibid.*, p. 279.

brethren in Ireland.[14] On those occasions when the American experience proved less inspirational or worthy of emulation he was not found wanting. Quick to denounce nativism in all its garbs, he appeared at a repeal meeting during the summer of 1844 to castigate the Philadelphia rioters whose violence had been aimed principally at the Irish. At a time when there were no more than 400,000 Irish-Americans, even if a fifth of them were to be found in Seward's own state of New York, it required political courage to challenge so unequivocally the swelling ranks of the nativist movement. Perhaps there was more than a grain of truth in Charles Sumner's later description of the Secretary of State as "rash and visionary with a wonderful want of commonsense." [15] Of course, Sumner could just as well have been describing himself.

Despite the evidence to the contrary, the British continued to cling to their one-dimensional view of Seward's relations with the Irish. They remained convinced that he was motivated entirely by political ambition. His concern for Irish votes explained his indirect support for the Irish Republican Union in 1848, they argued. The Union was no more than a precursor of the Fenian Brotherhood, for it advocated revolution in Ireland and raids into Canada; the British tied Seward to this organization through the person of Horace Greeley.[16] The "able but queer" [17] editor of the *New York Tribune* had combined with Seward and Thurlow Weed, the future Secretary of State's political mentor, not only to found a Whig organ—*The Jeffersonian*—in 1838 but ultimately to dominate

[14] *Ibid.*, p. 230.
[15] Sumner to John Bright, May 2, 1865, John Bright Papers, British Museum, London.
[16] Foreign Office memorandum, April 7, 1865, FO, 5/1334.
[17] Earl Schenck Miers, *The Great Rebellion: The Emergence of the American Conscience from Sumter to Appomattox* (New York, 1961), p. 46.

that party in New York. Thus his conspicuous support for the Irish cause, the British felt sure, had been designed to advance Seward's senatorial ambitions. Yet the filling of the senatorial vacancy in New York in March, 1849, was the work of the state legislature not the electorate, and Seward was not the only aspirant. In short, the British did Greeley an injustice when they attributed his concern for Ireland to the exigencies of domestic politics. Much the same could be said of their interpretation of Seward's conduct. Undoubtedly, as the volume of Irish immigration increased dramatically at mid-century, the thought of political advantage was never banished from his mind, but it was not an exclusive consideration. However, perhaps it was as well for their own peace of mind in 1865 that the British failed to plumb the full depth of the Secretary of State's compassion for Irish national aspirations. They would have derived little comfort from this knowledge at a time when they were already concerned about his general attitude toward Britain.

Seward's relations with the British government, in his capacity as Secretary of State, had been hampered from the first by the mistrust born of his cumbersome attempt at humor during the visit of the Prince of Wales to the United States in 1860. During a conversation with the Duke of Newcastle, who accompanied the royal visitor, Seward apparently remarked that if he became Secretary of State it would "become my duty to insult England, and I mean to do so." [18] Accepted at face value, the memory of this comment no doubt played its part in shaping the British response to his subsequent appointment. Lord Lyons, the British Minister to the United States, wrote home that Seward would be a dangerous man, prepared to seek domestic popularity "by displaying violence

[18] Ephraim Douglass Adams, *Great Britain and the American Civil War* (London, 1925), I, 80.

towards us." [19] This opinion was shared by Lords Palmerston and Russell, both of whom had entertained the American during his visit to England in 1859. Slowly, however, as they received more encouraging reports from their diplomatic representatives in the United States and their confidence grew in Charles Francis Adams, whose appointment as Minister to Britain Seward had insisted upon, the British ceased to regard the Secretary of State as a warmonger. Yet he still excited distrust because he was so difficult to classify. Lord Clarendon, soon to succeed Russell at the Foreign Office, complained privately that he could not decide whether the American was a lukewarm friend of England or a covert enemy. Eventually he concluded that Seward was an opportunist, bending with every breeze of public opinion.[20] Against the background of widespread American hostility toward Britain, there was little comfort for the British here.

In April, 1865, therefore, it seemed that the British had good cause to be uneasy about their relations with the United States. Although alarmist fears of a war had quickly subsided, the depth of American bitterness promised to prevent any escape from the abrasive and costly consequences of the defects in British neutrality and to encourage the growth of Fenianism. The American correspondent of the London *Times* must have surprised few of its subscribers when he reported that the Fenians believed "themselves strengthened by this general indeed universal encouragement." [21] Nor could there be any doubt that the end of the war had provided the Fenians with the means to pursue their ambition. Thousands of Irish-Americans, many indoctrinated with Fenianism and

[19] Glyndon G. Van Deusen, *William Henry Seward* (New York, 1967), p. 293.
[20] Clarendon to Bruce, February 24, 1866, Clarendon Papers, Bodleian Library, Oxford.   [21] September 30, 1865.

all trained in the arts of warfare, would soon be seeking alternative employment.

This state of affairs lifted the Fenian movement, or so the editor of *The Nation*, E. L. Godkin, insisted, "from the position of a little whiskey stained conspiracy in a Chatham Street grog shop into the ranks of a formidable association." [22] Undoubtedly, this was an incomplete analysis of the looming significance of the Brotherhood, but the possibility of a Fenian army being raised was a very serious development. Equally important in this respect were the consequences of the American government's decision to remove the restrictions they had imposed during the war on the purchase and exportation of munitions. No powers of clairvoyance were required to predict, as Archibald did, that arms would now be obtainable in large quantities and at low cost. [23] Thus the end of the Civil War found the Fenians in a position to staff and equip an army of liberation and in a favorable climate of opinion in which to mature their plans. Always inveterate enemies of the British, the Irish-Americans were about to become formidable ones.

The disturbed nature of their relations with the United States, of which the danger of Fenianism was but one aspect, impressed the British with the need for conciliatory overtures. The assassination of President Lincoln was grasped as one opportunity. Russell wrote to Queen Victoria suggesting that "a very good effect will be produced in conciliating the feelings of the United States if your Majesty would deign to write to Mrs. Lincoln privately, condoling her on her bereavement." [24] The Queen responded enthusiastically, anx-

[22] William M. Armstrong, *E. L. Godkin and American Foreign Policy, 1865–1900* (New York, 1957), p. 108.
[23] Archibald to Russell, May 5, 1865, FO, 5/1334.
[24] Buckle, *Letters of Queen Victoria*, I, 265, Russell to Queen Victoria, April 27, 1865.

ious as she was to pay tribute once again to the virtues of "dearest Albert," to play her part in preserving peace, and to "pour balm into wounded hearts." [25] Yet another chance to conciliate the Americans had been presented by the vacancy at the British Legation in Washington. Lord Lyons had returned to England in 1864, leaving affairs in the hands of a chargé d'affaires. In February, 1865, the appointment of Sir Frederick Bruce was announced. His selection was intended to be, and was interpreted by the Americans as, a conciliatory step. Indeed, for Charles Francis Adams it "marked the disposition of this Government to maintain friendly relations with us." [26]

An experienced diplomat, the new Minister had been attached to the Ashburton commission in 1842, had served as Lieutenant-Governor of Newfoundland, and had held a wide range of diplomatic posts in South America and Egypt. In 1857 he had accompanied his elder brother, Lord Elgin, to China when the former Governor-General of Canada was appointed Ambassador Extraordinary. Quickly promoted from his original position as his brother's principal secretary to that of Envoy Extraordinary and Minister Plenipotentiary, in 1860 Bruce added Superintendent of British Trade to this already impressive list of titles. He established an excellent relationship with his American counterpart, Anson Burlingame, and soon won the gratitude of the United States. His refusal to grant British registers to Confederate vessels in Asian waters denied the rebels the protection of British colors.[27] Thus, the new British Minister had much to recommend

[25] *Ibid.*, pp. 266–267, Queen Victoria to Mrs. Lincoln, April 29; Queen's Journal, April 29, 1865.

[26] Diary of Charles Francis Adams, February 28, 1865, Massachusetts Historical Society.

[27] Frederick W. Seward, *Reminiscences of a War-Time Statesman and Diplomat, 1830–1915* (New York, 1916), p. 380; Adams to Clarendon, December 28, 1865, Adams Papers.

him in American eyes, and the *New York Times*, well aware that it was regarded by the British as an administration organ, welcomed the appointment of a man who "may be expected to bring to his mission such requirements of character and such antecedents as will make that mission acceptable to the two Governments." [28]

Yet it would be naive to believe that the British government appointed such "a very amiable and excellent fellow" [29] merely to conciliate the Americans, important as that was in 1865. If Bruce was sent to woo the Americans, it was no doubt in the hope of persuading them to forego those demands for redress which stemmed from the imperfect enforcement of British neutrality during the Civil War. Formidable if not impossible as this diplomatic task already was, it was further complicated by the disruptive issue of Fenianism.

From the time he stepped ashore in the United States on April 7, 1865—appropriately enough from the steamer *China* —Bruce set to work to cultivate Seward. An indication of his success was a note Thurlow Weed received in September from the new Minister's erstwhile American colleague in China. "The British Minister, Sir Frederick Bruce," Burlingame wrote, "will be [in] . . . New York . . . where I hope you may make it convenient to meet him. He is sound on all questions and knows who are safe advisers. He believes in Mr. Seward and his friends." [30] Subsequently, there developed between Bruce and Seward a friendship founded upon mutual respect,[31] and this certainly helped to mitigate the international effects of Fenianism.

[28] March 14, 1865.
[29] Sumner to Bright, January 1, 1866, Bright Papers.
[30] Anson Burlingame to Weed, September, 1865, Thurlow Weed Papers, University of Rochester, Rochester, N.Y.
[31] Van Deusen, *William Henry Seward*, p. 497.

For a brief period after Bruce's arrival it seemed possible that the Fenians were already on the wane. Archibald, assuming an uncharacteristic and hence all the more reassuring air of optimism, forecast a division within the ranks of the Brotherhood and its formal condemnation by the Catholic Church, but he was premature on both counts. The schism did not occur until the end of the year, and Papal criticism was withheld until 1870. Meanwhile, the period of Fenian inactivity ended abruptly in August, and the British Minister was soon receiving reports of a prospective invasion of Canada. He immediately engaged more agents and informers, made arrangements to ensure that whatever information they reported was forwarded without delay to the Canadian authorities, and then called upon Seward. The American's reaction, however, was not very encouraging. In the informal atmosphere of an unofficial conversation, the Secretary did not hesitate to make it quite clear that the administration had no intention of jeopardizing its domestic position by opposing an organization that appealed to a significant band of Irish sympathizers and tapped the widespread hostility toward Britain [32] —certainly not as long as he and his supporters, such as Henry J. Raymond, editor of the *New York Times,* could persuade themselves that the Fenians were all "brag and bluster." [33]

Accepted by Bruce as an organ of the Johnson administration in general and Seward in particular, the conservative *Times* had first begun to take notice of the Fenians in July. Its initial reaction was one of resentment at the use of the territory of the United States to organize conspiracies against "friendly nations," but its fears that such activities would compromise the national character were tempered by the

[32] Bruce to Russell, August 8, 1865, FO, 5/1334.
[33] *New York Times,* July 26, 1865.

suspicion that the Fenian agitation was no more than Irish blarney. The *New York Times*, it seemed, hoped that the Brotherhood would quietly expire. Yet it remained sufficiently uncertain of this happy demise to attempt to hasten the end by deliberately advertising the hostility of important members of the American Catholic hierarchy. Similarly, it betrayed a certain measure of anxiety when it attacked the Irish, and the "demagogues" who pandered to them, for advocating war with England in retaliation for her conduct during the Civil War. Not content with this, it also conducted an inquiry into the motives of the Irish and reached the same conclusion that an earlier generation of conservatives at Hartford had, namely, that "the course of England is with them [the Irish] rather the excuse, than the real motive, of their hostility." [34] Having said all this, however, the *Times* was careful not to leave itself open to the charge of lacking sympathy for Ireland. It readily agreed that "the wrongs of Ireland are solemn realities which must some day be atoned for," but it continued to scorn liberating leagues of the Fenian variety as subjects of sport. [35]

If he failed to find the Fenians an object of fun, Sir Frederick Bruce did not agree either with the *New York Times*'s rather sanguine assessment of their political insignificance. Thus, in commenting on a report that Fenian strength had grown to two hundred thousand, the New York journal had observed: "One would think that such a body of men, consisting mostly of voters, would have in their power to exert a strong influence upon political parties and the government. Nothing of the kind shows itself." [36] Bruce differed sharply with the newspaper on this point, having emerged from his unofficial meeting with Seward in August understandably

[34] *Ibid.*, August 24, September 7.   [35] *Ibid.*, September 15.
[36] *Ibid.*, September 28.

convinced that the administration's inactivity was governed by the weight of Irish ballots. It was apparent, or so he reported to Lord Russell, that "the Irish party, owing to their compact organization, exercise, unfortunately for us, a powerful influence in American politics." [37] Just how powerful was indicated by the subsequent course of events.

The sudden elevation of Andrew Johnson to the presidency following the assassination of Lincoln had been greeted by some of the murdered President's erstwhile opponents as another example of the intervention of that divine providence that guides the affairs of the United States. Certainly, for those infuriated by Lincoln's expansive concept of executive powers and his stand on Reconstruction, the new President came as a godsend. His early statements, in which he disclaimed all thoughts of malice or revenge but declared "in the most forcible language that punishment must be visited upon the authors of the rebellion," [38] reassured some observers that he was "sound" on Reconstruction. This early enthusiasm began to wane after Johnson's own Reconstruction proclamations in May. The essential points of difference slowly emerging between the new President and the Radicals were enumerated as early as June 21 at a public meeting in Boston. The speakers, of whom Governor Andrew of Massachusetts was one, were generally agreed that Reconstruction was not the prerogative of one branch of the government but a joint function of the executive and legislative; that it was better to reconstruct the Union well rather than quickly; that all disloyal elements should be excluded from participation while no one should be excluded solely on grounds of race or color.[39] Ignoring these clear warnings of dissent, Johnson pressed on with his executive policy of haste and leniency, even extend-

[37] Bruce to Russell, August 8, 1865, FO, 5/1334.
[38] *New York Times*, April 20, 1865. [39] *Ibid.*, June 22.

ing it to prominent ex-Confederates. In fact it was apparent, at least to the correspondent of the London *Times*, that the President would continue on his course unless thwarted by the Radicals.[40] There was, of course, no foregone conclusion about the success of Radical opposition in the summer of 1865. For even if all Republicans who were vocal in their opposition to presidential Reconstruction were labeled Radicals, as indeed they were by British observers in 1865, they were still a minority within and without Congress and would remain so until Johnson pushed men of more moderate opinion into their arms. There were men like Horace Greeley, who, while they had not as yet made public their opposition to the President, called not only for amnesty but also for civil and political rights for the freedman.

One expression of the Radicals' displeasure with domestic developments, or so the British came to believe, was their unending assault upon the Secretary of State. Having lost the Republican nomination in 1860 partly as a result of an undeserved reputation for radicalism, Seward had quickly been identified as a luminary of the conservative faction after his appointment to the Lincoln Cabinet in 1861. Because he was considered laggard on emancipation and insufficiently thorough on the prosecution of the war by the Radicals, they attempted periodically to force his resignation but were always outmaneuvered by an artful President. With Lincoln's death, however, they fully expected a reorganization of the Cabinet that would include the dropping of Seward. Instead, he was retained and soon emerged as a strong supporter, and a very astute one,[41] of the new President's conservative Recon-

[40] *Ibid.*, July 10.

[41] John H. and LaWanda Cox, "Andrew Johnson and His Ghost Writers," *Mississippi Valley Historical Review*, XLVIII (December, 1961), 460–479.

struction policy. If frustrated by this turn of events, the Radicals remained fixed in their opposition to the Secretary and grasped every opportunity to embarrass him and the government he served.

It was evident from their attempt to magnify out of all proportion a report in the London *Times* that they would attempt to capitalize on any measure the administration adopted to check the Fenians. On September 19 the English newspaper alleged that Seward had provided the British authorities with information that had done much to ensure the stifling of Fenian activities in Ireland. The radical *New York Tribune*, its editor, Horace Greeley, having long since forsaken political alliance with Seward for inveterate opposition, and now slowly moving towards the Radicals as a result of Johnson's refusal to make the protection, let alone the enfranchisement of the freedman, a condition of Reconstruction, seized upon the report to berate the Secretary and the administration. Reminding its readers of British conduct during the Civil War, the *Tribune* caustically described the American government's Fenian policy "as one of heaping coals of fire upon the head of England." That country, it proclaimed, "was our greatest foe when we were in trouble; now when trouble threatens its possessions, we shall be its best friend." [42] Painful as such criticism was for Seward, it was mild in comparison to what he suffered at the hands of other Radicals. They denounced him as a British spy, some even going so far as to suggest that he had been paid for the information. [43] For Seward the most obvious way to counter such accusations was to deny the truth of the report on which they were based, and although, when asked publicly to do just this, he loftily replied, "I cannot depart from my habits of leaving my vindica-

[42] October 3, 1865.   [43] London *Times*, October 23, 1865.

tion against calumnies to an intelligent country and candid world,"[44] he went to some lengths to refute it. Thurlow Weed's *Albany Journal*, on which the Secretary's son and assistant, Frederick, had formerly been employed as an assistant editor, printed an authoritative contradiction.[45]

Meanwhile the administration at large took care to demonstrate a touching concern for Irish sensibilities. At the request of the Fenians, the President agreed to release John Mitchel from detention. He was an old Irish revolutionary who had won notoriety in the United States as a rabid Confederate. Johnson's incentive was implicit in the formal letter of thanks he received from a member of the Fenian convention then meeting in Philadelphia. "I have the honor of being delegated by the convention of Irish-American citizens," William Roberts wrote, "representing large social classes in thirty states and territories, to wait upon your excellency and express to you how deeply they feel the act of restoring to freedom a man who they love and venerate for his self sacrificing devotion to his native land."[46] The Fenians, it seemed, were growing self-conscious about their potential political power. Presumably it was no coincidence that their request for Mitchel's release was granted shortly before state elections in New York, for these promised to be of national significance. With Congress soon to assemble, the administration considered it important that the President's Reconstruction policy receive an electoral endorsement. Consequently, Johnson's conduct since succeeding Lincoln became a campaign issue in New York, albeit a somewhat confused one following an an-

[44] *Ibid.*, November 2.

[45] Bruce to Russell, October 17, 1865, FO, 5/1335.

[46] D. Appleton, ed., *American Annual Cyclopedia and Register of Important Events, 1865* (New York, 1866), p. 334.

nouncement of support for the President by the Democrats as well as the Seward dominated Union Republicans.[47]

Bruce had long predicted this involvement of the Fenians in the domestic politics of the United States and had speculated on the probable diplomatic consequences. He thought it likely that the Johnson administration would refuse to cooperate with the British against the Fenians. Such a refusal, in short, a policy of noninterference, might draw Irish-American political support to the administration and would certainly deny its opponents ammunition for further attacks. Confronted by this likelihood, the British Minister responded with a sophisticated policy. Obviously, it was crucial that he be well informed of Fenian activities; therefore he organized a more effective intelligence system. The specific information he now expected to derive from his network of informers he intended to lay before the American government in a manner that would "induce them to discourage these enterprises underhand, unless they are prepared to face the eventualities of a rupture." In return for not embarrassing the administration by presenting his evidence in an official dispatch and for confining himself to unofficial notes and conversations, Bruce evidently expected the government discreetly to restrain the Fenians. Failure to do so would clearly fasten upon the Americans the entire responsibility for any invasion of British territory and any subsequent rupture of relations.[48]

Here, then, was a policy well adapted to the needs of the British and the prevailing conditions of American politics. Bruce reasoned, cogently enough, that formal protests were futile. An official correspondence would attract publicity

[47] LaWanda and John H. Cox, *Politics, Principle and Prejudice, 1865–1866* (New York, 1963), pp. 68–87.
[48] Bruce to Russell, August 8, 1865, FO, 5/1334.

which might very well dissuade the American government from taking action against the Fenians. If left unhindered, the Brotherhood might embark upon adventures detrimental to Anglo-American relations. On the other hand, unofficial approaches would permit the Johnson administration to move quietly and carefully, and if overt anti-Fenian measures were required, they could be adopted without fear that they would be interpreted as concessions to British pressure—1865 was no time to be accused of friendship for or fear of Britain. If Bruce's policy was the one most likely to secure for the British what they wanted with respect to Fenianism, it had been formulated with an eye to other advantages as well. If the British Minister had been governed in part by a desire not to rock the American government's boat, his motives were more complex than a determination to frustrate the Fenians. He had "larger considerations" for working with rather than against Johnson and Seward, and these he defined when forced to defend his policy from Canadian attacks.

During September the Canadian authorities were deluged with reports of alleged Fenian preparations for a raid on the colony.[49] With the Governor, Lord Monck, away in England on leave, Sir John Michel, the Commander of the British military forces, was serving as his deputy. Michel's response to the reports was that of a military man. Sure that no more than five thousand Fenians could wreak considerable damage if they advanced simultaneously at several points along the colony's defenceless frontier, he lent a willing ear to those advis-

---

[49] Archibald to Monck, September 16, 1865, Archibald Papers, Public Archives of Canada (PAC), Ottawa; McMicken to Macdonald, September 25, 1865, Sir John A. Macdonald Papers, PAC. Gerald McMicken was a Stipendiary Magistrate appointed to head a special Canadian intelligence force, formed to keep the government abreast of Fenian activities.

ers who suggested an official correspondence with the United States. They reasoned, no doubt, that after a formal warning the American government would be unable to avoid taking whatever measures were necessary to frustrate the Fenians. Therefore Michel wrote to Bruce asking him to raise the matter of Fenian activities with Seward and to raise it officially.[50]

Instead of acceding to this request, the British Minister continued to follow the course he had already charted for himself. He certainly mentioned the fears of the colonial authorities to Seward, but during an unofficial conversation. For his part, Seward offered the opinion that the Fenian affair had been exaggerated and that "nothing would seem to give it importance than that it should become the subject of an official correspondence." While less phlegmatic than the Secretary, whose response after all was that of a politician whose anxiety to shirk a potentially unpleasant domestic and international issue had persuaded him to place his faith in the efficacy of procrastination, Bruce, without the specific information he needed to force Seward to act, had to be satisfied with this. If the alternatives at this point, he wrote in an explanatory dispatch to Lord Russell, were to do nothing or to protest officially, there was really no choice. A demand for a formal declaration by the American government against Fenianism was unlikely to solve anything. Even if it could be extracted from Seward, which was by no means certain, the same domestic political pressures that had driven him to refute the report in the London *Times* might now persuade him to accompany any declaration "with some expression of sympathy with the national aspirations which underlies the movement, rather than lose for his party the support of the Irish

---

[50] Bruce to Russell, October 31, 1865, FO, 5/1335.

vote at this critical moment." [51] The critical moment was polling day in New York, no more than a week away when Bruce wrote on October 31. Had Seward issued such a statement of sympathy, which would not have been an inaccurate reflection of his personal sentiments, the Fenians might well have interpreted it as an endorsement of their cause. Such encouragement would certainly have increased the danger of a crisis with England.

There was another critical moment approaching, however, and its significance for Britain had not escaped the alert Bruce. By the last days of October, presidential Reconstruction was almost complete, and while opposition had emerged and was still gathering force, there remained a possibility of Congress accepting the *fait accompli* when it assembled in December. For Bruce the speedy readmission of the Southern states and the return of their representatives to the national legislature would be doubly welcome. Reconstruction would be followed, he was sure, by the revival of the ante-bellum political alliance between the South and the West—a development of profound importance for his nation. Such an alliance held out the prospect of a more effective check upon the Fenians. He had been assured by no less a personage than Postmaster-General Dennison of the West's lack of interest in Fenianism. Thus he looked forward to its representatives and those of the South combining to restrain the belligerent elements of the North who were currently encouraging the Irish-American nationalists. The primary concern of these belligerent elements, however, was the unpaid war bills, particularly the account for the depredations committed by the *Alabama*. Yet the British might even escape these, Bruce thought, if the Union was speedily reconstructed. It "is hardly to be sup-

[51] *Ibid.*

posed," he wrote to Lord Russell, "that the Southern members . . . will support violent proceedings against England founded on her recognition of them as belligerents and on the doings of their vessels of war." [52]

The removal of the threat of the United States supporting her demands for redress with violent action would certainly have eased British resistance to those demands. The British government could have intervened in European affairs safe in the knowledge that there was no chance of the United States taking advantage of their involvement. They would have escaped the embarrassment to which Lord Clarendon gave expression when he wrote to Queen Victoria, against the background of increasing tension between Austria and Prussia: "In the present state of Ireland, and the menacing aspect of our relations with the United States, the military and pecuniary resources of England must be husbanded with the utmost care." [53] It was no coincidence that the British initiated the negotiations that led to the Treaty of Washington during another period of crisis in Europe. All this *might* have been different if those Southerners returned to Congress under the program of presidential Reconstruction had been admitted, and their admission was the hope Bruce could still hold out in October, 1865. Consequently he argued that it was inexpedient to risk embarrassing the President or the Secretary of State by raising the Fenian problem in a manner that might attract publicity. Bruce was particularly anxious not to jeopardize Seward's position further at a time when he was already under attack by the Radicals. The Secretary's attraction for the British Minister was his strong support of Andrew Johnson's Reconstruction policy and his success in persuading

[52] *Ibid.*

[53] Buckle, *Letters of Queen Victoria*, I, 315, Clarendon to Queen Victoria, March 31, 1865.

the Englishman of his peaceful attitude toward all Anglo-American problems.[54]

Having conceived this elaborate diplomatic strategy, Bruce undoubtedly expected the support of the home government. When he wrote to Russell stating his intention to confine himself "to communicating in a private and friendly manner" any specific information he obtained which appeared to call for vigilance on the part of the United States government, it was only as a formality that the Minister added "unless otherwise instructed." [55] These words were not intended to be interpreted literally, a fact that was evident from his response to the instructions he soon received from London ordering him to accede to the Canadian request for an official correspondence with the United States on the subject of Fenianism. Unknown to Bruce, a reorganization of the British government had placed his diplomacy in jeopardy.

On October 18, just two days before he completed his eighty-first year, Lord Palmerston died. He was succeeded by Lord Russell as Prime Minister, Lord Clarendon returned to the now vacant Foreign Office, and Gladstone assumed the duties of Leader of the House. Although little more than a reshuffling of familiar cards, it was widely believed that it would strengthen the hand of "the friends of a pacific and reasonable policy" toward the United States.[56] The *New York Times* was moved to conclude that it would facilitate a peaceful arrangement of Anglo-American difficulties, but it was a gross oversimplification to attribute, as this American newspaper did, all the serious disputes of the preceding quarter of a century to the late Prime Minister's brinkman-

[54] Bruce to Russell, October 31, 1865, FO, 5/1335.   [55] *Ibid.*
[56] "Bright-Sumner Letters," *Proceedings of the Massachusetts Historical Society*, XLVI (October, 1912), 148, Bright to Sumner, October 20, 1865.

ship.[57] Nor was there any reasonable ground for the belief that
Russell's position on the *Alabama* claims would soften with
his elevation to the foremost position in the government. As
for the new Foreign Secretary, although he was thought to be
"conciliatory to other powers,"[58] he had very definite opinions on the state of Anglo-American relations.

As he soon informed Bruce, Lord Clarendon looked upon
the Irish-Americans, whose "vote and interest are best obtained by unscrupulous abuse of England," as one of the two
primary obstacles to good relations with the United States.[59]
As for the Fenians, the fact that they had been permitted to
establish all the paraphernalia of a government in exile in an
American city, even though their announced purpose was to
subvert the territories of a friendly nation, he found almost
unbelievable. "This must surely be looked upon by the Government of the United States," he wrote, "as a proceeding not
only unheard of in the history of the world, but one incompatible with the dignity of the United States and with their
international obligations towards Great Britain."[60] However,
if the Irish, both as a result of their own activities and of the
willingness of American politicians to pander to them, were
one impediment to amicable relations with the United States,
Clarendon regarded the press on both sides of the Atlantic as
another. Unlike Palmerston he did not fuse these two malign
influences. The late Prime Minister had on at least one occasion indicted the press in the Northern states for the sorry
condition of Anglo-American relations. He attributed the

[57] *New York Times,* November 1, 1865.
[58] Buckle, *Letters of Queen Victoria,* I, 280, Queen Victoria to the
King of the Belgians, October 25, 1865.
[59] Clarendon to Bruce, November 25, 1865, Clarendon Papers,
Bodleian Library.
[60] Clarendon to Bruce, November 16, 1865, FO, 5/1335.

hostility of the American newspapers to the anglophobia of the Irish who he believed ran and staffed them.[61]

Clarendon was no stranger to Irish-American nationalism —he had been Lord-Lieutenant of Ireland in 1848 and Foreign Secretary during the brief diplomatic heyday of the Massachusetts Irish Emigrant Aid Society in 1855—but concerned as he was about the Fenians, his initial response to the news that Bruce had rejected the Canadian request for an official correspondence with the United States was to countermand it. Informed by the Colonial Office of the Minister's decision, he wrote on November 7, "I have to instruct you to call the attention of the Government of the United States to the intended raid into Canada of a force armed and organized in the territory of the United States." [62] However, when he received Bruce's dispatch of October 31, detailing the advantages to be secured from a less overt policy, the Foreign Secretary moderated his position somewhat. On November 16 he wrote to inform the Minister that he would not be required, "at all events for the present," to make official representations to the United States.[63]

Although this proviso was accompanied by a flattering expression of the home government's continuing confidence in the Minister, to whose discretion they left the manner of dealing with this problem in his communications with the American authorities, it was clear that the policy of Sir Frederick Bruce had been given no more than a conditional reprieve. "If proper precautions can be taken against the invasion of Canada by private and unofficial remonstrance," Clarendon wrote, "we have no wish to make a public flare up." [64] Natural as this reservation was, the tone of the instructions left no

[61] Herbert C. F. Bell, *Lord Palmerston* (London, 1936), II, 295.
[62] Clarendon to Bruce, November 7, 1865, FO, 5/1335.
[63] *Ibid.*, November 16.   [64] *Ibid.*, November 23.

doubt that the Foreign Secretary was authorizing the Minister to remonstrate officially as soon as it was necessary, and that he thought that moment was near. Therefore, Bruce's firm response to the instructions he received from London, which arrived at a time when he was already under severe pressure from Canada to be more demonstrative, illustrated his determination to exercise to the full his discretionary powers as a Minister.

Throughout October the colonial authorities in British North America had continued to receive reports of Fenian preparations for a raid on Canada. They responded to this danger with a variety of measures which ranged from the calling out of the militia and the alerting of British regulars to the removal of railway rolling stock from exposed positions near the border. Plans were also drawn up to render the railroad tracks unusable.[65] Undoubtedly these preparations would have impeded any Fenian advance, but it was far more desirable that a raid should be prevented from occurring, and that could only be guaranteed by the government of the United States. As a result, the colonial authorities were anxious to secure from the Americans a formal declaration of their intention to frustrate Fenian filibusters.

Canadian concern over the vigilance of the United States would not have been reduced had they, like Bruce, looked to the *New York Times* for an indication of the administration's attitude. In an editorial on November 9 the newspaper seized upon the colonial uneasiness about Fenianism, the abrogation of the Reciprocity Treaty, and the generally unhappy state of Anglo-American relations, to raise once again the specter of annexation. "We leave our colonial friends to draw their own

[65] Macdonald to C. J. Brydges (head of the Grand Trunk Railway), November 14, 1865, Macdonald Papers. Similar instructions were sent to the head of the Ottawa and Prescott Railway.

conclusions from the undeniable facts," it commented. "It is manifest that their great troubles, during more than half a century, have grown out of their present political dependence on a distant Power, which has unreservedly confessed its desire not to perpetuate the connection." Independence, which the *Times* was transparently encouraging, was viewed by many Americans of expansionist but pacific predilections, as was Seward, as the first step toward peaceful annexation. Had the members of the Canadian government been advised at this time by Bruce, as later they were, to subscribe to the New York newspaper on the grounds that it was an authoritative expression of Seward's policy,[66] they might justifiably have suspected that the American was going to unleash the Fenians as a means of impressing them with the need for independence. After all, the attraction of Canada for the Fenians was the British connection.

As it was, much of the Canadian irritation was directed against Bruce. In a letter to John A. Macdonald, Prime Minister of the colony, Dennis Godley, the Governor General's Secretary, commented:

Mr. Seward applied to this government on the vaguest rumours last winter, and we immediately made the strictest enquiries as to their truth. I think things have come to that pass that we are entitled to know what Sir Frederick Bruce is doing or not doing . . . and we should take care that the United States Government does not evade the responsibility for want of due warning on our part. If Lord Lyons had been at Washington now, I have no doubt that we should have had intelligence long before this of the intentions of the United States Government.[67]

[66] Bruce to Monck, June 15, 1866, Carnarvon Papers, Public Record Office.

[67] Godley to Macdonald, [?], 1865, Macdonald Papers.

Seeking an answer to these questions, Sir John Michel, who was still acting as Governor, telegraphed Bruce on November 18. Two days later, having received no word from Washington, he cabled again brusquely requesting a reply. When at last it arrived, on November 23, Bruce's personal expressions of confidence in the vigilance of the American government could not disguise the fact that he "had not procured any authoritative announcement from the President of his determination to perform his constitutional obligations, and to prevent the territory of the United States being made the base for hostile preparations directed against this Province" [68]—news that was relayed immediately to London.

Clarendon learned of Bruce's latest rebuff of the Canadians at a time when Archibald, the consul at New York, was advocating, certainly by implication, a more demonstrative British policy. It would seem, Archibald wrote to the Foreign Secretary, "as if the time had arrived when some action should be taken by the Government of the United States to proclaim the illegality as well as to repress the effort of the Fenian demonstrations against the territory of a friendly power." [69] Presumably the moment had also arrived for Clarendon to instruct Bruce to remonstrate officially against the continuance of Fenian activities. Yet it was obvious, even from the formal instructions he sent the Minister, which were forwarded to the Colonial Office and were evidently designed to soothe the Canadians, that the Foreign Secretary was not going to insist upon a more overt policy. "I have to state to you," he wrote, "that whether you obtain the required information unofficially or otherwise, Her Majesty's Government desire to be accurately informed, and also that the officers administering the Government of Canada should be equally

[68] Michel to Cardwell, November 25, 1865, FO, 5/1335.
[69] Archibald to Clarendon, November 29, *ibid.*

informed, whether proper precautions are taken by the United States Government to prevent Fenian raids into Canada." [70] Moreover, in his private correspondence with Bruce, Clarendon was effusive in his support for the Minister's policy. "I entirely agree with you," he wrote in a private note that accompained the official dispatch, "upon the *modus operandi* that you have hitherto adopted and I can only repeat that we wish you to act upon your own judgement and discretion with reference to the temper of the Government and people and the circumstances of the time of all which you must be a more competent judge than the Government at home can pretend to be." [71] This attitude was a far cry from that of November 7. What had happened in the interim to mollify the Foreign Secretary and transfer the direction of British policy from London to the Legation in Washington?

In truth it was Bruce rather than Clarendon who had been mollified. He had accepted the position of Minister to the United States on the condition that he be permitted to exercise his initiative, and he was prepared to be removed rather than surrender his independence. Thus, once confronted by the danger of being countermanded, he had offered his own government the choice of following the course he had suggested on Fenianism or withdrawing him from his post. [72] For a British government already uneasy about its relations with the United States, the consequences of removing a man whose appointment had been greeted as a mark of conciliation, and

[70] Clarendon to Bruce, December 16, 1865, Colonial Office (CO), ser. 537, Vol. 96, Public Record Office.

[71] Clarendon to Bruce, December 16, 1865, Clarendon Papers, Bodleian Library.

[72] Adams, Diary, May 25, 1866. Adams derived this information from Bruce's secretary, Thurloe, then in England on leave, and it was confirmed by the opponents of the British government's policy, who privately blamed Bruce for its continuation.

who had succeeded in establishing a friendly relationship with the American Secretary of State, were not appealing. In short, they could ill afford to lose Bruce. However, acceptance of his policy, both in Britain and Canada, was also eased by the subsequent course of events. Thus although opposition to presidential Reconstruction soon emerged when Congress assembled in December, and this obviously jeopardized Bruce's larger considerations, the contest was not decided; hence the considerations were not lost until the spring of 1866. Meanwhile, the Minister's decision not to discuss the Fenians officially with Seward was seemingly vindicated not only by his apparent success in persuading the Johnson administration quietly to discourage them, but also by a schism in the Fenian ranks. In both developments there was promise of an effective curtailment of the Brotherhood's disturbing activities.

3

Nemesis

While Bruce was successfully defining British policy towards Fenianism in the United States, his American counterpart, Charles Francis Adams, was forced to confront the diplomatic problems that arose out of Fenian activities in Ireland. There was never any real doubt that international difficulties would accompany and follow Fenian interference in the affairs of the island. The very limited participation of Irish-Americans in the Young Ireland fiasco had plainly indicated that even in defeat these frustrated revolutionaries personified the fundamental Anglo-American disagreement over nationality, and from their founding it was equally evident that the Fenians intended to participate to the full in revolutionary enterprises. Members of the Brotherhood were conspiring as early as 1859 to dispatch the New York (Irish) 69th Regiment on a "nostalgic tour" of their homeland.[1] Although this seditious excursion failed to materialize, there still remained for the British the irritating problem of Irish-American gifts of money and munitions to Irish nationalists. An unfortunate combination of lax American customs regulations and geography—the deserted expanse of coast in Western Ireland—ham-

[1] Hammond to Waddington, January 12, 1859, Home Office, Ser. 45, Vol. 6877, Public Record Office.

pered the effective control of this irritant, but the outbreak of the American Civil War eased the British task considerably. Both the Union and Confederate governments had their own uses for munitions, consequently export regulations were strengthened and enforced.

The American war failed to snuff out Fenian activities in Ireland, however. During the spring of 1864, the British Minister to the Vatican was warned confidentially by an influential priest that a conspiracy was being organized in the island by agents arriving from the United States.[2] This report was confirmed by the Dublin police, who kept a succession of Fenian emissaries under surveillance throughout the next few months. In October, 1864 a known Fenian, Philip Coyne, arrived and undertook a tour of the island before returning to the United States.[3] He was followed by Captain Thomas Kelly in April, 1865. Kelly's task was to establish contact with the local officers of the Irish Revolutionary Brotherhood, thus preparing the way for the training and leading of native revolutionary groups by Irish-American officers who had received their instruction during the Civil War.[4] Forewarned of Kelly's purpose, and informed by Archibald of the possibility of an imminent exportation of men and munitions now that the American war was almost over,[5] the Irish authorities might well have been expected to institute vigorous countermeasures. Yet, during the spring and early summer of 1865 their response was admirably restrained. They contented themselves with elementary precautions, such as searching those vessels the New York consul named as munitions trans-

[2] Odo Russell to Home Office, March 8, 1864, Samuel Lee Anderson Papers, State Paper Office, Dublin.
[3] Dublin Police Reports, October 31, 1864, State Paper Office.
[4] *Ibid.*, April 10, 1865.
[5] Archibald to Russell, January 16, 1865, FO, 5/1334.

ports and subjecting visitors from the United States to a careful scrutiny.[6] However, this moderation tended to be transitory because it was not founded upon a well-placed confidence in the government's ability to defeat an Irish-American invasion or faith in the loyalty of the Irish population. It was based, instead, upon reports that the Fenian leadership was torn by dissension.

The Dublin police were informed in April of a disagreement between Stephens and his American colleagues over the timing of the proposed insurrection. While the transatlantic revolutionaries wanted to postpone action until 1866, it appeared that Stephens, having already committed himself to his own supporters, was adamantly insisting upon a movement in 1865.[7] The arrival in July of a pair of investigators, instead of arms and warriors, illustrated the continuing resistance of the American leadership to precipitate action. Yet when this latest mission endorsed the earlier recommendations of Coyne and Kelly, that the time was ripe, action could no longer be evaded.[8] O'Mahoney issued the "final call" in the United States, and it was not long before the predicted disembarkation of Irish-American revolutionaries in Ireland began.

The reaction of the British and Irish authorities to the arrival of thirty Irish-Americans at the end of August, followed by another batch during the first week of September,[9] was swift. As most of the visitors were recently demobilized war veterans, they not unnaturally excited the suspicion that they were "agents either of the Federal government or the Fenian organization, well supplied with money, and well qualified to drill the militarily unsophisticated native popula-

[6] Larcom to Foreign Office, March 31, 1865, FO, 5/1334.
[7] Dublin Police Reports, April 10, 1865.
[8] D'Arcy, *Fenian Movement*, p. 70.
[9] Dublin Police Reports, August 31, September 5, 1865.

tion."[10] This fear provided the Cork County Magistrates—most of the visitors disembarked at the port of Queenstown in Cork—with the necessary incentive to convene a special meeting to determine their collective response. Concluding that discretion was the better part of valor, they decided to request police and military reinforcements.[11] Meanwhile, elements of the British fleet suddenly disappeared from the Channel only to reappear off the long, deserted stretches of coast in Western Ireland. Obviously, they were watching "for the expected Fenian cruisers loaded with men, arms and munitions of war from the United States."[12] Finally, on the evening of September 15, the Dublin police raided the offices of the Irish nationalist newspaper, the *Irish People*.

Founded by Stephens in 1863 to advocate Fenian views and to fill the organization's coffers, it had never been a financial success. Although the circulation had risen to eight thousand by 1865, costs far outran revenue; thus it was of indirect benefit to the British insofar as it further depleted the Brotherhood's already inadequate fiscal reserves.[13] Such subtleties, however, escaped the Irish authorities whose anxiety to clamp down upon the Fenians made the newspaper appear a tempting target. For not only was this nationalistic organ intimately involved in the preparations for an uprising, but a sudden raid promised to snare many of the Fenian luminaries who frequented its offices. In effect, this one blow presented the Irish administration with an opportunity to smash Fenian plans to raise a revolt, at least in 1865. There was no doubt of their success in the mind of William West, "a conceited, chattering Irishman" who was at that time acting American consul in

[10] *New York Times*, September 24, 1865.
[11] *Ibid.*, September 26.   [12] *Ibid.*, October 1.
[13] F. L. Crilly, *Fenian Movement: The Manchester Martyrs* (London, 1908), p. 34.

Dublin.[14] With this one act, he reported to Seward, the British had burst the Fenian bubble in Ireland.[15] This obituary not only proved to be premature but the British decision to act decisively threatened to resurrect another issue.

Among those detained during the raid was an American. According to newspaper reports, he had been carried away proclaiming his citizenship and invoking the name of the American Secretary of State.[16] He quickly appealed to West for assistance, but the acting-consul soon discovered that the man was at best a naturalized citizen. This was in itself a serious complication because British law did not recognize "any renunciation of allegiance by a native born subject found in the United Kingdom." In short, it was obvious that if he was brought to trial it would be as a British subject, and the American government would not tolerate that. Impressed with the delicacy of the situation, West prudently decided to turn to Charles Francis Adams for guidance.

The inquiry from West found the Minister in the middle of a report he was preparing for Seward on the general condition of Ireland. He was compiling it on the basis of his own observations during a recent visit. Conceived as a logical sequel to a similar tour by an earlier Minister, Lawrence, in 1851, Adams had landed in Ireland on August 13 and returned to England on September 2. By no means a whirlwind visit, he left the island fully aware of the existence of organized disaffection in the southern and western counties. Yet the knowledge that clubs had been formed for the purpose of drilling the dissident elements did not alarm the American Minister unduly. He was convinced that the countermeasures

[14] Adams, Diary, August 15, 1865.
[15] *House Executive Document*, no. 157, 40th Cong., 2d sess., p. 7, West to Seward, September 16, 1865.
[16] *New York Times*, October 8, 1865.

already adopted by the British, particularly the establishment of military garrisons in the larger towns and the stationing of naval vessels off the coast, would suffice. When he compared the situation in 1865 to that in 1851, he concluded that the disaffected class was not larger but "poorer, unarmed and generally wanting in the elements of moral power." [17] Who better than an Adams to pass moral judgment? Charles Francis Adams may not have stopped to salute his rectitude as often as his father or grandfather, but he carried it as high and as exposed to public acclaim. Nevertheless, in his apportionment of moral power, Adams may well have been influenced in this case by considerations other than the peculiar virtues of the cause of Irish freedom. Certainly he had no particular affection for the Irish. Although he had resisted the blandishments of the Know-Nothings during the 1850's because he disapproved of nativism,[18] Adams still experienced the fears common to many conservatives when he pondered the effect of the massive Irish immigration into the United States. Indeed, by 1867, the combination of a large Irish population "with Negro freedmen entirely unfitted for responsibility" made him despair temporarily for the future of American institutions.[19]

Of far greater significance in molding the American Minister's response to Fenianism, however, was his interpretation of the national interest of his country. Thus Adams' faith in the efficacy of the measures already adopted by the British in Ireland was always qualified by the possibility of the active involvement of large numbers of Irish-Americans. He realized that they might sustain the existing disaffection until the Brit-

[17] Adams to Seward, September 22, 1865, Adams Papers.
[18] Martin B. Duberman, *Charles Francis Adams, 1807–1886* (Boston, 1961), p. 105.
[19] Adams, Diary, March 19, 1867.

ish were provoked into the radical measures that might bring in their train Anglo-American difficulties.[20] And if the detention of an alleged American during the raid upon the offices of the *Irish People* illustrated this danger, diplomatic consistency and national interest—not mutually exclusive—dictated Adams' response. Having complained so frequently during the Civil War against those parties who had used English territory to conspire against the Union, he scarcely felt "justified in upholding similar proceedings on this side by citizens of the United States." [21]

Similarly, he believed that the treatment of foreigners by the United States government during the war hampered his activity. Having subjected them to hardships then, the United States was obligated, or so Adams thought, to "make reasonable allowance in cases of similar treatment here." [22] In effect, he accepted that even innocent people might suffer inconvenience, or side blows as he put it, as a result of the not unnatural suspicion all American strangers in Ireland excited. "The fact appears undeniable," he wrote in reply to West's request for guidance, "that many persons who have been engaged in the war have returned and are now in Ireland. It behooves . . . all such as desire to enjoy the benefit of their incorporation into the people of the United States to take particular care not to forfeit their rights by taking part in political struggles of what to them should be nothing but a foreign country." [23] Obviously, Irish-Americans detained by the authorities in Ireland

[20] Adams to Seward, September 22, 1865, Adams Papers.

[21] Moran to McCafferty, December 28, 1865, *ibid*. Benjamin Moran, Secretary at the American Legation in London, wrote at Adams' instruction to this Fenian prisoner.

[22] Adams to Young (American consul at Belfast), January 29, 1866, Adams Papers.

[23] Adams to West, September 20, 1865, *ibid*.

could expect little spontaneous sympathy or support from the American Legation in London. While the British interpreted this attitude as a mark of Adams' conciliation and friendliness, he was of course motivated by a determination not to punish his own country by succumbing to the temptation to use the Fenians as a weapon with which to chastise Britain. He was anxious not to weaken the American case against Britain by now failing to follow the course of action unsuccessfully demanded of that country during the Civil War. How could the United States continue to point an accusing finger and effectively maintain its demands for compensation if, when the roles were reversed, it followed a similar course? Consequently, in his mind, national interest demanded that the United States practice what it had preached.

The response of Charles Francis Adams to Fenian activities in Ireland bore a certain similarity, therefore, to the response of Sir Frederick Bruce to their activities in the United States, but the motives of the two men were the exact antithesis. Where the British Minister saw in what could be interpreted as a conciliatory and friendly policy the hope of Britain escaping the consequences of her conduct during the Civil War, Adams hoped to render escape impossible. Like his British counterpart, also, the American Minister always ran the danger of being overruled and his conservative policy being compromised by the government in Washington. They were more amenable to the political pressure of the Irish in domestic affairs.

The course Adams had marked out for himself and the consuls in Ireland was soon tested. The continued arrival of Irish-Americans, some carrying rifles and most handguns, and the persistent reports Archibald forwarded of the departure of squads of Fenians from New York, spurred the Irish police to adopt additional precautions. Anyone sporting a felt hat or square-toed boots was marked as an American and subjected to police scrutiny and surveillance. Such passengers landing from transatlantic steamers were searched, drill books and guns were confiscated, and if incriminating evidence was uncovered, such as a commission in the Fenian army, the suspect was detained. "He is lodged in jail," the *New York Times* commented, in a labored attempt at humor; "some informer will identify him as a raging Fenian, and swear that he threatened to smother the Queen under a feather bed and drink the blood of bishops and priests." [24] Yet this flippant attitude indicated the pervasiveness of the view, held for a short time during the autumn of 1865, that this tightening of police controls had stemmed the tide. The Fenian threat seemed to be subsiding, and certainly the suppressions and precautions smothered their plans for an insurrection in 1865. The overconfidence and facetiousness this success bred in England were illustrated by the London *Times*. "We are perfectly able to take good care of the Fenians at home," it proclaimed, "and if our brethren in America would come together in a fleet, instead of one by one in passenger steamers, it would save the police a good deal of trouble." [25]

The euphoria also permeated official and diplomatic circles. Adams was now more convinced than ever that the Fenian problem was something less than formidable, [26] and even Sir Hugh Rose, commander of the military forces in Ireland, believed that the danger had passed. The opposition of the Irish clergy, the suppression of the *Irish People*, and the arrest of several Fenian luminaries persuaded him that the crisis was over and that the Irish police were sufficient to maintain

[24] November 5, 1865.   [25] October 4, 1865.
[26] Adams to Seward, October 5, 1865, Department of State, General Records, *Diplomatic Despatches: Great Britain*, National Archives Microfilm Publications, NA/M30/86.

order.[27] But Adams and Rose had forgotten one very important factor. "You have omitted from your consideration," the Lord-Lieutenant, Lord Wodehouse, wrote to Rose, "the important point which the Irish in America play in this movement. The existence of a combination of Irish in large numbers in a foreign country for the purpose of stirring up rebellion in Ireland is unprecedented." Nor was their peculiar significance in any way lessened, Wodehouse argued, by the prevalence of anglophobia in the United States. The Fenians were an all too convenient nemesis for those anxious to be revenged upon Britain for all the injuries suffered during the Civil War. Equally disturbing was the fact that most of the returning Irish had acquired considerable military experience in that conflict.[28] Such skills, as the authorities were only too well aware, they intended to put to use directing rebellious enterprises in Ireland. In brief, it was as obvious to the Irish authorities as it had been to Adams earlier that the Irish-Americans held the key to the immediate Fenian problem in the island.

Some of these transatlantic revolutionaries had already been arrested by the police, and they quickly turned to the American diplomatic officials for help. Invariably they received short shrift. Adams had his reasons for assuming a "conciliatory" role, and West, echoing the sentiment of the Minister, believed that the inconvenience suffered by Americans in Ireland was just punishment for "their folly in abandoning the comforts and happiness of their American homes for the insane project of aiding revolution here." [29] Yet their appeals for

[27] Rose to Wodehouse, October 2, 1865, Sir Thomas Larcom Papers, National Library of Ireland, Dublin.

[28] Wodehouse to Rose, *ibid.*

[29] *House Exec. Doc.*, no. 157, p. 14, West to Seward, October 14, 1865.

assistance could not be completely ignored, because the possibility did exist that some were innocent. However, the problem confronting British and American officials alike was to distinguish between the few genuine visitors and the many who, as Adams privately admitted to Seward, it was impossible to deny were connected in some way with the Fenian conspiracy. Once the British resorted to indiscriminate arrests, this fundamental distinction would have to be drawn by the local diplomatic official of the United States, who was required to investigate each case as it was brought to his attention. Adams authorized American representatives in Ireland "to secure a proper share of protection for innocent persons who are citizens of the United States without attempting to interfere on behalf of those who have justly subjected themselves to suspicion of complicity with treasonable projects." [30]

Having instituted this policy of selective intervention, which in practice usually meant nonintervention, Adams ran the risk of its being countermanded by the home government. Indeed, during December, he received a dispatch from Seward in which he was instructed to make representations to the British government on behalf of a detained American, whose plight had aroused an ominous public interest in the United States. Under these circumstances his involvement with Fenianism was immaterial to the Secretary of State. Fortunately the Minister was able to sidestep this challenge because the man had already been released. [31] Here, then, was an illustration of one means by which an Anglo-American controversy over naturalization was avoided in 1865—the pragmatic willingness of the Irish authorities to release most of the men they had seized on condition they return immediately to the United States. Together with Adams' conservative

---

[30] Adams to Seward, December 28, 1865, Adams Papers.   [31] *Ibid.*

policy, this helped both countries evade a potential diplomatic pitfall. Thus James Murphy, whose arrest during the raid on the offices of the *Irish People* had first sparked fears of a controversy, was released once it was established that he was a naturalized American. Nevertheless, avoidance is not solution, and it was soon obvious that the issue had merely been postponed.

The rigorous enforcement of police powers and the suppression of the *Irish People* had been devised, in part, as a means of "persuading" Fenians, widely accepted as the trunk if not the root of the current difficulties in Ireland, to return to the United States. In this it failed, for it simply served to make them more cautious, which in turn bred further nervousness and frustration within the ranks of Irish society and government. As this atmosphere of crisis thickened, the possibility of the British government responding with more radical measures strengthened.

It is true that the capture of James Stephens in November raised for a fleeting moment the illusory hope that this would herald the collapse of Fenianism. Emboldened by the news, the London *Times* willingly returned to the congenial task of ridiculing the slow but steady Fenian infiltration of Ireland. "The scheme proposed by Napoleon I for invading England by means of 100 balloons, to carry 1,000 men, two guns and 25 horses each," it remarked, "was a more promising and reasonable device compared with the scheme of the Fenian Brotherhood for invading England from America with staff officers disguised as steamboat passengers, carrying artillery in carpet bags." [32] Unhappily, Richmond Bridewell had as many leaks as Napoleon's balloons, and Stephens was sprung before he had settled in. The inevitable investigation ended with the

---

[32] November 13, 1865.

dismissal of the Governor and the belated bolting of the prison gates, but this did not retrieve the Irish nationalist, nor did it revive the deflated spirits of the Anglo-Irish Establishment.

Significantly, John T. Delane, the editor of the London *Times*, was one of those who privately began to give expression to the fear which tightened its grip upon Ireland.[33] The Fenians soon dominated conversation in society, and Irish servants became the subject of the same nervous appraisal and doubts that had plagued some of Mary Chesnut's acquaintances, surrounded by Negro slaves, during the Civil War. Yet the Irish-Americans remained the principal cause of alarm. "As long as I see them busily at work," Wodehouse informed Lord Russell, "I cannot feel easy, although I am far from sharing the exaggerated fears of some of the Protestant gentlemen. Unfortunately these men have become so cautious that it is very difficult to get evidence sufficient to warrant their arrest." [34]

To calm the fears of the Protestant gentlemen, and in the hope that any Fenian uprising would be nipped in the bud, the authorities ostentatiously displayed their civil and military power. Rumors that disorders had been planned for Christmas Eve or Christmas night saw the police out on the streets in double strength and armed with cutlasses, while cavalry patrolled the suburbs, and elaborate preparations were made to defend the Viceregal Lodge, the Castle, and even the City itself. A few days later, on December 28, two regiments of infantry were ordered to the island. Such precautionary meas-

[33] A. I. Dasent, *John Thadeus Delane: His Life and Correspondence* (London, 1908), II, 143-145.

[34] G. P. Gooch, ed., *Later Correspondence of Lord John Russell, 1848-1878* (London, 1925), II, 342, Wodehouse to Russell, December 28, 1865.

ures were at best temporary expedients, of course, certainly as long as the crucial problem of the Irish-Americans remained unresolved. Even the outbreak of civil war within the ranks of the Fenian Brotherhood itself failed to disrupt their activities. The utter failure of the "movement of '65" had severely weakened O'Mahoney's position within the Brotherhood, even though he had been reluctantly dragged into action by Stephens. His opponents pressed their attacks upon him to a rupture. Their constitutional revisions at Philadelphia quickly led to a division of the American organization into two rival camps, each following its own policy. Under O'Mahoney's general leadership the Fenian Brotherhood had uncomfortably and unsuccessfully straddled the dual concepts of rebellion in Ireland and invasion of Canada. At least the schism in December of 1865 settled this problem. O'Mahoney now denounced all action other than that in Ireland, while the other wing, led by his former deputy, the President of the Senate, William Roberts, and the Secretary of War, Thomas Sweeney, committed all its energies to an attack on British North America.

If the schism in the American ranks was not accompanied by any relaxation of tension in Ireland, where the supporters of O'Mahoney naturally continued to abound, some of the decisions of a Special Commission which sat at Cork to try Fenians further intensified it. When the Commission adjourned on January 2 two Irish-Americans were freed for want of evidence of any overt act against the Crown. The decisions confirmed what some Englishmen had long suspected, namely, that any American citizen could join the Fenian conspiracy against British sovereignty in Ireland "and afterwards come here to help in carrying out the design. He may bring with him official instructions, drill books and credentials. He may land in Ireland with impunity and cannot be convicted under the treason felony act until he has committed some treasonable overt act after he has landed." [35]

Obviously, all measures that could euphemistically be described as normal had failed to stem the tide of Fenianism. The attempt to frighten the Fenians into silence had failed. They had not been struck dumb by the continuous trials at Cork or the imposition of harsh sentences upon those native Irish leaders arrested during the raid on the offices of the *Irish People*. On the contrary, Adams reported to Seward in January, 1866, "The Fenian organization is affirmed to be spreading in every direction carrying with it many of the more intelligent class of tenantry and even compelling the acquiescence of some of the priests." [36] The discovery of caches of arms became a daily event, and such evident signs of the growing disaffection brought two more battalions of British troops to the island early in the new year. Assaults upon the police occurred more frequently, and the frightened country magistrates quickly appealed to Dublin for assistance. County Kilkenny, lying squarely between Cork and the capital, was placed under the rigors of a Peace Preservation Act. A delegation from Galway, an outpost on the deserted coast of Western Ireland, called at the Viceregal Lodge to request troops. It was widely rumored that a Fenian cruiser had already sailed from New York, and the Galway delegation thought it might well reappear off their isolated town and unload its cargo there. Meanwhile, in the United States these indications of panic were greeted with unrestrained glee. "It would be interesting to see," the *New York Tribune* commented, "what effect the appearance of one, two or half a dozen *Alabamas*, sailing under Fenian colours, would produce upon the nerves,

[35] London *Daily Express*, January 4, 1865.
[36] Adams to Seward, January 18, 1866, NA/M30/87.

as well as the commerce of our English cousins." [37] The *Tribune* was not kept in suspense by the British.

At a meeting of influential persons in Dublin on February 1, presided over by the Marquis of Dowshue, it was agreed that the alarm the Fenian conspiracy raised was well founded and that it was the duty of the government to take whatever measures were necessary to crush the Brotherhood.[38] The very next day, as if in answer to their resolution, another five hundred British troops embarked at Liverpool for the island, but neither this nor any of the preceding measures effectively curtailed the activities of the Irish-Americans, the alleged core of any rebellion. They refused to return voluntarily to the United States; on the contrary, more arrived in Ireland. By the first week of February the Irish authorities estimated that there were more than five hundred in the island—one hundred and sixty of them in Dublin alone.[39] "They may be the leaders," the *New York Times* observed facetiously, "distributing themselves over the island, ready, at a concerted signal, to cry havoc and let slip the dogs of war." [40] Of this there was no doubt in the mind of the administration in Dublin, for whom the presence of large numbers of Irish-Americans was no joke. Confronted by the undeniable deterioration of the situation in Ireland, and convinced that the Irish-Americans were the ferment, the British were obliged to do something about them. As this was manifestly impossible within the normal framework of the law, some extraordinary measure was required.

On February 14, a harassed Lord-Lieutenant wrote to the Home Secretary, Sir George Grey:

[37] March 2, 1866.   [38] *New York Times*, February 19, 1866.
[39] *Hansard's Parliamentary Debates*, 3d ser., CLXXXI, 678, Wodehouse to Grey, February 14, 1866.
[40] February 5, 1866.

I have little hope of pacifying the alarm, which is doing most serious injury to every interest here, without seizing the agents, who are busily employed all over the country, sowing sedition and organizing this conspiracy. I have come to the conclusion, after much careful consideration, that the time has arrived when it is indispensable for the safety of the country that the Habeas Corpus Act should be suspended.[41]

The legislative vehicle for this drastic step was at hand. Parliament had formally reassembled on February 1. Yet in the Queen's Speech, five days later, the government alluded only in passing to the conspiracy and appeared to be satisfied with the effectiveness of the restrictions it had already applied. Wodehouse, however, continued to insist that the situation was grave. Convinced of the Fenians' determination to rebel during the spring, he remained uneasy about the efficacy of the existing precautions. Similarly, the malign influence of the Irish-Americans vitiated, in his opinion, the immediate effectiveness of any reform measures. "I must add that although I hope that remedial measures might lay the foundation of a better state of things," he wrote to Gladstone, "I am sure the old hatred of English rule fomented by the Irish in America burns too strongly for any measures to cure under a long time. It can only die out slowly, and will I fear survive the present century whatever we may do." [42] Therefore, unsure and pessimistic, the Lord-Lieutenant saw no alternative to a suspension of habeas corpus. But the implementation of his recommendation was delayed by a cattle plague, which left such extensive desolation in its wake that Parliament debated it before the plague of Irish-Americans. However, on Feb-

[41] *Hansard's Parliamentary Debates,* CLXXXI, 678, Wodehouse to Grey, February 14, 1866.

[42] Wodehouse to Gladstone, February 12, 1866, William E. Gladstone Papers, British Museum.

ruary 16, Wodehouse summoned Superintendent Ryan of the Dublin police to a special meeting at the Vice-regal lodge and instructed him to make the necessary preparations for a general and immediate seizure of Irish-Americans. At eight o'clock the following morning, a Saturday, squads of policemen raided private homes and lodging houses throughout the city, and by noon ninety-eight persons had been arrested. Thirty-eight of the prisoners laid immediate claim to American citizenship,[43] but their imprisonment was testimony to the success of Wodehouse's precautions. Forewarned of the British government's decision to push the suspension of habeas corpus through Parliament that same day, February 17, he had naturally been anxious to ensure that as many Irish-Americans as possible were snared before news of the suspension drove them underground.

In London there was little criticism of the suspension bill. Although the opposition attacked the government, it was for their delay in bringing this measure forward. Many members of Parliament had long been convinced not only of the political dangers but also of the threat the continuing excitement posed to the economic and business life of the island. The Landed Estate Court had virtually been compelled to suspend operations, trustees had refused to advance credit on Irish mortgages, and the value of land had dropped by as much as 8 per cent.[44] In short, Fenianism was proving expensive.

Yet, for all the provocation, economic and political, the British government had taken a calculated risk. Once the Irish-Americans were jailed, and that, as government spokesmen made clear in speeches to the Lords and the Commons, was the principal reason for the suspension, they were bound

[43] Dublin Police Reports, February 18, 1866.

[44] Andrew Lang, *Sir Stafford Northcote: First Earl of Iddesleigh* (Edinburgh, 1891), pp. 143–144.

to appeal vigorously to their government for protection and assistance. Indeed, Superintendent Ryan reported that "the Generals on their way to the police stations said this would cause a bloody fine row when the intelligence would reach their Government as they would not submit to John Bull." [45] Such appeals, coming as they did in many instances from naturalized Americans, were bound to revive the Anglo-American controversy over allegiance. Obviously, Charles Francis Adams did not need to tax his undoubted powers of perception to appreciate the difficulties that lay ahead for him. "There will be a strong desire on the part of the arrested," he wrote in his diary, "to bring on a complication with the government, or else raise popular sympathy at home. It will require a good deal of prudence. Luckily West is rather timid and consequently rather docile." [46]

The determination of the Fenians to capitalize upon events in Ireland in an effort to promote public sympathy in the United States was soon evident. Ironically, a mass meeting called for this very purpose was held in the American capital on February 17. Not content merely to protest the British imprisonment of Irish-Americans during 1865, those in attendance also passed a resolution denouncing Adams and his policy, and demanding his recall. A delegation then sought to present their recommendations to the President, but forewarned of their intentions, Seward advised Johnson not to receive any committee but to accept any communication in writing. [47] Naturally, news of the suspension of habeas corpus stirred the Irish-Americans to further activity, and on March 4 a crowd estimated to number one hundred thousand

[45] Dublin Police Reports, February 18, 1866.

[46] Adams, Diary, February 19, 1866.

[47] Banks to Seward, February 16, 1866, William H. Seward Papers, University of Rochester.

thronged Jones Wood to listen to and applaud impassioned denunciations of Britain.[48] For the conservative *New York Times* such activities were fraught with sinister implications. On the eve of the gathering in Jones Wood it concluded: "All the while they will be laboring to embroil this Government with that of Great Britain, to bring about some collision that may make England's necessity Ireland's opportunity."

These fears were shared by Charles Francis Adams. "They are quite astute enough," he warned Seward, "to contrive the means of raising complications between the two nations out of the questions that may follow from any abuse of the extraordinary powers of repression now resorted to here. This would suit their views exactly." [49] Of course it did not suit the views of the United States, at least as they were interpreted by the Minister in London. He was determined to prevent the Irish-Americans using the United States as a pawn in the contest for Irish independence, for this would certainly jeopardize American claims against Britain, if not peaceful relations between the two nations. Consequently, he ignored the abuse heaped upon him in the United States and sought to adhere to the cautious, conciliatory, and conservative course he had first marked out during the autumn of 1865. "The first business of a public servant in times of difficulty," he informed West, whose timidity in the light of developments in the United States might now prove to be a liability, "is to do his duty to the best of his ability without regard to what is said of him." He continued:

If I have done anything heretofore to avoid a direct conflict between the two countries on questions in which the merits were of the strongest character on our side, I am not likely to change

[48] *New York Tribune*, March 5, 1866.
[49] Adams to Seward, February 22, 1866, NA/M30/87.

my action now there is nothing to promote a rupture beyond the wishes of a combination of agitators laboring not for the interests of the United States, but to make them subservient to their designs against a foreign country.[50]

For Fenians detained as a result of the suspension of habeas corpus, Adams' attitude meant that it would still be pointless to look to the American Legation for support and sympathy. Anxious to avoid the potentially disruptive problem of naturalization, Adams determined to keep cool and prevent, if he could, the arrest of Irish-Americans from causing excitement. As in 1865 he ordered the consuls in Ireland to investigate each case and, if no substantial charges of complicity with treasonable activities could be made out, to raise the matter politely with the Attorney-General of Ireland. "You may also intimate quietly and carefully, avoiding all threat or emotion," Adams informed West, "that you are acting under instructions from me to report all cases of hardship that may arise, in the same manner as the British Consuls in America acted in behalf of British subjects, under instructions of Lord Lyons during circumstances in a measure the same in that country." [51] Through this policy, which he called "frankness and clear understanding," the American Minister expected to secure the release of the innocent while leaving the guilty to the British. This, together with what he was sure would be the desire of the Irish authorities not to stir up the hornets' nest of inalienable allegiance, would avoid the pitfall of naturalization, or so Adams thought.[52]

The successful implementation of Adams' policy was still dependent on others. First, he ran the risk of being overruled

[50] Adams to West, March 7, 1866, Adams Papers.
[51] Adams to West, February 19, *ibid.*
[52] Adams to Seward, February 22, 1866, NA/M30/87.

by Seward, a danger he did not forget. In fact, conscious of the extent to which he had already stretched his discretionary powers, when he wrote to the Secretary of State, Adams tactfully undertook not to implement his policy unless some crisis developed before "the moment when you have it in your power to furnish all that will be necessary for a decision." [53] As it happened, the crisis did develop, and it arose out of the second contingency upon which the American Minister had of necessity founded his response to the difficulties in Ireland. Adams had relied not only upon the consent of his own government but also upon the anxiety of the British to avoid any excitement over the problem of naturalization.

The crux of the matter was the inevitable distinction the Irish authorities drew between native and naturalized American prisoners. On February 28, Major-General Larcom, the Under Secretary for Ireland, informed West that he would be permitted to see any prisoner "who there is good reason to believe is an American and not a British subject." The full meaning of this statement was revealed when, on that same day, West was denied permission to see three men even though they all possessed certificates of naturalization. "This raises in the most unqualified manner," the alarmed consul wrote to Adams, "the issue between our Government and this in relation to our naturalized." [54]

The danger of this situation now getting out of hand was illustrated by the subsequent conduct of the "timid" West. Mindful of the recent public denunciations to which Adams had been subjected in the United States, and provoked by the firmness of the language used by the Irish authorities to reject his requests for evidence of the complicity of arrested Ameri-

[53] *Ibid.*
[54] *House Exec. Doc.*, no. 157, p. 162, West to Adams, March 1, 1866.

cans in the Fenian conspiracy, the acting-consul couched his own communications in demanding language. When rebuked by Adams for this violation of the unexcited and friendly course he had been instructed to follow, West invoked the weight of American public opinion. Thus, in a letter to Adams he defended his choice of words on the grounds that "99 out of 100 of our population will say that the case called for and justified an expression of demand made with firmness, and that the words were not unsuited or inapplicable to the situation." [55] West was obviously determined not to fill the role of a scapegoat, if the indiscriminate imprisonment of American citizens excited a public outcry in the United States and created a demand for a sacrifice. He hurriedly passed to the Minister the full responsibility for the plight of the imprisoned.

Faced by these developments, Adams had little choice but to implement his policy of frankness and clear understanding without waiting for Seward's approval. Consequently, he called at the Foreign Office on March 5 to discuss the problem with Clarendon. The atmosphere was not the most cordial. In his efforts to impress upon the Foreign Secretary the serious difficulties that might arise, if the British continued to hold Americans without providing evidence of their complicity in the conspiracy and continued to discriminate between the native-born and the naturalized, Adams unintentionally gave the impression of seeking to extend his "diplomatic mantle" over them all. To this Clarendon responded irritably. He drew a highly unfavorable comparison of the American attitude and the British policy of abstaining from remonstrance about Fenian activities in the United States. At this point it seemed likely that the interview would dissolve into recrimi-

[55] *Ibid.*, p. 169, March 8.

natory arguments, because Adams was in turn irritated by Clarendon's suggestion that the British policy had been motivated by some form of international altruism, and in his irritation he retaliated. He reminded the Foreign Secretary of the conduct of Lord Lyons, Bruce's predecessor in Washington, under similar circumstances during the Civil War, and drew an analogy between the current activities of the Fenian Brotherhood in the United States and those of the Southern Rights Association in England at that time. Adams pulled himself back from this abyss, however, and returned to the problem at hand. He sought to convince Clarendon that if given evidence of Irish-American complicity there would be no danger of his extending his protection indiscriminately over the guilty. Similarly, he expressed the opinion that it would be to the mutual advantage of both nations to avoid the problem of naturalization. Of course that was easier to suggest than achieve, but Adams did propose a compromise. He urged the British to act as they had in 1865, namely, release all the Irish-American detainees against whom they did not have substantial evidence, on the condition that such men return immediately to the United States. When he rose at the end of the interview, Adams was convinced that his arguments had "brought his Lordship to reason." [56]

Unknown to the American Minister, however, the possibility of a collision over the conflicting attitudes of the two nations toward allegiance was strengthened as a result of Clarendon's subsequent decision to turn the question over to the law officers. Their report, submitted on March 9, admitted of no compromise. "It is impossible," they wrote, "that Her Majesty's Government should recognize any title in a Foreign Power to interfere on behalf of natural born subjects of Her

[56] Adams, Diary, March 5, 1866.

Majesty whom it may be thought necessary to detain in custody in Ireland on grounds that such natural born subjects have become naturalized or otherwise entitled to rights of citizenship in a Foreign Country." [57] As ominous as this inflexible posture was the fatalism with which Clarendon apparently greeted the possibility of a further deterioration in Anglo-American relations. "I suppose," he wrote to the British Minister, "that this matter like every other will serve as a pretext for a quarrel in the state of men's minds which rapidly seems getting worse towards us in America." [58]

Yet nothing was to be gained from inviting unnecessary problems. Although he was satisfied that Fenianism had been sustained in Ireland since the suspension of habeas corpus only by shipments of money from the United States and the sympathy of the American government, whose tolerance of Fenian activity was interpreted as approval by "all reasonable persons in England" as well as the Fenians, Clarendon controlled his indignation. Anyway, he was soon mollified by the friendly and conciliatory attitude of Adams and the consuls under his direction. This spirit made a second interview between the two men on March 13 a far more amicable affair. Having assured the Englishman that he would confine his intervention to the cases of men against whom there was at best "feeble evidence of evil intent," Adams argued that "surely . . . it was no object of Her Majesty's Government to persevere in holding them, especially if the parties should prove willing . . . to pass without the limits of the jurisdiction." At this point Clarendon conceded the release of native-born Americans on the condition that they return immedi-

---

[57] Law Officers to Clarendon, March 9, 1866, Home Office (HO), 45/7799, Public Record Office.
[58] Clarendon to Bruce, March 10, 1866, Clarendon Papers, Bodleian Library.

ately to the United States. For his part, Adams, conscious of the desire of some of the prisoners to provoke a rupture, agreed that those who refused this offer did so at the cost of removing themselves from his protection.[59]

This compromise still left unresolved, however, the problem of the naturalized. During his conversation with the American Minister, Clarendon had specifically referred to those Americans whose citizenship was indisputable. Although a natural reservation, given the English doctrine of inalienable allegiance, it also reflected, or so Adams believed, British knowledge that many of the Irish-Americans had been improperly naturalized anyway.[60] It was a notorious fact that Irishmen were naturalized en masse by venal justices just before elections, whether they had fulfilled the legal residence requirement or not. The ceremony was performed, the *New York Tribune* was later moved to comment, "with no more solemnity than, and quite as much celerity as, is displayed in converting swine into pork in a Cincinnati Packing house." [61] Therefore the laxness of American naturalization procedures cast doubt upon the citizenship of many of those detained, although this was incidental to the British. Consequently, it must have come as no surprise to Adams when, on the essential problem of the naturalized, Clarendon would do no more than give him the ambiguous assurance that "in cases where the evidence of treasonable activities was slight, the prisoners would be dealt with liberally." [62] This assurance scarcely eradicated the danger of a confrontation. It left unresolved the crucial problem of nationality: Would the British treat

[59] Adams, Diary, March 13, 1866.

[60] Adams to Seward, March 15, 1866, NA/M30/88.

[61] Thomas C. Cochran and William Miller, *The Age of Enterprise: A Social History of Industrial America* (New York, 1961), p. 159.

[62] Adams, Diary, March 13, 1866.

naturalized Americans of Irish birth as subjects of the Queen? Fortunately the danger of a positive response was considerably lessened as a result of reports the British received from Ireland during the week following the interview. These must surely have impressed on them the futility of their current policy; certainly they did not justify the risk of an international controversy with the United States.

On March 15, Wodehouse wrote to Gladstone: "I hope things are looking somewhat better here. The arrests made under the Suspension Act have produced a salutary effect. The *bad* side is the increasing weight of evidence of a widespread feeling of disaffection, which only wants the opportunity to show itself actively." [63] An Anglo-American rupture over naturalization would have been a splendid opportunity. If this was not sufficient reason for the British to avoid a dispute with the United States, the inadvisability of antagonizing the Americans as the price of a coercive policy in Ireland was confirmed when a report from the Irish Police Commissioners raised serious doubts about the efficacy of that policy. On March 20 the Commissioners reported to the Home Office the disheartening news that since February 6, the date of the last report from Dublin, neither the "number of arrests under the Habeas Corpus Suspension Act, amounting in this district [Dublin] to 200 and upwards, nor the annoyance to which strangers, believed to be here for Fenian purposes, are subjected, appear to have produced the least effect on the numbers of that body [Fenians], in repressing their spirit or apparently disturbing their organization." When he saw this report, Waddington, the permanent Under Secretary at the Home Office, understandably commented that it was "as bad as possible." [64]

[63] Wodehouse to Gladstone, March 15, 1866, Gladstone Papers.
[64] O'Farrell to Waddington, March 20, 1866, HO, 45/7799.

Under these circumstances, the compromise proposed earlier by Adams and extended to embrace naturalized Americans had much to recommend it. If all the prisoners were permitted to return home, the danger of a collision with the United States would be avoided and this without any renunciation of British law. Thus, on March 22 the Attorney-General of Ireland announced to the House of Commons the British government's willingness to implement this expedient solution. Replying to a question about the Fenian prisoners, he stated that "if amongst those in custody there were persons who had come from America to promote the objects of the association he would be disposed to give a very favourable consideration to any application which they might make if they wished to leave Ireland and return to the place they came from." [65] Significantly, he avoided any mention of American citizens, for that might have precipitated a debate on the problem of definition. And if the issue of citizenship could not be completely evaded when American officials were informed of the release of prisoners, the British managed to devise a form of procedure that preserved the legal fiction of inalienable allegiance but at the minimum cost to American sensibilities. It became customary for the Irish authorities to state that as the prisoner was "a natural born subject of Her Majesty, no intervention on his behalf by any foreign authority can be admitted; but that His Excellency [the Lord-Lieutenant] has much pleasure, as a matter of courtesy, informing you that after consideration of the circumstances . . . he has found it consistent with this duty to direct his release on condition of his forthwith leaving Ireland." [66] British self-interest and the patient diplomacy of Charles Francis Adams had together

---

[65] *Hansard's Parliamentary Debates*, CLXXXI, 733.
[66] Larcom to Eastman, April 2, 1866, FO, 5/1337.

produced a compromise which promised to save the face of both nations.

Meanwhile, in the United States, Seward, whose information was of necessity between two and three weeks late, began to take an increasing interest in the problem. Initially he had been willing to do no more than confirm Adams' exercise of his discretionary powers and approve the conservative course the Minister had adopted.[67] But reports from West, detailing the rigidly legalistic attitude of the Irish authorities, suddenly stirred him to greater activity. On March 20, he asked Bruce to call at the State Department, and there they discussed the crucial problem of British discrimination between native and naturalized Americans. During the course of the conversation it became evident that Seward had no wish to join issue with Britain over this particular problem. He impressed Bruce with his good faith and "desire to arrive at a pacific solution of the Fenian difficulty." The American argued cogently that the time could scarcely be less propitious for a diplomatic confrontation over allegiance. He pointed to the widespread American resentment of British conduct during the Civil War and the peculiar inexpediency of wrestling with the problem when it applied exclusively to Irish-Americans, many of whom had fought bravely for the Union cause in that conflict. Finally, he warned that the rights of naturalized citizens was a traditional issue which, if forced, no American politician could afford to ignore. From all this he drew the conclusion that only the Fenians could gain if the two countries collided. Therefore, he pressed upon Bruce his own proposal, whereby the American consuls would be permitted to see and be of service to all Americans, as long as it was

[67] Seward to Adams, March 10, 1866, Department of State, General Records, *Diplomatic Instructions: Great Britain,* National Archives Microfilm Publications, NA/M77/79.

understood that in conceding this the British were not conceding also the doctrine of inalienable allegiance. At this point
Seward was evidently content to leave the treatment of the
Fenian prisoners to the British, just as long as the overt distinction between native and naturalized Americans ceased to
be drawn.

Bruce forwarded Seward's proposal to London along with
a strong endorsement. "I cannot conceal from myself," he
wrote to Clarendon, "the gravity of this question, and the
unfortunate influence that would be produced on public opinion here, if the Fenians are able to present themselves to
the American people as denied the privileges of American
citizens." [68] Obviously the British had little to gain if the
Fenians were permitted to cover themselves with this collat-
eral issue. However, if this explains Bruce's support for the
Seward formula, it does not in itself explain the American's
motives in proposing it. An indication of Seward's intent is to
be derived, perhaps, from his correspondence with Adams.

The Secretary of State carefully supplemented whatever
pressure Bruce brought to bear upon the British government
to be "reasonable" with the pressure he was able to exert
himself through Adams. Following in his correspondence
with his Minister much the same line he had pursued in his
conversation with the British Minister, he stressed the delicacy
and complexity of controversy that might now develop.
"From the very nature of the conflict," he wrote, "it is one
which, when practically raised, can find a friendly adjustment
only by concession on one side or the other, or both, in the
form of a treaty or of mutual legislation, or through some
form of arbitrament." Therefore, Adams was instructed to
submit Seward's views to Clarendon, emphasizing the inability

[68] Bruce to Clarendon, March 20, 1866, Clarendon Papers, Bodleian
Library.

of the United States to acquiesce in the existing discrimina-
tory attitude of the Irish authorities, and to ask for a reply "at
as early date as may be convenient." [69] Nine days later, on
March 31, he re-emphasized the urgency of the situation.
Delay in reaching a reasonable and friendly understanding, he
informed Adams, was unpropitious.[70]

Seward's anxiety to avoid the naturalization problem, indeed his evident desire to sweep it under the diplomatic rug
as quickly as possible, was probably a response not only to
the international situation but also to the state of affairs in the
United States. No doubt, he was genuinely alarmed by the
thought of the likely international consequences of any inter-
mingling of this issue with the postwar American hostility
toward Britain. The blend could lead only to a further deterioration of Anglo-American relations, bringing closer the dangers of an open rupture and removing further hopes of a
peaceful settlement of the war claims. Similarly, if the Fenians
were permitted to shelter behind the naturalization problem,
the base of their popular appeal in the United States would be
broadened and their international and domestic abrasiveness
heightened as a result, all of which would have been peculiarly inopportune in March of 1866.

The problem was that the threatened eruption of a naturalization controversy coincided with the threat of a Fenian
eruption along the Canadian border. Indeed, it was not incon-
ceivable that through skillful exploitation of the former, the
Fenians could certainly render more difficult the avoidance of
the latter. Thus on March 23, Seward, writing to Adams,
warned, "In my judgment the question of a possible disturbance of the peace of Great Britain, or her Provinces, has as yet

[69] Seward to Adams, March 22, 1866, NA/M77/79.
[70] *Ibid.*, March 31.

taken no serious aspect. It may acquire some, or even greater
importance from an error which shall be committed now in
regard to what in itself is merely an exciting incident." [71]
From the standpoint of the Johnson administration, a Fenian
assault upon Canada was doubly inexpedient. Not only would
it complicate relations with England but it would also inject
Fenianism into the deepening domestic crisis and to the disadvantage of the government. On March 27, President Johnson
vetoed the Civil Rights Act, thus failing to pass what was
generally regarded as the crucial test of his adherence to
Republican principles. Now, as the political lines were being
redrawn, the administration was anxious to secure the allegiance of any potential ally against "the violent party of the
North," [72] and conversely deny its political enemies propaganda with which to garner support.

A Fenian raid on the British colony would flush the administration out into the open, compelling it to forsake the refuge
it had sought in procrastination and "underhand" restraints.
And if overt restrictions on Fenian filibusters promised to
antagonize the large Irish-American electorate, the forcing of
the naturalization problem threatened to result in a similar
alienation. British discrimination between native and naturalized American citizens in Ireland was the kind of issue it was
in the best interests of the President to exclude from the
domestic political arena. Obliged to deal rationally with foreign governments, he and his colleagues would be unable to
compete with demagogues in any public discussion of this
problem. Therefore, if the "violent party" was to be denied
additional ammunition and the mass of Irish-Americans were
not to be politically alienated, it was imperative that Seward
secure from the British an assurance that the distinction they

[71] *Ibid.*, March 23.
[72] Bruce to Clarendon, April 17, 1866, FO, 5/1337.

drew between native and naturalized Americans would cease, and the sooner this was done the better.

It quickly became evident that Seward, anxious as he was to be rid of the issue, was in no way willing to jeopardize the American doctrine. Therefore only an explicit assurance from the British would satisfy him. He was not prepared to accept, as Adams was, Clarendon's vague assurances of the British desire to avoid an international debate on naturalization. During an interview on April 11 at which Adams read Seward's note of March 22 remonstrating against the forcing of this problem, "His Lordship," the Minister reported, "apparently saw the folly of this distinction, and waived further discussion of the matter, as it seemed to me, with an intention to quietly remove the difficulty." [73] This was not good enough for the Secretary of State. "It is to be regretted," he replied, "that we are left in uncertainty upon that subject. Should the desire of this Government still remain an open question when this communication shall have reached you I have to request that you ask for an understanding sufficiently explicit to enable the Government to define a policy." [74]

On May 29, Adams called once again at the Foreign Office to explain Seward's demand for an explicit assurance of the removal of the distinction between the two classes of Americans. Clarendon was puzzled by this turn of events because, as he told the American Minister, he had already written to the Irish authorities about the problem and assumed that it had been satisfactorily arranged. His confusion was the result of a natural underestimation of what was needed to satisfy the Americans. He had thought that the gradual and conditional discharge of proven Americans of both classes, as urged by Adams, would suffice. However, what the Secretary of State

[73] Adams to Seward, April 12, 1866, NA/M30/88.
[74] Seward to Adams, April 30, 1866, NA/M77/79.

wanted was an end to the discrimination practiced by the Irish authorities. He would not be satisfied until the British agreed that American consular officials could interview and intercede for naturalized Americans. This Clarendon reluctantly conceded on the understanding that it was not interpreted as a surrender of the English doctrine of inalienable allegiance.[75]

The domestic political considerations that may have done much to mold Seward's policy on the problem of naturalization also account for his reneging upon other aspects of the arrangement proposed by Adams and accepted by the British in March. The American Minister had agreed during his earlier discussions with Clarendon not to interfere in those cases where there was substantial evidence of complicity with the conspiracy, but Seward persistently sought the release of all prisoners. Continually petitioned by private citizens and politicians, he was anxious to place on record not only his sympathy for those who had been detained but his constant efforts to secure their release. As the battle for the electoral support of the Irish-American masses gained momentum, neither he nor the administration wanted to be caught napping by an expression of Congressional concern for Fenian prisoners in Ireland. The unanimous passage of just such a resolution on June 18 found Seward ready with the evidence of his and hence the administration's activity on their behalf. When President Johnson replied to Congress, four days later, his message described in some detail the persistent representations of the State Department which, or so he claimed, had resulted in the release of all but two of the prisoners. "It is believed, however," Johnson concluded, "that in consequence of the aforesaid representations, even the two persons referred to . . . have been set at liberty before the present time." [76]

[75] Adams to Seward, June 1, 1866, NA/M30/88.
[76] Bruce to Clarendon, July 2, 1866, FO, 5/1339.

In brief, the Secretary of State had diligently and successfully protected American citizens. In fact, this boast of total victory was a little premature. The two men in question, Condon and Burke, rejected the initial British offer of a conditional discharge. Commenting upon this development, in a dispatch to Seward, Adams observed, "Several of them appear discontented at their failure to create a misunderstanding between the two countries in regard to what they call their wrongful detention, but I have not yet heard of one person who persevered in refusing freedom." [77] In time, even a discharge conditional upon the humiliation of being escorted to and placed aboard a transatlantic steamer proved the better part of Fenian valor. By September 29, Seward was informed that "there is now no case before this legation of a proved American citizen being in custody in Ireland on suspicion of being concerned in treasonable practices there." [78]

When it came to the congenial task of recognizing those who had contributed to this successful negotiation of the Fenian difficulties in Ireland, the British did not forget the Americans. During a debate in the House of Lords, the Earl of Kimberley, formerly Lord Wodehouse, expressed his personal appreciation of the prudent, friendly, and moderate manner in which the American Minister, the consuls under his direction, and the American government had handled the problem.[79] But the prevalence of disaffection in Ireland, best illustrated perhaps by the Habeas Corpus Suspension Act Continuance Bill in August, and political developments within the United States, ensured that these qualities would be required again. Fenianism had not been eradicated in Ireland, nor had the attendant issue of naturalization been solved.

[77] Adams to Seward, August 2, 1866, NA/M30/88.
[78] Moran to Seward, September 29, *ibid.*
[79] London *Times*, August 7, 1866.

Meanwhile the domestic political considerations that in all probability had helped to shape Seward's response to these problems also shaped his response, and that of the British government, to the problems resulting from Fenian activities in North America.

4

Fenian Burlesque

By December of 1865, Sir Frederick Bruce, astutely combining reason and threats, had asserted his control over British
policy toward Fenianism in North America. Yet that control
was not unquestioned. The Canadian government on one side
of the Atlantic and Lord Clarendon on the other clearly
entertained misgivings about the Minister's self-determined
course of action. It was unlikely that Clarendon would be
restrained indefinitely by the threat of being compelled to
remove Bruce from his post in Washington, if he believed the
current Fenian policy to be inimical to British interests. There
remained also the danger that the Canadians might raise such a
howl of protest that the British government would be forced
to make concessions to them. The obvious solution to both
problems was to remove the doubts the Canadians and the
Foreign Secretary shared, and in his efforts to do this, Bruce
initially received powerful if unwitting support from the
Fenians and some assistance from the American government.

The fears of the colonial authorities were first allayed by
the reports they received from their own agents in the United
States. As early as November 25, a special detective sent to
New York to investigate Fenian activities had reported to
John A. Macdonald, the Canadian Prime Minister, "There is

not really any cause for apprehension of an immediate raid on Canada and that the chances of the Fenians being able to effect anything this winter are decidedly on the decline." [1] In addition, the widespread and apparently well-founded rumor that the Fenians planned to withhold any assault on the colony until a domestic insurrection had erupted convinced Sir John Michel, the acting-Governor, that "all thoughts on their part of hostile operations may be considered relinquished." [2] He and his colleagues in the Canadian government were further reassured as a result of Alexander Galt's visit to Washington. For although the Canadian Minister of Finance failed to effect a reconciliation over reciprocity—the Americans had no intention of reviving the 1854 agreement which Bruce's brother had negotiated with the help of a plentiful supply of champagne—he did report encouraging Fenian intelligence. He dined with Bruce and was assured that the Irish-American organization would quietly expire within a few months for want of active sympathy. While he did not say so explicitly, the British Minister was of course convinced that the Fenians would be denied active public sympathy only if his policy of publicly ignoring them was continued. The following day, December 5, the Canadian had an interview with Seward who was equally confident. He predicted that the Fenians had no intention of attacking Canada, but that if they did, the American government "would at once do their duty as neutrals." [3] The sarcasm implicit in this last remark, with its allusion not only to the British Proclamation of Neutrality during the Civil War but also to the apparent grant of belligerent rights to the Fenians, either missed its mark or failed to ruffle Galt.

[1] Canadian secret agent to Macdonald, November 25, 1865, CO, 537/96.
[2] Michel to Cardwell, December 1, *ibid.*
[3] Galt to Brown, December 5, 1865, George Brown Papers, PAC.

He left Washington much comforted by the universal ridicule with which informed and official circles in the American capital greeted Fenian activities and ambitions.

Further encouragement for those inclined to take a light-hearted view of Fenianism, interpreting it as a form of national burlesque, the comic relief for a country slowly recovering from four years of unrelieved tragedy, was soon forthcoming. On December 11, in bold, front page headlines, the *New York Tribune* announced derisively the outbreak of the Fenian civil war: "THE FENIANS IN A BOG—ERIN ARRAYED AGAINST ITSELF—THE GREEN ISLE OUT AT SEA." Not surprisingly, the fusion of this development with the reports from Galt and their special agents in New York provided the Canadians with enough confidence to ignore that alarmist Archibald. Unable to assess coherently the significance of this latest news, the consul would on one day forecast the inevitable and immediate demise of Fenianism and on the very next express concern for the security of the colony. Such mercurial changes of opinion would earlier have kindled anxiety in Canada, but now the colonial government simply concluded that they would have to send more of their own agents to New York if they were ever to obtain reliable information about what was really going on there.[4] However, within a short time even Archibald had apparently conquered his fears sufficiently to signify his unity with Bruce on the best means of counteracting Fenianism. He informed Macdonald early in January, 1866, that "to meddle with these miscreants would only give them importance and sympathy on the part of thousands now indifferent to them—our best expectations of their early discomfiture is from their own quarrels—I think the United States Government consider the best course to

[4] Marginal comments by Lord Monck on Archibald to Macdonald, December 21, 1865, Macdonald Papers.

give them rope and they will hang themselves." [5] He sent a similar assessment to Clarendon. Writing to the Foreign Secretary a few days later, the consul concluded that "reticence on the part of the Government rather disserves than helps the Fenian Movement. A public and official denunciation of it, the proceedings at law against individuals, would excite strong sympathy in favour, on the part of a very large portion of the community, now entirely opposed to the Fenians." [6]

Reassuring as the internal disruption of the Brotherhood undoubtedly was, and truly remarkable the sudden confluence of opinions emanating from Washington and New York, it was unlikely that Clarendon's misgivings about Bruce's policy could be quelled by anything less than proof of its success. There were encouraging signs in this regard. As early as November the London *Times* had published a report which suggested that the American government was unobtrusively attempting to restrain the Fenians. From one of its American correspondents this influential newspaper learned that the Brotherhood had been paralyzed by an "informal notice given to its President from the Government at Washington . . . that the proceedings of the Order in issuing bonds are calculated to embarrass the United States in her relations with foreign powers, and that the discontinuance of the movement would be accepted as new evidence of the loyalty of the numerous class of adopted citizens whom the Fenian organization professes to represent." [7] The movement referred to was the issuance of Fenian bonds rather than the Brotherhood itself, and the resultant paralysis was too brief to be perceived by other observers, yet this report did hold out the hope of the American government dissuading the Fenians from any act,

[5] Archibald to Macdonald, January 3, 1866, *ibid.*
[6] Archibald to Clarendon, January 9, 1866, FO, 5/1336.
[7] November 24, 1865.

including presumably an invasion of Canada, that might cause the United States international embarrassment. Even more encouraging was information forwarded by Bruce which lent weight to his argument that the Johnson administration could be persuaded to discourage the Fenians if its true purpose was cloaked.

One Fenian whose activities the British Minister found peculiarly objectionable was Thomas Sweeny. A Major in the United States Army, he also held the lofty rank of Major-General and acting-Secretary of War in the Senate wing of the Brotherhood. In this latter capacity he led a delegation to Washington to request surplus war materials from the Secretary of the Navy, Gideon Welles, and the Secretary of War, Edwin Stanton. Although there was no evidence of their having seen Welles, "It is well known," the London *Times* reported, "that they had an interview with Mr. Stanton." [8] Consequently when Sweeny, fresh from his Washington negotiations, informed a Fenian gathering in Philadelphia that President Johnson was a friend and Stanton "was more than a friend and a brother," [9] Bruce decided that the time had come to act. Confidentially drawing Seward's attention to Sweeny's activities in his dual capacity as an officer in the United States and Fenian armies, the British Minister concluded: "It seems to me that he ought to be called to choose between the North American and the Irish Republic. The effect of his acting as Secretary of War is to confirm the Fenian dupes in the belief that the Government of the United States favours the movement." [10]

Within two weeks Sweeny had been dismissed from the United States Army, ostensibly for being absent without

[8] January 9, 1866.
[9] Kortwright to Clarendon, December 5, 1865, FO, 5/1335.
[10] Bruce to Seward, December 26, 1865, Seward Papers.

leave. From this unhappy termination of an otherwise illustrious military career, the *New York Times* drew the conclusion that it was a common error "among a class of foreigners who have become citizens by adoption" that they could be citizens "at one and the same time, of two or more Republics, situated in different hemispheres." The *Times* was obviously quite ready to revive the familiar conservative complaint of divided allegiance. But anxious, as always, not to be stigmatized as an enemy of the Irish cause, for the independence of subject peoples was a traditional concern of the United States, the newspaper paraded its hostility under another banner. The Fenians were denounced for duping their fellow Irish out of their hard-earned money. Claiming that Irish-Americans had already contributed four million dollars to the Irish cause, it advised them to audit Fenian expenditures. How much of their money, it asked, was being used to support a fancy Fenian headquarters and a top-heavy staff in New York? [11]

Yet, if the dismissal of Sweeny was evidence of the American government's dissuasion of Fenian activity, the reports that he and his delegation had been received in Washington by members of the government suggested to at least one observer "that the Fenian organization is now a power, and one which cannot be scattered by the arrest of a few of its members in Ireland." [12] If this was the case, one question that came immediately to mind was, How responsive would the Johnson administration be to Fenian pressure, and what would be the effect upon Bruce's policy? Indeed, would the dismissal of Sweeny be the first or last attempt at "underhand" dissuasion by the American authorities? Significantly, Bruce chose this moment to compose an exhaustive restatement of his policy. His aim was to overcome Clarendon's earlier mis-

[11] January 10, 1866.　　[12] London *Times*, January 9, 1866.

givings and allay any fears now stirring in England about the probable reaction of the President and the members of his administration to the burgeoning political significance of the Fenians. If he could do this, the British Minister could avoid another confrontation with his own government over Fenian policy because he would be helping Clarendon to resist the temptation to embark upon a more demonstrative course.

On January 8, therefore, Bruce reaffirmed his personal belief in the American government's determination to fulfill its international obligations. However, if there was in his opinion no cause for alarm on this point, reasons other than the alertness of the American authorities convinced him of the inexpediency of attempting to press them into more overtly repressive measures than they had already adopted. Indeed, there was the best possible reason—futility. Even if the Johnson administration could be cajoled into bringing suit against Fenians, Bruce realized that "there would be little probability of obtaining in New York a conviction by jury against" them. "On the other hand," he cautioned, "a trial would give importance to the movement . . . and the members of the Government who from personal motives do not wish to lose the Irish vote would be tempted so to deal with the question as not to throw the Irish element on the side of the opposition." It would not be long before the identities of these members and the nature of their motives stood revealed. Under these circumstances, and convinced that the American government was more alert and better prepared to stop any Fenian foray than was generally supposed, and "assuming them to be sincere in their peaceful professions," Bruce reasoned that it was "better to leave them free to deal with this difficult question in their own way." [13]

[13] Bruce to Clarendon, January 8, 1866, FO, 5/1336.

If the British Minister hinged his policy upon the good faith of the American government, he was prepared to accept, for the purposes of argument, that it was insincere and to defend his policy as the one best suited to meet this eventuality. He recognized that the temper of American public opinion was a potential source of immense Fenian strength. Not only did the Irish excite the traditional American sympathy for "an oppressed nationality," but they also stood to profit from the anglophobia of most Unionists. "So strong is this feeling against Britain," Bruce warned, "that I doubt whether the Government would not have been powerless to prevent criminal enterprises on the part of sympathizers, if the cause had met with any considerable response in Ireland or the North American Provinces." [14] From this the Minister might well have drawn the conclusion that a settlement of the American war claims would also settle the Fenian problem, but in January, 1866, the widespread hatred of England merely served to re-emphasize for him the advantages of his quiet diplomacy. A diplomatic protest promised to achieve little unless it was a backlash of popular sympathy for the Fenians. Continued reticence, on the other hand, would avoid this pitfall, and it would not deter, as a more demonstrative policy certainly would, the growth of the feeling "that such associations are inconsistent with the duties of American citizenship and that sympathy with, and toleration of, their avowed objects are incompatible with a due discharge of international obligations." Bruce insisted that the pervasiveness of this sentiment was the only guarantee for the cessation of an agitation which he considered a standing menace to good Anglo-American relations. "I say it is the only guarantee," he wrote to Clarendon, "for no reliance is to be placed on the assurances and

[14] *Ibid.*

opinions of the men in power on any question unless they are endorsed by public opinion."

Although a somewhat pessimistic view of American statesmanship, Bruce did not deduce from this that the position was hopeless or that he was restricted to a purely negative role. He comforted himself and his government with the thought that "public men in the United States have unavowed channels by which they can foster, promote and change opinion on questions of importance." This meant that a sensible British policy was to be discerned "in judicious efforts calculated to make them work in that direction, not in attempts to force from them premature declarations which would give us no real security and would weaken their influence for good in their own country." [15]

One obvious channel, exploited by public men in all countries, was the press. Perhaps it was significant, therefore, that the *New York Times* continued to focus conservative opinion on the divided national allegiance of the Fenians and the extent to which they menaced the international reputation of the United States. The *Times* reacted sharply when it learned that the 99th Regiment of the New York State militia, a Fenian unit, had requested new uniforms. Consent might be interpreted as approval of their cause. "Great Britain has done us grievous wrong, we have abundant cause of complaint," it proclaimed, "but we can never be so wronged as to imitate her example, and permit upon our soil the organization of expeditions aimed at her safety." The newspaper might also have suggested, as had Adams, that the American demands for redress from Britain would not be strengthened "if the idea got abroad that we winked at, if we did not directly encourage the illegal organization." [16] When the Fenians actually

[15] *Ibid.*   [16] February 21, 1866.

attempted an invasion of Canada in April, the *Times* insisted that they were making war on the United States: "It is our interest and peaceful relations that they are attempting to interrupt." Naturally, such an obvious manifestation of divided allegiance, and divided unequally it appeared between Ireland and the United States, was not permitted to pass without comment. Carefully holding up as an example the vast majority of what it called "the good Irish-Americans," the *Times* concluded: "The sooner any immigrant followed their example of identifying himself with American institutions—became a citizen in all sincerity, which the Fenians are not—the better for them. The United States invites and has room for emigration from any quarter of Europe, but if it comes she claims the hands and hearts for her own service." [17] However, the seeds of nativism fell upon barren ground during this postwar period, which John Higham has called the "Age of Confidence." Meanwhile, the utter failure of the Fenian activities that provoked the *New York Times* into this outburst helped to turn aside the final and most sustained assault upon Bruce's policy.

Archibald was the first to sound the tocsin, but this necessitated another change of opinion so mercurial that it made even him pause to give an explanation. Having insisted on January 24 that all fears of a raid within the foreseeable future could now be safely dismissed, he was predicting the very next day an invasion within six weeks. This complete revolution in opinion he lamely sought to justify on the grounds of the fitfulness of Fenian plans—so fitful in fact "that one must be excused from entertaining varying opinions of their projects and of their ability to carry them into execution." [18] Although the Canadians had derisively dubbed Archibald

[17] April 24.
[18] Archibald to Michel, January 25, 1866, FO, 5/1336.

"the prominent alarmist," in this instance his warning was soon followed by ominous signs of mounting activity among the Fenians. On February 7 a man was apprehended in New York transporting a truckload of arms. He was discharged with a caution against violating the United States neutrality laws, while the arms were released to John O'Mahoney after he had proved ownership.[19] Five days later, a large Fenian rally was held in the Cooper Institute, and among the speakers was that prominent local politician, Fernando Wood. The champion of many causes, including the secession of New York City during the "Great Secession Winter," Wood concluded his speech with the promise: "So help him God, he would use all his influence, personal and political, for the furtherance of Fenianism."[20] It was political blarney but encouraging for the Fenians nonetheless.

A few days later, a Fenian Congress was held in Pittsburgh at which the "fighting element of the West" was conspicuously present, and a promise was given that material aid would be available for "carrying out the war programme."[21] News of the suspension of habeas corpus in Ireland provided the Fenians with additional propaganda, and they quickly organized mass meetings of protest and sympathy in those areas of the United States where the Irish had settled in large numbers. Public denunciations of the British flowed in Boston, Philadelphia, and New York. Meanwhile, less public but more sinister were the meetings of the O'Mahoney and the Roberts-Sweeny Military Councils. While both declined to release an official statement, it was widely rumored that "General" Sweeny planned to establish his base of operations upon British soil.[22] The danger to Canada seemed imminent.

Against this background, Archibald worked himself into a

[19] *New York Tribune*, February 8, 1866.   [20] *Ibid.*, February 13.
[21] *Ibid.*, February 20.   [22] *Ibid.*, March 5.

feverish state by the beginning of March. His agitation was evident from the credence he placed in reports of a Fenian plot to set fire to London in several hundred places before attacking the prisons and looting the banks. As for Canada, the consul was now convinced that the colony would be attacked by a force of five thousand Fenians unless the American government intervened, and he warned that if the initial foray proved successful, thousands of reinforcements would rally to the Fenian colors.[23]

The response of the Canadian government to these reports of Fenian militancy, confirmed by Gerald McMicken, head of the colony's own counter-Fenian force, was suitably dramatic. On March 7, just six weeks after Archibald penned his first warning of an impending raid, the government decided to call out ten thousand men of the Volunteer Militia. In addition, two regiments of British regulars about to embark at Halifax were detained, and elaborate precautions were re-adopted to protect railway rolling stock located at exposed points close to the frontier. The trains remained intact, the engines were kept warm, and the engineers slept on them.[24] Finally, Lord Monck, the Irish-born Governor-General, requested that British gunboats be put on the St. Lawrence. Under Canadian pressure, the British government agreed to station a naval force above Montreal, but it was a full calendar month before this decision was implemented by an inordinately lethargic Admiralty.[25]

The pace of the Canadian response was dictated by the thought that if the Irish-Americans did indeed plan to invade

[23] Archibald to Clarendon, March 6, 1866, CO, 537/97.

[24] Monck to Cardwell, March 9, March 15, 1866, CO, 42/654; *Senate Executive Document*, no. 42, 40th Cong., 2d sess., p. 39, Thurston (U.S. consul at Toronto) to Seward, March 9, 1866.

[25] Monck to Cardwell, March 15, Cardwell to Monck, April 14, 1866, CO, 42/654.

the colony, they would, with typical Celtic imagination, select March 17. Yet if the Canadian haste was understandable,
the scope of their response puzzled at least one observer.
Writing to Clarendon on March 10 before he had received
word of all the Canadian preparations, Archibald observed,
"The attitude of defence which Canada has suddenly assumed
. . . [is] perhaps out of all proportion to any hostile attack
which, in my judgement, can be brought to bear upon that
Province." [26] If the consul made no attempt to unravel this
British North American mystery, the *New York Tribune* did.
"Many assert," it reported, with an obvious reference to Canada East, "that this hubbub is got up for political reasons to
unite the opposing factions in a sense of their danger, so that
the Annexationists be silenced and the Confederation carried
next month." [27] The Canadian government, however, explained its actions, insofar as it felt obliged to do so, as a
natural reaction to the considered opinion that the United
States had insufficient power to prevent a large body of
Irish-Americans crossing the international line. Such pessi-
mism was not entirely unwarranted, as time would prove, and
it could hardly have been dispelled by the arrival of no more
than two hundred troops at Buffalo, just across the Niagara
River.[28] Denied the effective restraint a large body of American troops would have imposed upon the Fenians, the Canadians may well have reasoned that only massive precautions by
the colony would deter filibusters.

   If these were the ostensible reasons for the extent of the
Canadian preparations, this dramatic response to the Fenian
alarm undoubtedly advanced the national cause in the British
colonies. Certainly it encouraged the condemnation of the
United States for tolerating within its jurisdiction a group

[26] Archibald to Clarendon, March 10, 1866, FO, 5/1336.
[27] March 10, 1866.   [28] *Ibid.*, March 16.

whose publicly avowed purpose was to attack a peaceful neighbor. "It is poor repayment to the Canadian Government for its action during the rebellion in the Southern States," the Toronto *Globe* complained, "to be now compelled to spend money and blood in resisting outrages planned in the States of the neighbouring republic." [29] In short, the excitement, deliberately exaggerated or not, encouraged antiannexationist sentiment. In addition, it helped to stimulate nascent Canadian nationalism. It reminded British North Americans of the need for greater unity, for it revealed the doubtful wisdom of relying upon Great Britain rather than a new national organization for protection. The British government's refusal to modify its Fenian policy, a decision Gladstone announced in a Commons speech that was widely reported in Canada, could have brought little cheer to those colonial particularists who saw no need for greater Canadian unity so long as the colonies were sustained by Britain. As it happened, Gladstone's statement, to which the colonists took marked exception,[30] that the North American situation was not serious enough to warrant representations to the American government, had been evoked by the most sustained attack to date upon the British government's Fenian policy.

A parliamentary challenge had been brewing for some time when E. W. Watkin, the member for Stockport, rose to speak on February 23. He had given notice of his intention to ask a question more than two weeks earlier, but a lengthy debate on the current cattle plague prevented him from putting it until the evening of the twenty-third. However, by this time, the crisis in Ireland, necessitating the suspension of habeas corpus,

[29] *Ibid.*, March 10.
[30] C. P. Stacey, "Fenianism and the Rise of National Feeling in Canada at the Time of Confederation," *Canadian Historical Review*, XII (September, 1931), 255.

had strengthened both his personal conviction and his argument that the British government would be better employed striking at the American roots of the Brotherhood. In effect, to accept as Watkin did that the Fenians were responsible for the disturbances and that the origins of this movement were American, then the logic of the situation demanded that the American government should be required to enforce its neutrality laws and thus suppress the conspiracy. What Watkin wanted from Gladstone, as the government's spokesman in the House, was the assurance that every means of representation and remonstrance had been exhausted in an effort to prod the Americans into activity.[31] But the long delay between Watkin's notice of his intention to ask a question and his ability to do so, while it saw the full development of an emergency that strengthened his case, also gave Gladstone more than enough time in which to consider his reply.

Clarendon provided the Chancellor of the Exchequer with the letters that had passed between Bruce and the Foreign Office upon the subject, and a commentary upon the Minister's reasons for exercising his discretionary powers to the extent of refraining from official representation. Bruce had taken this course, Clarendon observed, on the advice of Seward, "with whom he is on friendly terms, but who at the same time gave him to understand that the Government was on the watch to prevent any breach of the law or raid upon Canada." As for Watkin, the Foreign Secretary suggested that it would be advisable to avoid a discussion of his interpellation. Consequently, he thought that the best line of approach would be for Gladstone to express the government's continuing confidence in the government of the United States "to prevent any breach of the law or hostile actions upon British

[31] *Hansard's Parliamentary Debates*, CLXXXI, 1036.

possessions, upon the good sense of the American people to treat such a conspiracy with the contempt it deserved, and the certainty that the Fenians would quarrel among themselves about the money they had levied upon the dupes, and that the result had justified this course of proceedings." The result to which Clarendon referred was not only the civil war that had erupted within the Fenian ranks but the dismissal of Sweeny. "We have every reason to believe," he informed Gladstone, "that Sweeny was dismissed the United States service for the part he was taking with the Fenians but the reason publicly issued was his absence without leave from his Regiment and we must not impute to the Government a motive different from that which they themselves have given." As a final caution he added, "It would be manifestly improper to publish any portion of the correspondence that I now send you."[32] Gladstone was well prepared if not overwhelmingly well armed, therefore, when he rose to reply to Watkin.

In his reply Gladstone admitted that the root of the mischief lay in the United States, but he insisted that it was not the fruit of American sentiment or the American mind, and he rejected Watkin's demand for official representations. He maintained that the British government could expect action from the United States in one of two eventualities: first, if American law was violated, or second, if the Fenians attempted to raid Canada. As neither of these had occurred, he answered, "we have not made any representations." He then concluded with the plea: "Let us trust to a friendly Government which has not yet failed in its duties, and which we feel will not fail."[33] During the ensuing discussion of the question and Gladstone's answer, the government was supported by Lawrence Oliphant, the Member for Stirling. Before the de-

[32] Clarendon to Gladstone, February 14, 1866, Gladstone Papers.
[33] *Hansard's Parliamentary Debates*, CLXXXI, 1044.

bate he had called at the American Legation to discuss the matter with Adams, and to him the American Minister had expressed the opinion that a British request for suppression would merely make martyrs of the Fenians. Nor did he forget to remind Oliphant that a British remonstrance, in the light of the unhappy events of the late war, would not be well received in the United States.[34] In his short speech the Scottish Member followed much the same line of thought; indeed, he followed it until he reached the conclusion that the only way to defeat the Fenians was to alleviate American bitterness by settling the war claims.[35]

If Oliphant's radical solution was ignored, for it involved the admission of crimes to which the British still refused to plead guilty, Gladstone's oratory failed to stem the tide of criticism. Within the House, one member drew a sinister analogy to Anglo-Russian relations in 1853. Had the Russian Emperor then been formally acquainted with British opinion, he claimed, the Crimean War might well have been avoided.[36] Meanwhile, outside the Commons, the press was by no means uniform in its support of the government. The London *Herald* had called for official representations on the day of the debate, while the influential *Times* wavered between support of the government's course and recognition of the apparent need to prod the Americans into action. Thus, to the suggestion that Britain could not afford to remonstrate for fear of the American response it replied, "We have always protested that we were sincerely active and energetic in doing our duty and we ought not, therefore, to hesitate to ask the American government to do theirs." [37] In fact, two days earlier, on February 24, when it announced its approval of the govern-

---

[34] Adams, Diary, February 11, 1866.
[35] *Hansard's Parliamentary Debates*, CLXXXI, 1046–1051.
[36] *Ibid.*, p. 1045.   [37] London *Times*, February 26, 1866.

ment's course, the *Times* had seized upon the Fenians as a convenient yardstick for measuring British wartime activities of which the United States complained so bitterly and for which she now sought compensation. "What damage done by the escape of a single steamer," it inquired, "can be compared with the miseries which might be inflicted on the United Kingdom by a treasonable conspiracy openly carried on in every chief town of the Union?" Yet the newspaper was not unwilling to concede that the law of the United States was "powerless to prevent such measures." However, having made this concession, the English journal was able to reject American claims that their law has "a superiority to our own, when it is unable to prevent proceedings so manifestly contrary to comity of friendly nations." Later, when the news of the mounting Fenian activity in the United States reached England, the tone of the editorials in the *Times* changed. Forgetting its evident intention to use the American government's inability to restrain the Fenians as an offset to the British failure to restrain Confederate agents in England, the newspaper gave expression to a sentiment similar to that voiced by the Americans during the Civil War. On March 31 it complained: "At present the Fenian agitators are able to whisper to their dupes that the Government of the United States is really on their side. It needs nothing but plain language to [counter] this, and if this is withheld it will be difficult to acquit the American Government of neglecting the most ordinary offices of mutual amity."

Adams had quickly detected the continuing disapproval of the British government's Fenian policy, an attitude he considered "pretty cool" when he reflected upon what had taken place during the Civil War. And while he was convinced that fear of the American reply would inhibit any British disposition to remonstrate with the Americans on this subject, he thought it as well to inform Seward of the "growing dissatis-faction . . . among a certain class of political men with the sluggishness manifested by the Government in making repre-sentations and remonstrances touching the Fenian organiza-tion in the United States." [38]

The American Secretary of State responded to these devel-opments in England, and the uneasiness in North America, with a long dispatch on March 10. Significantly, the *New York Times* had published the day before a long account of the Fenian debate in the Commons and what it termed Glad-stone's eloquent defence of American good faith. Seward's dispatch, written against a background of reports and rumors of Fenian preparations to invade Canada, massive precaution-ary measures by the colonial authorities, and evidence of the increasing intrusion of Fenianism into the politics of Recon-struction, was a model of diplomatic sophistry. Undoubtedly, he did not want to engage the British government over Fenian activities, for once involved in a public correspondence he might find himself and the administration he represented im-paled upon the horns of an uncomfortable dilemma—either to deal with the issue rationally and diplomatically or to court the Irish-American electorate. To choose the former course was certain to antagonize the Irish, while the latter would simply encourage the Fenians to think that the government would tolerate any assault they made upon Canada. The closer the Fenians drew to the border, the nearer the moment of decision came for the administration. If a raid against Canada was organized, the American government would be faced with the choice of opposing it or running the risk of a break with Britain. In this situation, a policy of "masterly inactivity" must have appeared the most expedient. Thus,

---

[38] Adams to Seward, March 2, 1866, Adams Papers.

while fear of antagonizing the Irish certainly inhibited the government, restraining any impulse to check those Fenians who were allegedly already preparing to invade the British colony, the hope that the Fenians' belligerence would subside, and that their ardor for conquest would cool if they were given enough time and were denied publicity, encouraged Seward and some of his colleagues to believe that they could escape this predicament without political loss. There remained, of course, the possibility of the British government pressing for a more positive American policy in the light of the domestic criticism of its conduct, thus initiating the correspondence Seward was anxious to avoid. Consequently, in his dispatch to Adams on March 10, he appears to have skillfully utilized Gladstone's speech to rationalize his government's intention to do nothing about the Fenians. Following the line of Gladstone's statement that the Fenians did not reflect genuine American sentiment or mind, he went to some lengths in an attempt to prove that, since the Fenians were motivated by sentiments they cherished as Irishmen, the problem was British not American. As a sympathizer with the plight of the Irish, Seward might well have gone on to say that the only solution lay with remedial measures in Ireland. But it was far from his intention to be argumentative, so he contented himself by grasping the excuse Gladstone had inadvertently proffered with his other admissions—namely, that the Fenians had not violated any American law or attacked Canada—to announce that the United States government would not interfere with them "as long as they confine themselves within the limits of moral agitation." [39]

On April 11, when Adams read this dispatch to Clarendon, the Foreign Secretary expressed pleasure at its tone and even

[39] Seward to Adams, March 10, 1866, NA/M77/79.

borrowed Adams' copy to show his colleagues. After all, it accorded so well with the latest public announcement of the government's position. However, all pleasantries aside, he then went on to impress upon the American Minister how badgered the Cabinet had been to demand some overt action by the American government. He claimed that the pressure had been resisted and that no word had been or would be written to Bruce on the subject, because the government had every confidence that the President would do his duty. This, Adams replied, was the wisest course, for a more demonstrative stand would inevitably arouse public sympathy for the Fenians in the United States.[40] Clarendon prevaricated, however, when he told the American that not a line had been written to Bruce on the subject of Fenianism. In actual fact, the clamor in England for a more assertive policy had merely been heightened by the news of Fenian preparations for a raid on Canada, and the Foreign Secretary had responded to it. On March 20, while still paying lip service to his confidence in the American government's good faith and determination to prevent hostile incursions into British colonies, Clarendon asked Bruce to secure "some sure proof of it." [41] Of course, that was something the Johnson administration, plagued by the problem of Reconstruction, was virtually incapable of providing.

Fenianism had been discussed by the Johnson Cabinet on March 9. The massive response of the Canadians to the alleged danger, along with the suspension of habeas corpus in Ireland, appeared to call for some action by the American government. Although Seward was not present at the meeting (he was unwell, and therefore it was not known whether the British had requested action), it was decided that some appro-

[40] Adams, Diary, April 11, 1866.
[41] Clarendon to Bruce, March 20, 1866, FO, 5/1336.

priate measure should be adopted. However, at this point all agreement ceased. The root of the ensuing controversy was suspicion. When Stanton suggested a presidential proclamation denouncing any Fenian invasion of the British colonies, Gideon Welles, suspecting some dreadful political conspiracy, demanded that all the members of the administration be associated with it. The inevitable political odium that would accrue should be shared by all, he argued, including Stanton and the General of the Army, U. S. Grant. When the Secretary of War opposed this, Welles was convinced that he had unmasked his colleague. Stanton's motivation in proposing a presidential proclamation, the Secretary of the Navy thought, was to furnish the opponents of the President's Reconstruction policy with more political capital—in effect, throw the Irish-Americans into the camp of the opposition. Eventually, on March 13, over the protests of Welles, the Cabinet decided to send out circulars, exhorting all District-Attorneys and Marshals to increased vigilance.[42] These circulars scarcely fulfilled the United States' international obligations, for they were unlikely to inconvenience the Fenians. For that reason, there was no chance of political embarrassment, and this was the overriding consideration in Washington.

If the hypersensitive Welles suspected Stanton, Sir Frederick Bruce had his doubts about Seward. Although the Secretary of State had been absent from the indecisive Cabinet meeting on March 9, the British Minister was well aware of his opposition to the adoption of any effective anti-Fenian measures. This reluctance, which Seward's dispatch to Adams on March 10 merely re-emphasized, the British Minister attributed to the presidential ambition he believed still motivated the American. "With reference to Canada and the Fenians,"

[42] Howard K. Beale, ed., *Diary of Gideon Welles* (New York, 1960), II, 450–453, March 9, March 13, 1866.

he reported to Clarendon on the same day Seward wrote to Adams, "I look upon his influence as unfavourable toward us. He will play the uncertain game as long as he can in hopes of some event which he can turn to his own political advantage." [43] Bruce soon discovered that the current occupant of the executive mansion was equally reticent.

Andrew Johnson was now locked in a struggle with Congress over Reconstruction. The veto of the Freedmen's Bureau bill had been followed by an unfortunate speech to a group of serenaders on the anniversary of Washington's birthday, which illustrated perfectly what the President meant when he said of himself, "I have to seize on fugitive thoughts as they pass through my mind, make the best application of them I can, and express them in my own crude way." [44] Consequently, he was looking to every possible quarter for political support. Whether or not any doubt still lingers about his and Seward's efforts to engineer a new political alignment in 1865, the attempt was clearly made in 1866 and culminated in the National Union Convention. Seward may have had ambitions to be Johnson's successor, as Bruce suspected, perhaps marching at the head of a conservative coalition to the White House, but in March, 1866, he, like Welles and the President, who planned on another term himself, was in all likelihood responding to the more immediate need not to alienate potential supporters of a conservative Reconstruction policy. With the Democratic party supporting the presidential program, and given the traditional political allegiance of the Irish, it was to be expected, as the British Minister recognized, that the administration would go to considerable lengths to avoid antagonizing the Fenians. It was

[43] Bruce to Clarendon, March 10, 1866, Clarendon Papers, Bodleian Library.
[44] Miers, *The Great Rebellion*, p. 110.

assumed that they represented if they did not command the Irish-American electorate, a force of increasing significance in the shifting coalitions of Reconstruction politics. For the British, what this all meant was that the President and his adherents would continue to delude themselves as long as they could that the Fenians were not violating any American law. If this was the situation before March 27, it was not improved when Johnson vetoed the Civil Rights Act and thus failed to pass what was widely accepted as the final test of his allegiance to the Republican cause. Now, the seemingly irreparable breach with his own party promised to compel the President to look even more to the Democrats for political assistance, and to be even more circumspect in his handling of the Fenians.

This dependence was candidly admitted by Johnson himself. When he agreed to give an interview to a reporter of the London *Times*, Bruce grasped this opportunity to acquaint the President, in a very informal way, with the growing irritation in England at the American government's failure to make any positive effort to control the Fenians. Although at first reluctant to discuss the problem with the reporter, Johnson eventually conceded the inconvenience and impropriety of Fenian activities, mentioned the discussions that had already taken place in Cabinet, and stated his determination to put down any overt act of Fenian aggression. Having claimed that this was all the law would permit, he then "frankly admitted that the Government, surrounded by difficulties in its internal policy, and anxious to obtain support from any quarter against the violent party in the North were desirous of avoiding, if possible, any collision with the popular sentiments of the Irish masses." [45]

[45] Bruce to Clarendon, April 17, 1866, FO, 5/1337.

As the exigencies of domestic politics increasingly dictated American policy, even Bruce grew uneasy over the situation, for he had long feared the consequences of the Fenians capitalizing on their political influence in the United States. Yet worried though he was, the British Minister could discern no advantage from any substantial modification of his Fenian policy. Although he had long forsaken the argument that Seward should be supported because he in turn supported the President's Reconstruction policy—the swift return of the Southern States daily appeared more and more improbable—the British Minister still preferred the Secretary of State to his Radical opponents. Convinced that he was no more unfriendly to Britain than they and was as pacific as any likely successor, Bruce saw no benefit in helping them unseat Seward. Certainly he had no intention of providing them with additional ammunition by attempting to force Seward's hand over the Fenians. "He is more likely to thwart the Fenians by unavowed and indirect methods," the Minister informed Clarendon, "if I confine myself to friendly and unofficial representations, and neither he nor the President would be obliged to me if I were to increase their difficulties at the present critical movement." [46]

Clarendon, however, less impressed with the awkwardness of the American political scene, moved relentlessly toward a more demonstrative policy. The confidence he had announced in the good faith of the American government on March 20 was short-lived. Just four days later further news from the United States had persuaded him that the Fenian army was tolerated and maintained there, and unpleasant feelings fostered against Britain, "in order that the Government

[46] Bruce to Clarendon, March 16, 1866, Clarendon Papers, Bodleian Library.

may be able to speak louder and more insultingly to us whenever the time comes for representing the Alabama bill." [47] By
March 31, he was expressing sarcastic approval of Bruce's
decision not to abandon his policy of official reticence, because a formal remonstrance would have provided the Americans with an opportunity to make "more manifest, if possible,
the favour with which the movement is viewed and the satisfaction with which Mr. Seward contemplates a fine Irish
corps de reserve in readiness for the quarrel which he means
to pick with us whenever it suits his electioneering purpose."
The doubts about the Secretary of State, to which Bruce had
given expression on March 10, had obviously found a receptive audience. "The conduct of the United States government
throughout the whole business," Clarendon concluded, "ex-
cites surprise and indignation on this side of the ocean and
European diplomacy regards it all but a declaration of war
against England." [48] Since he was in this state of mind, the
Foreign Secretary's next step was predictable, and he took it
on April 7.

When he was informed that the Fenians had purchased
thirteen steamers for the purpose of either interfering in the
sensitive Canadian-American fisheries dispute or transporting
an expeditionary force against Canada, Clarendon decided
that if these reports were accurate, "the time will have fully
arrived for making official remonstrance." The policy of abstaining from remonstrance had been judicious to this point,
he conceded in a dispatch to Bruce, but he believed that there
now existed a distinct possibility of its being taken too far. If
Canada was invaded, if any disaster occurred which precipitated a rupture with the United States, the Foreign Secretary
warned Bruce, the government would be blamed in Parlia-

---

[47] Clarendon to Bruce, March 24, *ibid.*   [48] *Ibid.*, March 31.

ment for being too passive. Perhaps he had not forgotten the analogy to 1853. Equally important was the need to ensure that if a raid occurred, but failed to provoke a rupture, Seward should not be permitted to deny his country's responsibility with the embarrassing diplomatic rejoinder that the United States was not bound to protect British interests when the British themselves exhibited indifference. Therefore, Clarendon suggested to Bruce that he hit upon some act, such as the purchase of the thirteen steamers, about which the British could remonstrate. If the report of the purchase of the steamers was inaccurate, the Minister was advised to consult the best legal authorities in an effort to discover some convenient violation of American or international law on which to base a remonstrance. In the interim, Clarendon wanted a full report of the measures adopted in the United States to counter the Fenians. He considered this indispensable if the government was to ward off successfully the parliamentary agitation for a report on its efforts to secure the suppression of Fenianism.[49]

That Bruce still opposed a more demonstrative course was evident from his dispatch to Clarendon on April 17, in which he reported on the interview given by Johnson to the correspondent of the London *Times*. The Minister stressed that the Fenians and the Radicals welcomed the prospect of an official exchange over the former's activities. For the Fenians, a formal diplomatic correspondence would bring free publicity and an enhancement of their prestige. For the Radicals, it would be one more weapon with which to beat the administration and conciliate the Irish vote. The chasm separating the Irish and the Radicals in domestic social policies, at least as they related to the Negro, could be bridged, it seemed, with a

[49] *Ibid.*, April 7.

shaky but passable structure woven from sympathy for Ireland and anglophobia.

Whether Bruce could have resisted the pressure from England once again, without help, is debatable. His dispatch of April 17 was sent before he received Clarendon's note of April 10, in which the Foreign Secretary had based the need for a change in British policy upon the doubts and evidence of political chicanery expressed and supplied by the Minister himself. But debate is academic, for at this critical juncture the Fenians came to Bruce's assistance. They attempted, with farcical results, to seize the Canadian island of Campobello. This fiasco apparently vindicated Bruce's decision to rely upon the good faith of the United States government, which gave the appearance of moving vigorously to enforce the American neutrality laws. Yet, the image of the Johnson administration acting quickly and decisively was no more than an illusion; its members were too concerned with the Irish vote to take any step that might prove precipitous.

It is not improbable that the earlier concessions of the Lincoln and Johnson administrations to domestic expediency encouraged the Fenians to undertake the kind of enterprise that merely heightened the danger of the government's being compelled to move against them, something it was desperately anxious to avoid. Toleration of Fenian activities during the war, when they had been permitted to construct their own military framework within that of the United States, their purchase of war surplus after its conclusion, and the conspicuous absence of any announcement of the government's disapproval of their filibustering ambitions could all too easily be interpreted as tacit approval of their cause. The existence of just such an interpretation outside the United States was evident from Clarendon's notes, while its prevalence within was explicit in Bruce's request for the dismissal of Sweeny. Who could blame the Fenians for drawing this conclusion when it was widely reported that their leaders had been received by prominent members of the Johnson administration? Whatever his motives, it was public knowledge that Stanton had received them, while Johnson and Seward had given at least one interview when they agreed to release John Mitchel. Access to leading members of the government, and their ambiguous expressions of general support for any people struggling to secure republican institutions, provided Sweeny and other Fenian agitators with excellent copy. When Sweeny told a gathering of Fenians in Philadelphia that Stanton "was more than a friend and a brother," his credibility was not questioned. In fact, there can be little doubt that the Fenians interpreted the government's circumspect handling of them as an implied assurance that the march to Canada would not be impeded by the United States.

Strangely enough, the first advance was undertaken by the O'Mahoney faction whose rallying cry had always been "action in Ireland." Alarmed by the success of the Roberts-Sweeny faction in the contest for Fenian allegiance, and attributing it to their call for the more realizable goal of quick and dramatic action against Canada, O'Mahoney was persuaded by his advisers that the corrective lay in an assault upon Campobello. This one blow, it was thought, would steal the thunder of the opposition and attract much-needed financial and physical support. The island of Campobello was selected for several reasons. The Fenian General Staff believed it to be disputed territory; consequently, its seizure promised to irritate further an already sensitive Anglo-American problem. The master planner of this grand Fenian strategy, B. Doran Killian, the man who had played a prominent role in securing the release of John Mitchel, also considered the island a natural springboard for an invasion of Ireland and a base from which privateers, licensed by the duly constituted Fenian government, could prey upon British commerce.[50]

The possibility of an attack on Campobello had long been apparent to the British authorities. Even as the Canadians prepared for a raid on St. Patrick's Day, the Lieutenant-Governor of New Brunswick was writing to the Colonial Secretary: "Campobello I own I think a very likely place for a Fenian descent. It has capital harbours—it is close to the United States and its population is small—and it has no means of defence." [51] Ironically, the Fenian decision to launch an attack was taken on March 17. That same day, Bruce reported to Clarendon that "attempts will be made to seize either some port in New Brunswick or Nova Scotia, or some island off the coast on which to hoist the flag of the Irish Republic and to send out privateers." He was not at all sure of the response of the Johnson administration should a raid prove successful. He realized that "great pressure would be brought to bear upon the Government to recognize these adventurers as belligerents as a means of justifying damage on British commerce in retaliation for the losses the Confederate cruisers inflicted upon American shipping during the Civil War." [52] Consequently, he suggested to the Foreign Secretary that "the presence in the waters of British North America of a considerable naval force is at this moment of great importance." Shortly afterwards the British government reinforced the North American

[50] Archibald to Clarendon, April 18, April 24, 1866, FO, 5/1337; D'Arcy, *Fenian Movement*, p. 135.

[51] Gordon to Cardwell, March 12, 1866, Edward Cardwell Papers, Public Record Office.

[52] Bruce to Clarendon, March 20, 1866, FO, 5/1336.

squadron with H.M.S. *Tamar* and H.M.S. *Simoon,* and each vessel brought troop reinforcements as well.[53]

Of course it would be far better if the raid were frustrated, thus removing the danger of all these additional complications. To that end, Bruce warned the Lieutenant-Governors of New Brunswick and Nova Scotia of the likelihood of a Fenian attack.[54] The British response to the sinister concentration of Fenians in Portland, Maine, on April 7 was swift and massive. One thousand men of the New Brunswick Militia were called out, and although contemptuously dismissed by the War Office as "useless for all practical purposes," [55] their presence undoubtedly had some psychological significance for New Brunswickers as well as Fenians. By April 11, with the Fenians massing at the border town of Eastport, two British warships were conspicuously stationed off that Maine town with their gun ports open, and in little more than a week, there were five British ships and five thousand British and New Brunswick troops in the vicinity.

The reaction of the American government to the danger of a raid was naturally more restrained, forced as it was to keep a weather eye on the Irish electorate as well as the Fenians. However, for a time, it threatened to be completely hamstrung by the same mutual personal suspicion that had delayed action in March. Thus as it became increasingly evident that something was afoot along the Maine-New Brunswick frontier, the government moved hesitantly into action. On April 13 the American correspondent of the London *Times* reported that "the Government is desirous of avoiding coming into conflict with the Fenians as long as it possibly can, but it

---

[53] P. B. Waite, *The Life and Times of Confederation, 1864–1867* (Toronto, 1962), p. 267.

[54] Bruce to Clarendon, March 20, 1866, FO, 5/1336.

[55] Cardwell to Gordon, April 28, 1866, Cardwell Papers.

will not suffer any violation of the laws of neutrality to be attempted." Of course, the danger was that the laws would be violated while the government procrastinated. The Fenians had assembled in Portland on April 7, yet it was April 13 before Seward formally informed Attorney-General Speed of their activities and was in turn informed that the officers of the courts would take action if it became necessary.[56] That same day Welles ordered the steamer *Winooski* to Eastport and on April 14 instructed the commander to enforce the neutrality laws.[57]

Three days later it seemed probable that these modest and not as yet politically incriminating measures would be insufficient. News that a vessel, the *Ocean Spray*, had arrived on the scene with a cargo of five hundred stands of Fenian arms excited another minor crisis among Johnson's cabinet officers. On April 17, soon after he had received the news from the commander of the *Winooski*, Welles was approached by Seward's son and assistant, Frederick. He brought with him copies of telegrams Bruce had received from the British authorities in North America, warning him of the arrival of the vessel and her cargo, and a covering note from Bruce to the Secretary of State urging that the Fenians and the arms be kept apart. Seward had first approached Stanton, suggesting that he order the seizure of the arms, but the Secretary of War evaded the responsibility with the excuse that as General Meade was already on his way to the frontier, further instructions would only warn the Fenians of his impending arrival.[58] This was not a convincing argument, particularly from a man whose call for a presidential proclamation in March has been

[56] D'Arcy, *Fenian Movement*, p. 137.
[57] Welles to Cooper, April 14, 1866, Gideon Welles Papers, Library of Congress.
[58] Beale, *Diary of Gideon Welles*, II, 486, April 17, 1866.

described by his biographers as a sincere effort to prevent a crisis that might provoke war with Britain.[59] In fact, Stanton had already roused the suspicions, for what they were worth, of the correspondent of the London *Times*. In a report printed in London on April 26, but dated thirteen days earlier, he concluded: "Mr. Stanton would let the Fenians make war how they pleased, and even give them help, so intense is his bitterness towards England." Meanwhile, Seward, having been rebuffed at the War Department, turned to Welles with the suggestion that he order the commander of the *Winooski* to seize the munitions. However, Welles was not anxious to shoulder a responsibility others had shirked.[60]

The seizure of the *Ocean Spray* promised to be the kind of overtly anti-Fenian measure that political enemies would utilize to considerable advantage, and having observed the lengths to which, in his opinion, Stanton and Seward had gone to avoid it, the Secretary of the Navy took refuge behind a strict interpretation of his duty. He refused to telegraph further instructions to the naval commander, leaving the matter to that officer's personal discretion until Meade arrived. Presumably, Seward continued his search for someone to assume the responsibility and met with success at the Treasury Department, for instructions were sent to the Collector of Customs at Eastport to seize the *Ocean Spray*—a seizure Meade confirmed when he arrived on April 19. Thus, the Johnson administration's enforcement of domestic law and its fulfillment of international obligations had scarcely been marked with decision. The Fenians had been allowed to gather near the border while the government attempted to persuade itself that nothing serious would occur. The arrival of a vessel

[59] Benjamin P. Thomas and Harold M. Hyman, *Stanton: The Life and Times of Lincoln's Secretary of War* (New York, 1962), p. 486.
[60] Beale, *Diary of Gideon Welles*, II, 486, April 17, 1866.

loaded with Fenian munitions saw an uncomfortable evasion of the personal responsibility for its seizure. Although Meade, on his arrival April 19—a full twelve days after the Fenians had begun to assemble—proclaimed his determination to enforce the neutrality laws and confirmed the seizure of the arms, the fact that the Fenians had restricted themselves to infantile pranks, such as the theft of a British flag, was a reflection of their own incompetence and the inhibiting presence of the British. In short, the affair was a warning of future American procrastination and its consequences. Yet the British chose to interpret it as an indication of the American determination to enforce their laws.

Although he realized that the Johnson administration had carefully avoided any formal declaration against the Fenians or their objects, confining itself instead "to the simple object of enforcing the laws of the United States," Bruce thought that this was all to the good. "Taking into account the ignorance which prevails here as to the real cause of Irish discontent," he wrote to Clarendon, "and the sympathy felt by the people generally for those whom they consider oppressed and the extent to which that feeling is worked upon by politicians with the view of obtaining the Irish vote, I am inclined to think that the Government will be more heartily supported in its efforts." Similarly, the British Minister was reassured by the belief that the activity of the administration would "tend to undeceive the Fenian dupes as to the supposed favour with which according to their leaders the Government of the United States look upon these hostile demonstrations." Therefore, despite nagging doubts about the effectiveness of the American neutrality laws and concern over the burgeoning political influence of the Fenians, he declared himself satisfied that "the Government of the United States has shown that it will not tolerate far less lend itself to these criminal enterprises." [61] For Bruce, of course, such optimistic opinions vindicated his policy of reticence, a fact that may well have influenced the firmness with which he offered them.

Yet everyone else appeared to be satisfied as well. Clarendon accepted the Minister's assessment of the situation and instructed him to pass on to Seward the British government's satisfaction. However, he did warn Bruce, it is to be hoped with a touch of irony, not to be too effusive in his congratulations lest he give Seward the impression that he had pleased Britain so much that he must have been false to his own country. Finally, the Minister was praised for his handling of the affair. "You have dealt very skillfully with him [Seward] about the Fenian question," wrote the Foreign Secretary, "and I am sure that no written application still less remonstrance would have led to the same results." [62]

Similar satisfaction pervaded government circles north of the American border. For the Governor-General, Lord Monck, the Campobello episode had served to illustrate "three things which together deprive the Fenian threats of their significance. They are," he wrote to his Prime Minister, John A. Macdonald, "First, our power at very short notice to turn out a large body of troops and turn them on any threatened point—Second, the certainty that the Government of the United States will permit no invasion of Canada from their soil nor export of munitions—Third, the inability of the Fenian leaders to get together any number of men without our knowledge." [63] Events were to play a cruel jest on Monck.

All in all, the Campobello affair bred overconfidence. The belief that this fiasco would herald the collapse of Fenianism proved as seductive as the misplaced faith in the vigor of the

[61] Bruce to Clarendon, April 30, 1866, CO, 537/98.

[62] Clarendon to Bruce, May 19, 1866, Clarendon Papers, Bodleian Library.

[63] Monck to Macdonald, April 29, 1866, Macdonald Papers.

United States government. The correspondent of the London *Times* unilaterally and unwisely declared, as early as April 27, that "there need no longer be the slightest apprehension of the Fenian Movement in America." Even the ability to discriminate between the O'Mahoney faction, responsible for the Campobello disaster, and the Roberts-Sweeny group, still preparing for an invasion, failed to dissipate the euphoria. The *New York Times* ridiculed reports of belligerent activity by the latter group. "At their headquarters whispers of contemplated movements are rife," it reported on May 19, "but nothing tangible can be got at. Another Quixotic expedition under General Sweeny is said to be in the course of preparation, but whether the objective point be Campobello or the Fejee Islands is not disclosed."

The arrival of James Stephens in the United States early in May aroused among the British the fear that he would reunite the Fenians, but when he failed to entice Roberts and Sweeny back into the Irish action group, now pruned of O'Mahoney and Killian, such fears quickly evaporated. Meanwhile, further cause for confidence was the apparent success of Bruce's policy of securing the "underhand" frustration of the Fenians by the American government. The British Minister passed information to Seward concerning the location of depositories of Fenian arms along the Canadian border and seizures soon followed.[64] Unfortunately, the principal arsenal at Buffalo was not raided. Yet Monck, still holding fast to the three conclusions he had drawn from the Campobello affair, wrote to his son on May 31, "Mr. Sweeny is still swaggering about attacking Canada but I don't think he can do much." [65] In the early hours of the following morning, June 1, a force of several hundred Fenians crossed the Niagara River into Canada.

[64] Seward to Bruce, May 14, 1866, NA/M99/44.
[65] Baron Monck to Henry Monck, May 3, 1866, Baron Monck Papers, PAC.

5

A Policy of
Delay and Lenity

Portents of an imminent Fenian assault upon British North America passed unnoticed in Washington, New York, and the Colonies. The post-Campobello euphoric interlude was not conducive to concern. The Brotherhood's internal divisions, verbally illustrated by a campaign of denunciation waged against Roberts and Sweeny by James Stephens, and the rumored bankruptcy of their faction helped to sustain even the faintest of British hearts. There was also the comforting fact that Fenian gatherings had traditionally been accompanied by nothing more terrifying than Celtic brag and bluster. Thus, when Irish-Americans began to congregate in the city of Buffalo at the end of May, neither British nor American officials could bring themselves to believe that these men seriously intended to cross the Niagara River into Canada. "It has been the fashion for the last few months for Fenians to assemble in all our cities and make a great splutter, and then disperse," wrote an American correspondent of the London *Times*, "and the Buffalo gathering was thought to be no more than one of these boisterous meetings."[1] This time it was

[1] June 20, 1866.

different, however, and the location of this point of Fenian concentration, separated from the British colony by a narrow band of water only, might well have shaken someone's confidence. Yet it was not until May 31 that the British finally awoke to the danger.

Reports of Fenian preparations for a raid into Canada from St. Albans, Vermont,[2] which Sir Frederick Bruce received at the eleventh hour, put an entirely different complexion on their activities at Buffalo. In effect, what had earlier been casually dismissed as Irish tomfoolery suddenly assumed the character of an extensive and aggressive conspiracy. Buffalo now acquired strategic significance, either as the site of a diversionary maneuver while the main body of Fenians struck north from St. Albans, or as another base for the simultaneous attack at different points along the border long feared by Sir John Michel, commander of the British troops in the colony. Naturally, Bruce immediately warned Monck by telegraph of this disturbing turn of events, while the mayors of the Canadian cities of Toronto and Hamilton were privately informed of what was taking place at Buffalo by their American counterpart there.[3] As a result, the Canadian authorities made somewhat belated provision for the Province's defence. The Volunteer Militia of Upper Canada was called out to service on May 31 and a battalion ordered to travel by rail to Port Colborne the following morning.[4] From here it would have to advance on foot to Fort Erie, a deserted outpost opposite Buffalo and for that reason an obvious beachhead for any Fenian expeditionary force. But in the absence of any opposition, American or Canadian, during the early hours of the

[2] Archibald to Clarendon, June 2, 1866, FO, 5/1338.

[3] London *Times,* June 20, 1866.

[4] Garnet Wolseley, *The Story of a Soldier's Life* (London, 1903), II, 157.

morning of June 1, "Colonel" John O'Neill and his army crossed the river into Canada.

The response of the American government to the Fenian advance was even more dilatory than that of the Canadian. Although it had been warned by its own agents at the end of May that a raid was imminent, it did not order Meade back to the border until it had received the news that the Fenians had crossed into Canada. Nor was it able to provide him with a force of more than twelve hundred men. The modest size of his command shaped the general's strategy; he reasoned that as he would not impress them with his power, he would have to overawe the Fenians with his presence.[5] However, even as Meade travelled to the border planning his campaign, local officials were already seeking to frustrate the Fenians.

At Buffalo the commander of the naval steamer *Michigan*, Captain Bryson, and the local District Attorney, Dart, cooperated to prevent reinforcements crossing the Niagara to support O'Neill. Two tugs were pressed into service, armed, and together with the *Michigan* patrolled the river.[6] Meanwhile at St. Albans the United States Marshal for the area, H. H. Henry, with the assistance of a meager army detachment of one officer and twenty other ranks, vigorously applied himself to the task of seizing all munitions and suspicious packages. But with an estimated five hundred Fenians already crowded into the small Vermont town and another eight hundred reportedly on their way, the Marshal asked Washington for reinforcements before the Fenians succumbed to the temptation to test his authority.[7] Similarly, General Meade, once he

[5] Meade to Stanton, June 2, 1866, Andrew Johnson Papers, Library of Congress.

[6] Dart to Seward, June 2, 1866, Seward Papers.

[7] Henry to Stanton, June 2, 1866, Johnson Papers.

had seen for himself the situation at the frontier, sought additional powers from the Federal government. He wanted martial law to be proclaimed there and the authority to call upon state authorities for assistance if further disturbances created a need for reinforcements.[8] Meade was granted neither request by a government that was once again confronted by the delicate task of balancing its international obligations with the exigencies of domestic politics.

In Washington, the events along the frontier revived mutual suspicion at the highest level of government. When Bryson and Dart requested more tugs to help patrol the river, Seward forwarded their request to Welles. Unfortunately, the hypersensitive Secretary of the Navy decided that this step would be widely interpreted as "war on the Irish"; consequently he was as keen as any of his colleagues to evade the responsibility for it. As in April he quickly sought refuge behind an inelastic definition of his duty. Arguing that he had no constitutional authority to intervene unless a state of war existed, Welles insisted that the Fenian activities called for simple police action. This meant that the chartering of additional vessels was the responsibility of the State and Treasury Departments. Not content with this, he also suggested that the situation emphasized the need for a presidential proclamation warning American citizens not to participate in activities that violated the nation's neutrality laws. However, such an overt declaration of "war on the Irish," which the Navy Secretary had himself opposed earlier unless it received the unanimous and public support of the entire administration, was still resisted by Seward.[9]

For a few days after the initial Fenian foray, this stand did

[8] George G. Meade, ed., *Life and Letters of George Gordon Meade* (New York, 1913), II, 286.

[9] Beale, *Diary of Gideon Welles*, II, 518–520, June 2, 1866.

not appear unreasonable since it seemed possible that the movement would collapse without the proclaimed intervention of the government. Meade visited Buffalo and St. Albans and, in addition to being mistaken by the Fenians for "General" Sweeny, left troops with instructions to prevent reinforcements crossing the border.[10] On June 3, after a brief but successful skirmish with elements of the Canadian Militia, O'Neill, hearing of the advance of British regulars, prudently ordered a retreat to the United States. As they ferried themselves back across the Niagara, the Fenians were arrested by the *Michigan* and her little flotilla; their detention raised another embarrassing problem for the Johnson administration.

When Seward and Attorney-General Speed consulted with the President and later with Welles on June 4, the main topic of conversation was the prisoners. Johnson, conscious of the fact that his besieged administration had a political elephant on its hands, could suggest nothing more constructive than procrastination. Yet the detained Fenians were a physical as well as a political embarrassment. From Welles, Seward and Speed learned that the Navy did not possess the facilities needed to guard them, and Stanton was not anxious to assume the responsibility; therefore, the Secretary of State suggested that they be permitted to run away. Although the most expedient solution for both domestic problems, physical and political, it was vetoed by the Attorney-General. He raised an obstacle that should have occurred to Seward, namely the possibility of acute international embarrassment if the American government permitted the Fenian prisoners to escape and then received an application from the British for their extradition. Eventually, the three men reached a settlement that satisfied the legal and diplomatic niceties: Seward took charge

[10] Freeman Cleaves, *Meade of Gettysburg* (Norman, Okla., 1960), p. 343.

of the arrested Fenians as prisoners of state and then released them on nominal bail.

The same domestic political considerations that undoubtedly aroused the Secretary of State's anxiety to be rid of the prisoners also prompted his continued opposition to a presidential proclamation. Thus, when Welles revived his suggestion during their meeting on June 4, Seward still insisted that "it was not necessary." Indeed, he expressed the belief that the existing situation "was just right." "He felt," he said, "very happy over it." [11] Unfortunately, Sir Frederick Bruce soon ceased to be quite so pleased, and under his urgings Seward modified his opinion.

Bruce had been kept apprised of developments at Buffalo by the British consul there, Hemans. In the wake of O'Neill's withdrawal, for example, he received the satisfying news: "There can be no question that the surveillance of the *Michigan* which was reinforced . . . by a Revenue Cutter, and the patrolling of the river by the armed tugs effectively cut off the Fenian reinforcements and operated powerfully in frustrating their plans." [12] In short, the British Minister was not quite as poorly informed as he claimed when he wrote to Seward on June 4 to request an interview because he was "anxious for to-days mail to tell Lord Clarendon what measures you are taking to put a stop to the incursions into Canada, a point on which I am entirely ignorant." [13]

In his report to the Foreign Secretary, Bruce did his best to be constructive and conciliatory. Thus, the unpreparedness of the American authorities on June 1 he attributed to the false sense of security that everyone, including himself, had shared after Campobello. He then went on to describe the Fenian

[11] Beale, *Diary of Gideon Welles*, II, 521, June 4, 1866.
[12] Hemans to Bruce, June 4, 1866, FO, 5/1338.
[13] Bruce to Seward, June 4, 1866, Seward Papers.

expedition, its retreat, and the effective intervention of the *Michigan*. Finally, he endorsed the conduct of the United States government. "Since the information reached this government of a raid being intended," he wrote, "they have taken such measures as were in their power to thwart it." He did concede that the American means might not be equal to the task. "The regular forces of the United States in the north are . . . inconsiderable," he admitted, "and inadequate to prevent a movement if the Fenians attempted it in force." Still, he remained unshaken in his confidence, or so he would have Clarendon believe, "that vigorous efforts will be made to put a stop to the proceedings, and to assert the authority of the United States along the frontier where at this time it may be said to be in abeyance." [14]

As it happened, Bruce played a crucial role in stimulating the assertion of American authority he so confidently predicted in his dispatch to Clarendon. During his interview with Seward on June 4 he pressed for the arrest of the more prominent Fenians, and two days later instructions to this effect were sent to Meade and forwarded by him to his local commanders. The subsequent arrests, together with the seizure of large quantities of Fenian arms, convinced Meade briefly that the entire affair had been crippled. Unfortunately, the Fenians refused to draw the same sensible conclusion. They continued to move up to the border in considerable numbers, undoubtedly encouraged by the political tomfoolery in Congress. Representative Clarke, from Ohio, introduced a resolution on June 4 which, reminiscent of the British extension of belligerent rights to the Confederacy, proposed that the Foreign Affairs Committee "be requested to inquire into the propriety of recommending such action as may be

[14] Bruce to Clarendon, June 4, 1866, FO, 5/1338.

proper to secure" belligerent status for the Fenians.[15] This kind of political opportunism, and the knowledge that Fenian reinforcements were still arriving at the border, swelling to five thousand those who were still milling around Buffalo merely awaiting an opportunity to launch another raid across the inadequately defended frontier, prompted Bruce to address a candid private note to Seward on June 5. "You must allow me to say," he wrote, "that I do not understand why the United States Government does not issue a proclamation warning people against joining these proceedings. There are many in their ranks who would be deterred from going further in the face of an official warning. It would, moreover, produce a good effect on opinion in the Provinces." [16] The following day President Johnson issued a proclamation which helped to mollify the British Minister who was beginning to show signs of uncharacteristic irritation with the American government. "I trust this public step taken by the President," he commented in a dispatch to Clarendon, "will have some effect in stopping the despatch of men from different points to the frontier. It is high time in the interests of peaceable citizens of the United States that the supremacy of the law should be vindicated." [17]

The situation along the border stabilized within a few days of the publication of the proclamation. The arrest of Roberts, Sweeny, and O'Neill, the issuance of a General Order by Meade which denied the Fenians the means of communication and transportation, and the President's proclamation convinced most of them that the jig was up. Too poor, however,

---

[15] *Congressional Globe*, 39th Cong., 1st sess., part 4, p. 2946, June 4, 1866.

[16] Bruce to Seward, June 5, 1866, Department of State, Notes from Foreign Legations: Great Britain.

[17] Bruce to Clarendon, June 7, 1866, FO, 5/1338.

to finance their own way home, they suffered the indignity of being compelled to beg the federal government for assistance. When it was clear that this was the only way of removing an unruly mob from the frontier—a mob that terrified American residents and jeopardized relations with Britain—the assistance was soon forthcoming. By June 15, seven thousand had been transported home at public expense, having first given their parole to desist from further adventures in Canada.[18]

The sudden collapse of the Fenians as a military power brought little relief for either the British or the American authorities. Bruce had long recognized that "if the Irish agitators instead of attempting piratical raids and enterprises confine themselves to constitutional proceedings, and make the adhesion of the Irish vote contingent on the adoption by some party of a war policy towards Great Britain, the maintenance of friendly relations between the two countries will become very difficult." [19] The political force of the Fenians was always potentially powerful in the United States, particularly if D'Arcy McGee, the great Irish-Canadian of this period, was correct when he estimated "that the whole number of electors in the United States likely to be influenced by the Fenians do not fall far short of a million." [20] There was, unquestionably, a large Irish-American electorate, and its significance was certainly not diminished by the politics of Reconstruction. Long at odds with the majority of his own party over this issue, Johnson had been forced to turn increasingly to the Democratic party for support. The crucial test of this political realignment, as both the President and his opponents fully appreciated, was bound to come in the fall elections, when the

[18] Hemans to Bruce, June 19, *ibid.*
[19] Bruce to Clarendon, April 17, 1866, FO, 5/1337.
[20] Isabel Skelton, *Life of Thomas D'Arcy McGee* (Gardenvale, Que., 1925), p. 442.

entire House of Representatives and a third of the Senate would be elected. Therefore, with so much at stake, Johnson and his adherents were very keen to hold the Irish to their traditional support of the Democratic party, and thus to the administration, while the Republican opposition was just as anxious to win converts to their standard. The struggle for the Irish vote, contested over the treatment of the Fenians, was the larger political battle in microcosm.

The administration had attempted for a long time to avoid antagonizing potential supporters of the President's Reconstruction policy by ostentatiously pursuing a policy of laissez faire toward Fenianism, but this necessarily collapsed with the June raid. However, once the government had been compelled to take action, its supporters sought to minimize the political liability by denigrating the ambitions, achievements, and character of those against whom it had acted. In the vanguard of this crusade came the *New York Times*. News of the Fenian success in seizing Fort Erie prompted the *Times* to remind its readers that this was no more than a "deserted dunghill." As for the participants in the raid, the newspaper accorded them every term of opprobrium bequeathed by the Civil War. They were described as heroes, but "heroes of the stamp of those who bravely led the retreat at Bull Run, who helped to make up the great army of bounty jumpers . . . who are the curse of American society." But it was for O'Neill, the Fenian commander, that the newspaper reserved the ultimate vilification. Not only was he a Confederate but he was a confederate "of the infamous Wirtz of Andersonville." [21] He was being tarred with the same brush as the only man executed for war crimes.

While guilt through association was utilized to condemn

[21] June 2, 1866.

the Fenians, the administration's supporters fastened upon a more novel policy of innocence by association to defend its course. If the Fenians were Confederates or cowards, the *New York Times* was careful to identify the living symbol of Unionism with the administration's policy. General Grant's orders ensured that the Fenian war was treated as an insurrection against the United States, the newspaper reported, "and the President's proclamation" gave "the matter specific and unmistakable expression." Finally, the *Times* went to some lengths to plead the government's innocence to any prospective charge of having been inspired in its enforcement of American neutrality laws by friendship for Britain. "On the contrary," it protested, "the feeling in regard to the bad faith of the British authorities, the sense of the insulting tone of the statesmen of England, and the abuse of the Tory press in times of our misfortunes, is as bitter as ever." [22] Quite understandably, its supporters preferred to explain the government's conduct in terms of national integrity, not anglophilia.

This campaign of defamation notwithstanding, there was never any real chance of the Fenians being ignored by the politicians. The administration's efforts to isolate them from the bulk of the Irish-American electorate were bound to be challenged. First, they offered Congressmen in an election year too splendid an opportunity to score off the detested British. Thus, the Clarke resolution was soon followed by that of Robert C. Schenck, another Representative from Ohio, which was even more transparent in its hostility to Britain. Later to be sent to London by President Grant as American Minister—an unhappy experience for everyone—Schenck proposed that Johnson follow in the Fenian crisis a course comparable to that pursued by Britain during the Civil War:

[22] June 8.

in short, recognize both parties "as lawful belligerents" and observe between them "a strict neutrality." [23] For such politicians, particularly those opposed to the administration, the publication of the President's proclamation opened up new possibilities. Bruce had been deliberately obtuse of course when he informed Seward that he was mystified by the American government's unwillingness to issue a proclamation. The political dangers were always evident, and they accounted for Seward's prolonged opposition to this step. Indeed, if Welles can be believed, political chicanery exaggerated its ill effects when it did appear. Speed, an alleged Radical who was soon to be replaced as Attorney-General by Henry Stanbery, circulated a preliminary draft which both Johnson and Welles considered unnecessarily offensive, presumably to Irish-American opinion. Yet he ignored their objections, publishing it unrevised—a decision which drew from the Secretary of the Navy the comment: "The effect will be likely to throw the Irish against the Administration, or make them at all events indifferent towards it, whereas all this might have been different." [24]

Criticism of the President's course was implicit, perhaps, in the resolution submitted to the House of Representatives by S. E. Ancona of Pennsylvania on June 11. He recommended "that the Committee on Foreign Affairs be instructed to report a bill repealing [the Neutrality Act of 1818] under the terms of which the President's proclamation against the Fenians was issued." [25] There was, however, a more explicit line of attack to which the administration was vulnerable and against

[23] *Congressional Globe*, 39th Cong., 1st sess., part 4, p. 3085, June 11, 1866.

[24] Beale, *Diary of Gideon Welles*, II, 524, June 7, 1866.

[25] *Congressional Globe*, 39th Cong., 1st sess., part 4, p. 3085, June 11, 1866.

which the faithful *New York Times* had already sought to defend it. In an editorial on June 9 the *Times* attacked the Radical *New York Tribune* for accusing the President of not playing fair with the Fenians. In effect the *Tribune* argued that the proclamation should have been issued before, not after, the raid. Indeed, the persuasive and sympathetic argument of the Republican opposition, to which the *Tribune* had given expression, was that, by permitting their activities in the army, by tolerating their public organization and the formulation of their plans without comment, by allowing them to purchase arms from government arsenals, and by uttering ambiguous political assurances of sympathy with their republican aspirations, the government had tacitly encouraged the Fenians to launch their assault on the British colony only to crush them as soon as they sought to implement their plans.[26]

In one sense, the government was now hoist with its own petard. Procrastination had ended, as Bruce was quick to point out to Clarendon, in "a collision with the mass of the Fenians instead of a mere handful of individuals." [27] For the want of more political courage earlier, the administration had helped to precipitate a confrontation on a dimension that promised to render the Fenians "more hostile at the forthcoming elections." [28] Accurate as Bruce's estimate of the subsequent political developments was, it is not difficult to understand why the government followed the course it did. Surrounded as they were by domestic political enemies, any positive and overt action against the Fenians threatened to be very costly to Johnson and his colleagues on polling day. Therefore, procrastination was the easiest and conceivably the

[26] *New York Tribune*, June 7, 1866; Gibson, *Attitudes of the New York Irish*, pp. 186–187.

[27] Bruce to Clarendon, June 7, 1866, FO, 5/1338.   [28] *Ibid.*

most expedient policy, for there was a chance that Fenianism would fizzle out.

If the demise of the Fenian movement was the only eventuality that could have rescued the government from its predicament, it was also the only development that could have prevented the Republican opposition from profiting from the administration's dilemma. For had the President adopted explicitly anti-Fenian measures earlier, these would have been trumpeted by his enemies as proof of the government's hostility to the aspirations of Irish America. When the events in June forced his hand, the policy of toleration returned to haunt him. He was now exposed to the charge of bad faith, of duping the naive Fenians, and the article in the *New York Tribune* was merely the opening shot in what promised to be a long struggle.

The sensitivity of the government to the charge of bad faith was soon evident, for it found itself confronted by a potentially disastrous development. A new session of the Canadian Parliament opened on June 8, and it quickly made provision for the Fenians seized during the raid. Habeas corpus was suspended, and a bill was passed which authorized the trial by Militia General Courts Martial of persons taken in the act of attacking the Province.[29] What the opponents of the Johnson administration would have done with the propaganda that the Fenians had been duped into attacking Canada by the government, only to be frustrated by it or, what was even worse, martyred by drumhead courts martial in the British colony, left little to the imagination. Consequently, Seward moved quickly to bolster the government's defenses.

Seizing upon an unconfirmed report that British troops had

[29] *New York Times,* June 9, 1866.

pursued the Fenians across the border into the United States, the Secretary of State hastily emerged as a stout defender of American national sovereignty. However, it was the treatment of captured American citizens that really exercised him, and this was the issue he emphasized in a note to Bruce. The British Minister was informed that the American government "could not look without serious concern upon the practice of unnecessary severity and especially upon the exercise of retaliation or other illegal proceedings upon the persons of such of the offenders as have fallen or shall hereafter fall into the hands of the Canadian Authorities." Seward concluded with an expression of his hope "that even the customary administration of law will be tempered with special forbearance and clemency." [30]

To Sir Frederick Bruce the purpose of Seward's note was obvious. He was clearly attempting to checkmate any move to saddle the administration with the responsibility for the fate of the Fenian prisoners in Canada. Written for domestic consumption, it would be published at the appropriate time. Therefore, Bruce responded to it with characteristic calmness and moderation. He questioned the accuracy of the rumor that British troops had violated American territorial sovereignty and defended the Canadians' treatment of their prisoners. Indeed, he praised their "humanity" in holding the raiders for trial rather than summarily disposing of them, and expressed the belief that Seward's suggestions would "receive the respectful consideration of the Canadian Authorities." [31]

The spirit in which Bruce handled this American exercise in "domestic diplomacy" was a clear indication of his determination to hold to the guidelines of his earlier Fenian policy. Naturally, in the wake of the raid, that policy was in the

[30] Seward to Bruce, June 11, 1866, NA/M99/43.
[31] Bruce to Seward, June 11, 1866, FO, 5/1338.

process of redefinition. Yet it continued to be one of unofficial cooperation with the American government. There remained, of course, the possibility of opposition. Perhaps it occurred to Bruce that the raid might have undermined his influence in London: certainly it could be interpreted as a defeat of his policy of "underhand" dissuasion of Fenianism. No matter the reason, the British Minister evidently believed that it was necessary to justify his course to his own government.

While the situation along the American border remained confused, he confined himself to appeals for room in which to maneuver. Accordingly, he wrote to Clarendon on June 7, "I think it desirable to delay discussions or specific instructions in reference to matters on the Canadian frontier until those matters are at an end, and until we know precisely the effect of the measures taken by the United States Government." [32] Then, as the smoke cleared, he began to press for a policy of cooperation with the Johnson administration. "Whatever may be thought of the conduct of the Government in allowing the Fenian agitation to be publicly carried on without any check," he observed, "one thing is certain, that the best course to pursue is to act in concert with the President in preventing fresh issue . . . from arising out of the proceedings on the frontier." [33] More specifically, Bruce advocated lenity for the prisoners in Canada, and re-emphasized the wisdom of holding fast to his policy of confining all representations to unofficial correspondence. Both he and Archibald dwelt upon the danger of Fenianism, as a diplomatic problem, being brought within the reach of Congress.

The politicians' natural anxiety to capitalize on the Fenian problem had long been evident. The "important considerations to which the House really addressed itself" with the

---

[32] Bruce to Clarendon, June 7, *ibid*.   [33] *Ibid*., June 11.

Ancona and Schenck resolutions, Archibald reported, "were the securing of the Irish vote in the autumn elections and depriving the President and the Democratic party of the support of a section so numerous and influential. It was indeed to prevent, if possible, so serious a defection that the minority of the House—the Democrats—seemed willing to concur in the justice of the argument on which Mr. Schenck's resolution was based." [34] The consul might well have concluded that most Unionists followed Schenck's reasoning, such was the strength of anglophobia. However, examples of Congressional opportunism certainly did nothing to undermine Bruce's argument that "it is of importance that this subject should be kept exclusively in the hands of the Executive and should not be made the theme of discussion in Congress where there are not wanting men who for various reasons would take up the Fenian cause." [35] The lengths to which some Congressmen were prepared to go to take up the cause momentarily threatened to nonplus even the urbane British Minister.

One of the more prominent Fenians arrested during the turmoil along the Canadian border had been William Roberts, President of the Senate wing of the Brotherhood. The government made half-hearted efforts to prosecute him, but these were quickly rendered futile by the refusal of his associates to testify, on the grounds of the familiar constitutional sanctuary, and the intimidation of those witnesses who had been prepared to give evidence.[36] After this dubious reprieve, and despite his evident complicity in a terroristic raid on an inoffensive neighbor, Roberts was serenaded in Washington by a large, admiring crowd which included a considerable number of politicians. On June 21, he appeared on the floor of the

[34] Archibald to Clarendon, June 13, *ibid.*
[35] Bruce to Clarendon, June 11, *ibid.*
[36] *New York Times*, June 18, 1866.

House of Representatives and was introduced to several members, and the following evening he occupied his time "returning the visits of prominent members of both Houses, who had called upon him." Flattering as all this was to Roberts personally, and noteworthy as evidence of the politicians' assessment of the importance of the Irish vote, a reporter for the *New York Tribune* also thought he discerned during this exchange of courtesies a significant change in the attitude of the Irish in the capital. He dated it, however, from the administration's adoption "of extreme measures against the bold move into Canada." As a result, he concluded: "Even those who have never been Fenians and who have always been 'Democrats' are now among the most violent anti-Administration men. They say they were foolish to believe that men who have no sympathy for the loyal slave would evince any for the crushed Irish people." [37]

This identification of their interests with those of the American Negro must have been a novelty—and one of dubious merit for most Irishmen. Their lowly position in the American social hierarchy had traditionally made them peculiarly sensitive to the possible economic and social challenge of an emancipated Negro population, and this sensitivity had been tragically evident during the New York draft riots in 1863. Indeed, the apparent anomaly of claiming Irish political support for Republicans who were committed to an extension of Negro rights eventually persuaded the *Tribune* to offer an explanation. It claimed that the Irish were split. On one side there were the old Irish who had voted Copperhead during the war and "burned the Colored Orphan Asylum, mobbed a great tobacco manufactory in Brooklyn because colored persons were employed in it, and chased poor, frightened Negro

[37] *New York Tribune,* June 23, 1866.

children through our streets, seeking to kill them because of their color." These people, the *Tribune* proclaimed, would still vote Copperhead, and thus for the administration, but opposed to them were those Irishmen who "now comprehend that the direct and sure way to win liberty and opportunity for that race [Irish] is to concede . . . that [there] are . . . natural, inalienable rights, not of superior races, but of every race." [38]

In June of 1866, however, this marriage of Radical and Fenian, whether to be later consummated on a bed of principles or not, was still in the throes of ardent courtship. For Bruce, its most unseemly manifestation was the introduction of Roberts to a "National Fair" by Schuyler Colfax, a Radical and the Speaker of the House of Representatives. "It is a singular spectacle," the Minister wrote to Clarendon on June 19, "that of the Speaker presenting himself in the character of patron and introducer of a man who is about to be prosecuted against for a breach both of the municipal law of the United States and its international obligations and I fear it argues badly for the termination of this Fenian agitation." Indeed, viewing the affair as "proof of the great influence the Irish vote will exercise in the elections," he prepared his government for the likely response of the American. "It is not at all improbable," he wrote, "that the *Alabama* claims will be pressed in some shape, as this Government may find it necessary to atone for their opposition to the Fenian raiders, by bringing forward afresh these claims." [39] Of course, the Johnson administration did not require additional incentives to resubmit the *Alabama* account, but the Fenian imbroglio encouraged expedition.

If it was inevitable that the claims would have to be faced

[38] August 25, 1866.
[39] Bruce to Clarendon, June 19, 1866, FO, 5/1338.

once again by the British government, Bruce's more immediate concern was to minimize the diplomatic disruptiveness of the Fenians, and it was to this end that he urged upon his government lenity for the prisoners in Canada. Such a policy, he believed, would strengthen the hand of the American government in its struggle with the opponents of the President's Reconstruction policy—a group that had already indicated the lengths to which it was prepared to go to secure the Irish vote or at least deny it to the supporters of Andrew Johnson. Similarly, lenity promised to place the administration, or so Bruce reasoned, in direct opposition to the "violent" element of the Irish-American population and morally obligate it to prosecute the Fenian leaders arrested in the United States. To his mind, punishment of these men by the American government would be the most effective discouragement to another raid.[40] The Fenians might well leave Canada alone if they were given clear notice that they could not be assured of sanctuary in the United States.

If mercy had much to recommend it, severity was valueless except as balm for aroused British opinion. In the United States it threatened to weaken the government's position and strengthen that of its Republican opponents and the Fenians. It also promised to permit the government to seize upon the sophistry that British punishment had been severe enough to evade its obligation to punish the Fenians. Finally, a policy of severity would only intensify Irish animosity towards Canada, reproducing "on this continent," as Bruce put it, "that antagonism between the Irish race and British rule from which we suffer in Great Britain." Therefore, "in dealing with this delicate question it is security for the future and the effect on opinion here which are the main points to be considered, and

[40] *Ibid.*, June 18.

the question of punishment to be inflicted on these misguided dupes that have fallen into our hands should be decided in view of these considerations and not of the very natural resentment these proceedings call forth." [41] Yet even as this very sound advice was being dispatched to England, the British Minister was forced to protect the policy of lenity from the "very natural resentment" the recent proceedings had called forth in Canada.

Bruce had approached Lord Monck about the crucial problem of the treatment of the prisoners as soon as he received Seward's note of June 11. To describe the problem as crucial was no overstatement, at least in the opinion of the Minister. He expressed the belief that "the future relations of Canada [with the United States] and its deliverance from any chance of becoming a battlefield of Fenianism will depend in a great measure on the tact and temper with which this question of the prisoners is managed." Not content with generalities, he made three specific suggestions: First, any prisoners taken on the American side of the international line should be turned over to the American authorities. Second, all the Canadians' prisoners should be tried in the usual manner. Third, "considering the grave and important interests involved in the question," capital punishment should not be inflicted without due deliberation and consultation with the home government. Of course, to advise consultation with the Imperial government was to press for delay, and Bruce was quite prepared to make this more explicit, for above all he wanted a cooling off period during which the prevailing excitement in Canada might subside, thus permitting mature consideration of the most expedient course.[42]

It was the fear that political haymaking of the Ancona and

[41] *Ibid.*   [42] Bruce to Monck, June 11, 1866, FO, 5/1338.

Schenck variety would only increase Canadian resentment that prompted Bruce to write to Monck again the very next day, June 12. However, not content merely to explain the resolutions, the British Minister also turned them to his diplomatic advantage. Thus if to Canadians the choice between Johnson and his Congressional opponents looked remarkably uninviting, for Bruce the resolutions redounded to the credit of the President. They emphasized, he thought, the difficulty of the American government's position and Johnson's "pacific intentions." Therefore, "our true policy," he went on, "is to aid him by our course." The object to be obtained "is the enforcement of the law against the agitators here— That is the way to cut off the root of the evil and to release Canada from future danger." Finally, he seized upon the resolutions as additional evidence of the need for delay. Not only should the delicate problem of the prisoners be postponed until the Imperial government had been consulted and "the present excitement has passed away," he argued, but also, if possible, "until Congress is no longer in session." [43]

The success or failure of Bruce's policy obviously hinged in large measure upon the reaction of Monck and the Canadian government to his warnings and blandishments. Unfortunately, the Governor's attitude was complicated by considerations other than expediency. Yet his judgment was not impaired by anger toward the United States over the raid. On the contrary, although a certain ambiguity crept into the language he used to describe the American determination to check infractions of international obligations "from the moment that it became evident that an invasion of the Province by Fenians had actually taken place," in his letters to his son Henry, his speech opening the Canadian Parliament, and his

[43] *Ibid.*, June 12.

report to the Colonial Secretary, Edward Cardwell, Monck freely acknowledged that the "determination of the Government of the United States to stop the transportation of men and supplies to the places of assembly, rendered even the temporary success on the part of the Fenians impossible." [44] Despite this acknowledgment, his reply to Bruce's notes was essentially negative.

The Governor's unfavorable response was probably provoked by his irritation with Bruce and the highly offensive nature of Seward's note of June 11. Monck was certainly upset by what he considered to be the Minister's failure to keep him abreast of developments in the United States. Thus, he learned of the President's proclamation and the Attorney-General's order authorizing the arrest of prominent Fenians from the public press, not the British Legation in Washington.[45] This personal dissatisfaction was also representative of a wider suspicion of Lord Lyons' successor. The Canadian government had never been convinced of the wisdom of Bruce's attitude toward Fenianism, and his policy had only been executed over its prolonged opposition. Consequently, the Minister's suggestions could only have lent further credence to the belief that he was willing to pander to American pressure and interests at the expense of those of Canada. In this atmosphere, the tone and content of Seward's note, a copy of which Bruce had forwarded to the colony, must have been doubly intolerable. In his reply, Monck informed the British Minister with some asperity that "the course of justice cannot be interfered with at the dictation of a foreign power." [46]

Undaunted by this uncompromising response, Bruce wrote

[44] Monck to Cardwell, June 14, 1866, CO, 42/655.
[45] Monck to Bruce, June 11, 1866, CO, 537/98.
[46] Bruce to Monck, June 13, 1866, FO, 5/1338.

yet another letter to Monck, and it was a model of tact and diplomacy. First, he attempted to smooth the ruffled feathers in the colony by agreeing that the Governor's reply had been "both in itself just and not uncalled for by the language in some parts of Mr. Seward's note." Then, as on June 12, he cleverly turned this to his advantage, re-emphasizing the point he had made on that occasion. Seward's note, he argued, "is only of value as testimony of the difficulties in which the Government is placed and the pressure that is brought to bear upon them by Congress and powerful party influences." Finally, and probably as a result of an awareness of the suspicion with which he was viewed in the colony, Bruce made it a point to defend his course as the one best suited to Canadian interests.

Once he had completed the defence of his own and the American government's conduct, Bruce turned to the task of prosecuting his policy. Carefully, he increased the pressure on the Canadian authorities. Pointing to the large number of unemployed ex-soldiers as a potential source of Fenian recruitment, he stressed the danger of another and more serious raid if any incident took place that aroused public sympathy for the Fenians in the United States. Little intelligence was required to perceive in the martyrdom of the Fenian prisoners in Canada the necessary incident. In pressing home this point, Bruce raised the alarming possibility that in the event of another raid the widely recognized inadequacy of federal forces might compel the government to turn to the state militias for assistance. "If the Militia of . . . New York is called out," he wrote, "the affair will get mixed up with the politics of that State where the Irish are powerful, and I for one will not answer for their conduct." [47] Obviously, to pro-

[47] *Ibid.*

voke the calling out of the militia, an organization well infiltrated by the Irish in general and the Fenians in particular, was to court disaster. Indeed, the perils were all too clearly revealed on July 4 when a group of British soldiers was fired upon across the Niagara River by members of the 74th Regiment of New York militia, one company of which was exclusively Irish.[48]

For Bruce the solution to all these crises, present and prospective, was self-evident. "There are no two opinions," he warned Monck, "on the danger of creating a false sympathy and a fresh excitement if the proceedings of the Canadian government are not marked by great calmness and temper." Under the circumstances he strongly recommended that the Fenian prisoners be tried by the ordinary courts, that the trials be delayed until the prevailing excitement had abated, and that "no blood be shed." If procrastination for this length of time proved impossible, Bruce was willing to settle for a period of delay that corresponded to the current session of Congress. The great object, he wrote, "is to keep things quiet until Congress adjourns, for some member who represents an Irish constituency can always be found to move an incendiary resolution which serves to keep up the excitement among the Irish." [49]

If in essence, then, Bruce's diplomacy was a reversion to the traditional statecraft of enjoying "the benefits of time," cooperation with the Johnson administration was also an essential ingredient. He made no bones about this in his correspondence with the Canadian government. He warned the Governor that it was not safe "to disregard the wishes of the Government" in this matter. "They have acted as fairly as could be expected," he observed, "and nothing but the Presi-

[48] Hemans to Bruce, July 6, 1866, FO, 5/1339.
[49] Bruce to Monck, June 13, 1866, FO, 5/1338.

dent and his advisors stand at this moment between us and a
more serious movement. We must strengthen his hands by acting in concert with him or we must be prepared to see him
carried by the current and entirely passive in his attitude." [50]

This was how the problem rested until the Fenians inadvertently questioned the soundness of Bruce's arguments. One
weapon he had deliberately utilized in his correspondence
with the Canadian government was the threat of another raid.
Unfortunately for him, by June 15, Roberts had blunted it by
publicly urging all Fenians to return to their homes. Perhaps
concerned that the Canadians would interpret this news as
carte blanche for the treatment of their prisoners, the British
Minister now wrote to Monck for the fourth time in five
days. Skillfully minimizing the relief Roberts' remarks offered
the colony, he carefully pointed out that the Fenian leader
had spoken of the project as being postponed only. Similarly,
he drew the attention of the Canadian government to the
Fenian leader's sinister comments about the activities of a
"sympathetic group" in Congress. To his mind both considerations indicated the wisdom of a policy of cooperation with
the Johnson administration. Describing the American government as one that had no wish to see any Anglo-American
complications arising out of Fenianism, and then, more ques-
tionably, as one that had no sympathy for the Irish element or
genuine interest in the prisoners, he insisted that its real concern was the "risk of exciting the sympathies of the masses
and the use that would be made of it by unscrupulous politicians." Consequently, when the Americans advised delay and
lenity," Bruce concluded, "they advise what is best for their
interests as well as ours." [51] This coincidence of British Imperial interests with the domestic political interests of the be-

[50] *Ibid.*   [51] *Ibid.*, June 15.

leaguered Johnson administration was no reason, or so the Minister thought, to jeopardize the former.

Still, conscious of the persistence and unflagging zeal with which he had pursued his course during the last five days, Bruce evidently believed that it needed further justification; therefore he informed the Governor that his aim throughout had been to strengthen the hand of the Canadian government. Indeed, the very urgency of his representations, he argued, could be used to overcome the probable opposition in Canada to a policy of "delay and lenity." If "you wish anything in a more official shape," he wrote, "I am quite ready to give it." [52]

This offer to accept publicly the responsibility for a policy Canadian public opinion might reasonably enough find unpalatable was unnecessary. The very day it was made Monck was writing to Bruce to inform him of the Canadian government's decision to postpone the trials of their Fenian prisoners. Despite Monck's apparently boorish insistence that this decision had been taken before a line from Bruce had been received, the Minister greeted the news gratefully. "I am glad to see," he wrote to Lord Clarendon, "that Lord Monck fully appreciated the matter in its political bearing." [53]

One political bearing Monck had not overlooked, which may have spurred him to antedate officially the Canadian decision, was the probable reaction of the Canadian public to further procrastination in bringing the Fenians to trial, certainly if it got abroad that this had been dictated to their government by the United States. It was in an effort to head off just such an impression that the Governor attempted to pry from the Americans, through Bruce, an assurance that Seward's note of June 11 would not be published. This was impossible, however, for it would have defeated the note's

---

[52] *Ibid.*   [53] Bruce to Clarendon, June 18, 1866, FO, 5/1338.

very purpose which, as the Minister explained to the Governor, was to "checkmate the Radicals in Congress who think they can abstract the Irish vote from the President's candidates at the next elections by professing strong sympathy with the Fenians, and by accusing the Government of having allowed them . . . to be sacrificed."

Yet anxious to sweeten the pill of this setback, Bruce also reported that he had informed Seward that such offensively worded communications did little to improve the situation in the colony, and perhaps as a result of this, the Secretary of State's one subsequent note had been perfectly inoffensive. As further consolation, the Minister reminded Monck that the note had been addressed to him, and as he had sent a copy of it to the Governor in a private letter, the latter could always defend himself against attack with the face-saving argument that only its substance had reached him. In effect, he could plead ignorance of its offensiveness.[54]

The alacrity with which Bruce once again volunteered to bear any odium associated with the policy of "delay and lenity" in Canada testifies to his faith in it. Still another believer now, despite the certain publication of Seward's note, was Lord Monck. Yet, one vital question remained unanswered: Would the British government endorse the Minister's course?

The earliest reports of the Fenian raid to be published in England, on June 14, were too brief to provide adequate information for comment, but two days later the London *Times*, in a marked break with its recent policy, was to be discovered eulogizing the American government:

Before congratulating ourselves and the Canadians on this satisfactory result, we hasten to express our sense of the ad-

[54] Bruce to Monck, June 24, *ibid.*

mirable spirit displayed in these transactions by the Government of the United States. It would be impossible to exaggerate the good faith, the friendliness, the sincerity, and the regard for mutual obligations which have prompted these energetic and decisive measures.[55]

In this atmosphere, Charles Francis Adams found himself showered with praise of his government. So impressed was he by these expressions of appreciation that he concluded, "At no time since the revolution has the reputation of the country stood so high in Europe as it does now." [56]

What really mattered, however, was the reaction of the British government to the news from the United States. Of course, the public and official responses could not be disassociated, for it would be difficult for any government to take a firm line against another when its own people professed a highly favorable opinion. Even Lord Clarendon admitted that the American handling of the Fenian raid had produced an enormous change in British public opinion, which was now well disposed toward the United States.[57]

The first intimation of the government's official attitude was given by Edward Cardwell. Replying to a question in the House of Commons on June 14, the Colonial Secretary stated that "he had no reason to change his belief that the Americans were doing all they could to uphold the law." [58] As for the Foreign Secretary, although it was his personal belief that the Americans had done only "that which they should have done long ago for their own interests as well as honour," [59] he

[55] June 16, 1866.
[56] Adams to Seward, June 21, 1866, NA/M30/88.
[57] Clarendon to Bruce, June 16, 1866, Clarendon Papers, Bodleian Library.
[58] London *Times*, June 15, 1866.
[59] Clarendon to Gladstone, June 23, 1866, Gladstone Papers.

declared himself satisfied with the American response in a note to Bruce. The American government "seems to have acted in a most friendly and efficient manner with respect to the Fenians," he wrote on June 16. "We only as yet know what has been done by telegram but without waiting for your official report I do not hesitate to ask you to convey to Mr. Seward and the President, if you can see him, the best thanks of Her Majesty's Government." [60]

Yet something more formal than this was required. From the Colonial Office where Monck's dispatches were now coming in, Clarendon received a note expressing "the very great satisfaction felt by Mr. Cardwell at the friendly and efficient assistance by the Government of the United States in repressing such unjustifiable invasions of British territory." [61] Then, on June 22, he was politely but firmly prodded into activity by his permanent Under Secretary, Hammond, who inquired, "Should not some despatch be written to Bruce to-morrow thanking for measures against Fenians?" [62] The following day a formal note of thanks was prepared expressing the British government's pleasure at finding "that the confidence which they . . . placed in the friendship of the United States has been so fully justified by the result." [63]

Although such formal accolades are traditionally designed for public bestowal, when a copy of the British dispatch was sent to the Colonial Office it was accompanied by a warning that "this was not to be made public on any account." [64] The

[60] Clarendon to Bruce, June 16, 1866, Clarendon Papers, Bodleian Library.

[61] Monck to Cardwell, June 8, 1866, marginal comments, CO, 42/655.

[62] Hammond to Clarendon, June 22, 1866, FO, 5/1338.

[63] Clarendon to Bruce, June 23, *ibid.*

[64] Monck to Cardwell, June 21, 1866, marginal comments, CO, 42/655.

inevitable question is: Why? The logical answer would seem
to be that this secrecy was governed by the British government's anxiety to save its American counterpart from any
unnecessary domestic embarrassment. Secrecy was obviously
not a concession to English sensibilities, while little was to be
gained by keeping the note back out of deference to Canadian
opinion. Monck had already paid public tribute to the United
States in his speech opening the Canadian Parliament and
tendered a formal note of thanks on June 11. Only in the
United States would reference by a British government to the
"friendship of the United States" have detonated a political
explosion. In the summer of 1866 few Englishmen were ignorant of American sentiment toward Britain or the domestic
plight of the Johnson administration. In fact, on the very day
that the official note was sent out, the London *Times* published a revealing report from its American correspondent.
"The firm and praiseworthy vindication of American neutrality," he wrote, "while it, no doubt, will meet with unqualified
praise abroad, has had a strange effect upon politics at home.
The Conservatives endorse the action of the Government, but
the Radicals and other English haters join the Fenians in
denouncing its interference." [65] Naturally, the British government, now receiving more complete analyses of American
developments from Bruce and Archibald, had no desire to
provide "English haters" with additional ammunition. The
effusive British note of thanks, had it been published, would
certainly have been seized upon by the President's opponents
and paraded as proof of his anglophilia. In the aftermath of
the Civil War there were few offences as heinous as this in the
entire catalogue of American political crimes.

[65] June 23, 1866.

The significance of the British government's cautious handling of the note was its obvious implication for Bruce's policy of unofficial cooperation with the Johnson administration. A decision to endorse the Minister's recommendations was logical enough, for if the American government hardly deserved the lyrical praise it received in the English press, it was certainly less objectionable to the British than its opponents. If its response to the raid had lacked decisiveness, as had its attitude toward Fenianism throughout, it had helped to cripple the Fenian offensive eventually. Lukewarm assistance was better than none at all, and this threatened to be the result of any domestic embarrassment it suffered at British hands. Therefore, conscious of the fact that the Fenians were, despite their military setbacks, by no means politically impotent, Clarendon endorsed Bruce's stand on the treatment of the prisoners in Canada. Indeed, as a further concession to American opinion, he wrote to the Lord-Lieutenant of Ireland suggesting the immediate release of any Americans still imprisoned there.[66]

The Colonial Office, meanwhile, moved to restrain the ardor of the Canadian government. Discussing the emergency measures adopted in the colony, particularly the provision for the trial of Fenians by Militia General Courts Martial, Cardwell wrote to Monck: "I rely on your discretion for the use you will make of these extensive powers, and do not doubt that you will have recourse in any case in which it may be possible to do so to the ordinary tribunals for the punishment of offenders." Finally, the Colonial Secretary expressed the hope that the prisoners would not be treated in a manner which gave "any appearance of precipitation or undue

[66] Clarendon to Bruce, June 30, 1866, Clarendon Papers, Bodleian Library.

severity." [67] "Delay and lenity" as a policy had won endorsement in England.

The decision of the British government was informally revealed to Charles Francis Adams on July 1. During a conversation with Lord Russell, the American Minister referred to the strain his government's actions during the Fenian crisis had placed upon American opinion and urged forbearance in the treatment of the prisoners. In reply, the British Prime Minister was able to reassure him that Monck was fully impressed with the delicacy of the situation. However, the satisfaction this news would normally have given Adams was probably tempered by the knowledge that Russell's government, having been recently defeated, was about to be replaced by a Conservative administration. Consequently, the Prime Minister was unable to give any assurances "about the future." [68]

[67] Cardwell to Monck, June 30, 1866, CO, 537/97.
[68] Adams, Diary, July 1, 1866.

6

The Election of 1866

As soon as Lord Derby and his Conservative colleagues
filled the offices of government, they confirmed the late administration's Fenian policy. Conscious, however, of the difficult position in which the Canadian government found itself,
caught between the public indignation the raid had naturally
provoked in the colony and the domestic "American pressure
upon Mr. Johnson and his Government," the Earl of Carnarvon, Cardwell's successor at the Colonial Office, addressed a
formal dispatch to Monck in which he advocated leniency for
the Fenians in even more emphatic terms than those used by
his predecessor. His intention, as he informed the Governor
confidentially, was "to facilitate you to carry out the policy
of Moderation with which you are already impressed, and
which appears to me especially necessary at this moment."[1] In
effect, the British government accepted full responsibility for
the implementation of this policy, and subsequently both
Cardwell's note of June 30 and that of Carnarvon a week later
were forwarded to the Canadian Parliament and then published.[2]

[1] Carnarvon to Monck, July 7, 1866, Carnarvon Papers, Public
Record Office.
[2] Bruce to Stanley, July 24, 1866, FO, 5/1339.

The new Colonial Secretary explained the Imperial government's policy in more depth in a private note which accompanied his official dispatch. From this it was evident that the need to avoid any unnecessary domestic embarrassment of the Johnson administration, upon whom the British would have to rely for help in the event of further trouble, was as important a consideration for the new government in London as it had been for the old.

The President and his Government appear to be desirous of acting fairly by us though at the same time so liable to pressure from Domestic opponents that I would regret much to see recourse had to exceptional remedy of a court martial for the Prisoners unless some new circumstances or urgent necessity arise, and even when you come to the question of punishment I hope you will find yourself able to use your influence in the direction of leniency.

Leniency was only one side of the coin, however; delay was the other, and this Carnarvon re-emphasized. "Under all circumstances," he continued, "our principal object at this moment should be to secure the interposition of whatever delay is possible. Angry feeling on both sides of the border will thus have time to cool and the final decision, whatever it may be, will be more easily carried out." [3]

Monck, of course, had already conceded the wisdom of procrastination in his correspondence with Bruce, and his reply to the Colonial Secretary's notes reflected the discussion he had had with the British Minister. "I think you may safely dismiss from your mind," he answered reassuringly, "all fears of any difficulties arising from the treatment of the Fenian prisoners. I am resting on my oars with regard to these prisoners until Congress shall have adjourned—which will probably

[3] Carnarvon to Monck, July 7, 1866, Carnarvon Papers.

take place in a few days and we shall then try them in statutable felony before the ordinary courts." [4]

If the Canadian government had been persuaded and prodded into a policy of delay and perhaps leniency by Bruce, it alone selected the charge upon which the Fenians would ultimately be indicted. Anxious to plug up legal loopholes and, by denying the Americans any cause for resentment, diplomatic ones as well, it astutely permitted the prisoners to claim whatever citizenship they chose. The Canadians had no intention of following the British example in Ireland and confusing two issues, the punishment of Fenian prisoners and the American naturalization of British natives. To try any prisoner for treason, Monck observed in a report to Carnarvon, although perfectly correct if the British law of inalienable allegiance was rigidly adhered to, "might be open to misconstruction on the part of the masses in the States and would probably lead to the excitement of angry feelings. It would be alleged that we were falling back on their original allegiance to the Queen and leaving altogether out of account their acquired rights as United States citizens." [5]

The wisdom and necessity of the British course of avoiding difficulties with the United States was further emphasized by subsequent developments in Europe. Lord Stanley, Derby's son and Clarendon's successor at the Foreign Office, was soon too deeply immersed in continental affairs, where the Prussia of Bismarck was annihilating the tattered remnants of the Hapsburg claim to hegemony in Central Europe, to invite the discussion of thorny Anglo-American issues. Of course, the danger was always present that the issues would be forced by the American government which was engaged in a critical election campaign.

[4] Monck to Carnarvon, July 21, *ibid.*   [5] *Ibid.*

That Fenianism and the Johnson administration's attitude toward it would be dragged into the election was never in doubt. Indeed, as the political struggle gained momentum, it appeared to at least one English observer that this issue would assume an importance second only to that of Reconstruction. "The Radicals," the correspondent of the London *Times* reported, "are making most strenuous exertions to use them [Fenians] against the President. He is now abused almost as heartily for his vindication of neutrality as for his friendship towards the South." [6] This political involvement was not, however, solely the work of the Radicals. William Roberts, the Fenian "President," played his part "in making every possible effort to convert the Fenian business into a political lever against" his American counterpart. In preparation for a mass indignation meeting in New York, to protest the government's enforcement of the law, he traveled to Washington "to procure Radical members of Congress as speakers." They in turn "made a great fuss of him," inviting him onto the floor of the House of Representatives once again and introducing him to interested members. "These demonstations of sympathy for Fenianism by the ruling Congressional faction" began to excite fears of "renewed cause for trouble with Great Britain." [7]

Seward had warned Bruce on June 26 that as the end of the session and the election drew nearer, Congress would become more "pestiferous" and violent in its language than ever. Bombast was one way of enticing the Irish-Americans to commit political adultery, and the language of seduction was the Congressional resolution that ostensibly brought aid and comfort to the Fenians. Clark, whose earlier proposal to extend belligerent rights to the Irish nationalists had been quietly defeated after a prudent interval, now proposed that the President be

[6] June 28, 1866.   [7] *Ibid.*, July 3.

requested to urge the Canadians to release their prisoners. Carried by an overwhelming majority, it was forwarded to the executive mansion, along with a resolution submitted by a fellow Ohioan, Rufus Spalding, which requested that the President discontinue the prosecution of Fenians in American courts.[8] Here was the eventuality for which Seward had prepared on June 11, and when Johnson's reply to the resolutions was received in Congress, it included the Secretary of State's abrasive note to Sir Frederick Bruce. Once sent to Congress, the note was quickly published, and the faithful *New York Times* immediately used it for the intended purpose: to counter Congressional thunder. Thus the newspaper emphasized how well the resolutions harmonized "with the spirit of the letter." [9]

Although Seward's foresight prevented the government from being immediately priced out of this public auction for the Irish-American vote, the Radicals had already decided to raise their bid substantially. General N. P. Banks, a Representative from Massachusetts, had given notice that on July 26 he would "introduce into the House a report from the Committee on Foreign Affairs which will denounce the President for interfering with the Fenian raids and recommend great modifications of the neutrality laws." [10]

As might be expected, the initiative for much of this Congressional activity came from men representing districts with large Irish populations. Clarke, Spalding, and Schenck all came from Ohio, which had a substantial Irish citizenry. The same was true of Massachusetts, but while the three Ohio men may have been inspired by a natural concern with the interests of their constituents and the traditional American sympa-

[8] *Congressional Globe,* 39th Cong., 1st sess., part 4, pp. 4047–4048, July 23, 1866.
[9] July 27, 1866.   [10] London *Times,* August 7, 1866.

thy for subject peoples, it is difficult to believe that principle played any part in shaping Banks's conduct. Although his proposed neutrality bill did not "disguise the strong sympathy of Americans with all suffering nationalities," there appears to be no reason to challenge the assessment of the correspondent of the London *Times* when he described the measure as "this electioneering document, most elaborately prepared." [11]

A political charlatan, Banks had been elected to Congress in 1854 as a member of the American or Know-Nothing Party, and there he had stridently voiced that party's demand for government of the United States by "Americans." Subsequently, he transferred his allegiance to the Republican Party and served in the army during the Civil War—one of the many "political" generals whose record was not marred by outstanding success. The end of the war found him back in Congress where he was appointed Chairman of the Foreign Affairs Committee. It was from this position that he sought to command the vanguard of those championing the rights of Americans who were motivated by a sentiment that was more Irish than American. He was now defending those who would have been grist for his nativist mill little more than a decade earlier. It was this checkered career which drew from Charles Francis Adams a scathing if bewildered description.

Dissolute in habits and feeble in conduct the wonder is that he is able to hold up his head at all. Yet he has been elected to Congress by the ruling party in our moral and religious state and he has been the exponent of their foreign policy during the past session. Alas, alas for the folly and wickedness of political adventurers.[12]

Banks's first sally into Irish-American and expansionist politics was vainglorious nonsense. On July 2 he introduced a

[11] *Ibid.*   [12] Adams, Diary, August 23, 1866.

bill into the House under the terms of which the British possessions in North America were invited to enter the United States in the form of four states and three territories. His supreme contribution, however—in 1866, that is—was to propose a reform of the neutrality laws. To recommend the emasculation of the American laws until they corresponded to the manifestly inadequate British equivalent, the Foreign Enlistment Act of 1819, promised to be a clever move. First, the analogy to the British measure could not fail but to reinvigorate the anglophobia the Civil War had greatly intensified if not generated. Second, Banks offered an aroused public a form of retribution and, at the same time, proclaimed the soundness of the Congressional group to which he belonged on this issue. Third, the measure offered the Radicals another weapon with which to beat the administration. The government's interference with the Fenians, they argued, benefited the British alone. Thus, the appeal of this measure was both general and specific. At a time when it was politically expedient to be an ardent anglophobe, Banks expressed the general American bitterness against Britain, but his bill also served the more specific purposes of encouraging the alienation of the Fenians and the mass of Irish-Americans from the administration and of proving to them who their true friends were. All of this was to be achieved by promising to remove what many Fenians had come to believe was the principal obstacle to their success.

The leaders of the abortive June raid had publicly and understandably argued, "Were it not for the interference of the United States Government officials no power which England could bring to bear could impede the triumphant advance of our brave boys." [13] Indeed, this conviction was so

[13] *New York Tribune*, July 6, 1866.

strong that Roberts may have sought the alteration of the neutrality laws, upon which the government had based its intervention, in exchange for the Fenian vote in the fall elections. James Stephens certainly believed that this was the plan, and he loudly condemned Roberts and Sweeny for their conduct.[14] However, his righteous indignation at this alleged bartering of Irish-American votes sprang not from principle but from the realization that to facilitate further raids into Canada was to strengthen the Roberts-Sweeny faction and thus render more remote than ever the organization of a massive rebellion in Ireland—the course he favored.

For all its virtues as an electoral gambit, the Banks bill still incurred criticism in committee. Representatives Raymond of New York, a staunch supporter of Johnson and Seward and editor of the *New York Times*, and Patterson of New Jersey wrote a dissenting opinion to the measure in which, while agreeing that the laws stood in need of reform, they argued that "for the present the laws should stand as they are." [15] This was a forlorn effort, and the majority reported the Banks proposal to the House where it passed without one vote being cast against. With Roberts ostentatiously present on the floor of the House, often "in earnest conversation with several prominent members," [16] even Raymond prudently decided to leave the chamber just before the vote was taken. This unanimous demonstration of sympathy for the Fenian cause quickly brought its reward. In a public letter, published three days later, Roberts declared:

I trust that the noble action of the great American House of Representatives in the passage of a just and republican law on our neutral obligations towards monarchical nations will meet

[14] Bruce to Clarendon, June 26, 1866, FO, 5/1338.
[15] London *Times*, August 9, 1866.
[16] *New York Tribune*, July 27, 1866.

with the warm approval of my countrymen everywhere, and that the noble and eloquent words of that great statesman Nathaniel Banks . . . will secure him the love and lasting friendship of all Irishmen.[17]

Yet if, as this letter suggests, the Irish-American vote had been promised, at least to Banks, in exchange for less stringent neutrality laws, both sides were offering more than they had the ability or the inclination to give. It was unlikely that the Brotherhood, even had it been united on a policy of political activism in the United States, could have "delivered" the Irish vote en masse. This probability was transformed into a certainty by the lack of Fenian cohesion. Similarly, it is doubtful whether Banks expected his measure to make its way through both Houses of Congress before the end of the session. Indeed, had it done so, it would still have been open to a pocket veto by the President. Understandable doubt about the sincerity of Banks was voiced, therefore, by some contemporary observers. Commenting on the developments in the United States, the London *Times* concluded:

The Radicals are determined to get the vote [Irish-American] on their side at any cost; hence they memorialize the President on behalf of the Fenians and hence they bring in this Bill as a bait to catch the Irish vote all over the country. But it may be questioned whether Mr. Banks is not acting treacherously towards his dupes, for it is observable that he kept back his Bill until the eleventh hour of the Session, and when he knew there was no chance of its passing the Senate.[18]

In the Senate, Zachariah Chandler of Michigan, as unattractive a Radical as Banks, had attempted to persuade the Foreign Relations Committee to consider alterations to the neutrality

[17] Bruce to Stanley, July 30, 1866, FO, 5/1339.
[18] August 11, 1866.

laws before the Banks measure came up, but to no avail. Both proponents of change were frustrated by the fiercely independent Charles Sumner, another Massachusetts man, who retained his sense of proportion throughout the entire affair. The strength of his personality and his position as Chairman of the influential Senate Foreign Relations Committee lent considerable weight to his opinion. Few could have doubted his determination when he announced that any attempt to "railroad" the neutrality bill through the Senate would precipitate a filibuster. He intended to see that the measure was reported to his committee where it would die of inattention. Any attempt to by-pass him, he warned, would compel him to speak until the end of the session, thus bringing the Senate to a standstill. Sumner had his way.[19]

To describe the Banks bill as madness, as Sumner did in his private correspondence,[20] was no exaggeration. Had the Senate passed this measure, it would have placed the President in an uncomfortable dilemma, and this no doubt was the intention of the framer. Either Johnson would have had to accept it, with all the implications that decision would have carried for Anglo-American relations, or reject it and thus provide his opponents with more ammunition. And the struggle between Executive and Congress over Reconstruction was so desperate that presidential acquiescence was not entirely beyond the bounds of possibility. Yet this would have invited a further exacerbation of relations with Britain, and for this reason alone would have been inimical to American interests. It would also have been a peculiarly inappropriate step for a nation still determined to collect compensation from Britain for her conduct during the Civil War. This point did not

[19] Sumner to Bright, August 17, 1866, Bright Papers.
[20] *Ibid.*, September 3.

escape the London *Times*, and no matter the facetiousness, there was logic in its observation:

The American Government declare we ought to be made to pay for having bad laws. But even while these claims are pending the House of Representatives destroyed all pretence for making them by affirming that our laws are so blameless that those of America ought to be made to resemble them, only allowing greater latitude for such depredations of commerce of other powers as the *Alabama* committed.[21]

For just this reason Adams had always opposed any action inspired by revenge, for however sweet initially it would ultimately prove very expensive.

If British interests might have been served in some perverse manner by the passage of the Banks bill into law, the introduction of this measure was still a subject of concern for them. For admirers of the United States like John Bright, the affair was a sorry indication of an American willingness to sink to the level of Britain instead of setting her an example.[22] While for an American correspondent of the London *Times* it proved "that the Radical party are the real fomentors of the ill-feeling often expressed in America towards Britain."[23] Of more immediate concern to the British government, however, was the response of its American counterpart to this Congressional activity. How would President Johnson and his colleagues react to the development of an alliance between the Roberts section of the Brotherhood and the Radicals? How would the administration respond to a new Fenian crisis which Congress by its activity might well incite?

[21] August 11, 1866.
[22] Bright to Sumner, August 16, 1866, Bright Papers.
[23] August 9, 1866.

The closest observer of the American scene was far from confident. Sir Frederick Bruce was not at all sure that the President would have the strength of purpose to take the necessary preventive measures if confronted by the choice of sacrificing the Irish vote or permitting the Fenians to take their chance at the border. He had not changed his opinion that Johnson was honest and Seward pacific, but he thought that the President's honesty might be put to "too severe a trial," while the Secretary of State might be unable to cling to office unless progress was "made towards an amicable settlement of the questions in dispute" with Britain. In short, having repeatedly prepared his government for the reappearance of the *Alabama* claims, Bruce was now suggesting to Lord Stanley that some arrangement of these claims might be necessary to hold the administration up to the mark on Fenianism. In effect, whether prompted by his own observations of the situation in the United States or subtle pressure exerted by Seward, the British Minister was suggesting that the American government be permitted to recoup its ebbing political fortune at the expense of the British.[24]

It was this same nagging doubt about the response of the Johnson administration to another Fenian crisis that prompted Bruce to offer advice to the Canadian authorities as well. Reminding Monck of the British government's decision to release American Fenian prisoners in Ireland rather than run the risk of a collision with the United States, he suggested that the same policy might be even more desirable for the British Provinces, sharing as they did a common border with the Republic. Aware, however, of the suspicion with which his recommendations were greeted in Canada, the Minister emphasized that they were based upon what he believed to be the

[24] Bruce to Stanley, August 2, 1866, FO, 5/1339.

best interests of the Province. Indeed, he repeated the argument he had, by implication at least, used in his dispatch to Lord Stanley, namely, that it was not punishment of the prisoners by Canada or Britain that would stamp out the Fenian threat but good relations with the United States.[25] For the British government this meant concessions on the *Alabama;* for the Canadian, the liberation of their Fenian prisoners.

To this point Bruce had always carried the day, at least with regard to the handling of the Fenian problem in North America. He had defined British policy both before the raid into Canada and in its aftermath. However, he was asking a great deal not only of the Canadian government, which had never been an enthusiastic supporter of his policy, but of his own government as well. Simply to have released the Fenian prisoners, as Bruce advocated because they were Americans, would undoubtedly have provoked a storm of protest in the British colonies where the understandable popular hostility toward them had only been strengthened by the activity in Congress and the publication of Seward's note of June 11. Insofar as the press reflected public opinion, the Canadians were anxious that an example should be made of the hapless men who had fallen into their hands.[26] Yet, prudent deference to popular sentiment was not the only restraint upon the government's exercise of the power of amnesty. The familiar and ominous rumblings of Fenian activity south of the border had also to be considered. What greater incentive could the Fenians require to attack the colonies again than proof that even if caught by the Canadian authorities they would quickly be released?

[25] Bruce to Monck, August 6, *ibid.*
[26] Lester B. Shippee, *Canadian-American Relations, 1849–1874* (New Haven, 1939), p. 234.

Reports of Fenian plans to hold a giant "pic-nic" in Buffalo evoked all too familiar memories of similar reports during the last days of May to be ignored. Determined not to be caught napping again, the Canadian government ordered gunboats to the neighborhood and stationed some three thousand troops, Volunteers and Regulars, at Fort Erie. Although these preparations were ridiculed by one American consul in Canada as "Falstaffian," they served some purpose, as he admitted, in that they helped to reassure a public "really alarmed in anticipation of another raid." [27] The alarm also permeated official circles, and not without reason. As the American election campaign gained momentum, the doubt Bruce had already voiced about the American government's response to a new raid must have strengthened its hold upon the mind of the Canadian government. If, as appeared possible during the second week of August, 1866, the Fenians did launch another attack during the fall elections, could the Canadians rely upon the American government to do even as much as it had in June?

The political pressures to which the Johnson administration was already subject, and which in the event of a raid might become irresistible, were illustrated by a giant Fenian "picnic" held in Chicago on August 15. There a large gathering of Irish-Americans were entertained by a galaxy of speakers. Governor Oglesby of Illinois shared the platform with Senator Trumbull, Congressmen Logan and Schuyler Colfax, and "General" John O'Neill. Their remarks followed a familiar and relentless pattern—English tyranny, the courageous record of the Irish in the Civil War, the treachery of President Johnson in tacitly encouraging the raid and then preventing it

[27] Fitnam to Frederick Seward, August 20, 1866, Seward Papers.

from continuing to its inevitable triumph, and finally but by
no means least, the wisdom of voting Republican.[28]

While their opponents attempted to seduce the Irish-Americans with an ardent courtship of the Fenians, first in Congress
and then on the hustings, Johnson and Seward were being
pressed by their supporters to take steps to counter this political cuckolding. An obvious expression of affection was to
cancel the prosecution of those Fenians first arrested during
the June raid. James Dixon, a conservative Senator from Con-
necticut and firm supporter of Andrew Johnson, urged this
course upon the President as early as July 8. "How would it
do to pardon all the Fenian prisoners?" he inquired. "I wish
you would. The Radicals are making some capital on that
point."[29]

Shortly thereafter Seward received similar advice from
his political crony Thurlow Weed. "Can you not let up [on]
the Fenians? If they must be tried should not the pardoning
power be exercised?"[30] The answer of course was that they
would not be tried. On August 20 it was announced that the
government intended to enter a nolle prosequi in cases pending against Fenians at Buffalo.[31]

These results of the contest for the electoral allegiance of
the Irish-Americans did nothing to reassure the nervous Canadians. Indeed, it "has produced an impression both in Canada
and, I have reason to think among the Fenians," Monck reported to Carnarvon, "that the Government of the United

---

[28] *Speeches of Hon. Schuyler Colfax and General J. O'Neill, Delivered at the Great Fenian Pic Nic, Chicago, August 15, 1866* (undated
pamphlet).
[29] Dixon to Johnson, July 8, 1866, Johnson Papers.
[30] Weed to Seward, July 25, 1866, Seward Papers.
[31] *New York Tribune*, August 21, 24, 1866.

States will not interfere energetically should another invasion be attempted as they did on the former occasion." His personal belief that the Americans would fulfill their international obligations notwithstanding, the Governor agreed that the abandonment of the prosecutions against the Fenians in the United States lent countenance to the popular fears in Canada. It also reinforced the necessity of the Canadians making an example of the captured Fenian terrorists, for it was now manifest that they could not rely upon the Americans to punish them. More immediately, however, these disturbing developments persuaded Monck not only to delay the departure of himself and several of his ministers for London to discuss the final stages of confederation, but also to appeal to the home government for military reinforcements.[32]

The Canadian appeal prompted the Tory government in Britain to examine critically its relationship with colonies now in transition to dominion status, while at a personal level Carnarvon grew alarmed at reports of habitual drunkards holding positions of power in Canada.[33] His concern could not have been lessened by Monck's information that "the worst feature of the case is that the principal delinquent is not only the ablest man in the Province but so completely dominates all other politicians that his ejection from the Ministry is impossible. It is neither easy nor agreeable to work with such tools, but for the present unfortunately for me it is inevitable." [34]

The notorious intemperance of John A. Macdonald, which Carnarvon thought could be best offset by Monck retaining in his own hands the direction of affairs in the event of another Fenian raid, was not the principal concern of the Imperial government. More serious was the defensive capability of the

[32] Monck to Carnarvon, August 27, 1866, Carnarvon Papers.
[33] Carnarvon to Monck, September 7, *ibid.*
[34] Monck to Carnarvon, September 27, *ibid.*

Colonies. In short, the Canadian application for assistance provided the home government with an opportunity to express its displeasure with the colonists' inadequate contribution to their own defence. Deeply concerned, as one would expect, with expenditures, particularly when the beneficiary was a virtually autonomous state, Benjamin Disraeli, Chancellor of the Exchequer, wrote to Lord Derby: "It can never be our pretence or our policy to defend the Canadian frontier against the United States. If the colonists can't, as a general rule, defend themselves against the Fenians, they can do nothing . . . what is the use of these colonial deadweights which we do not govern?" [35] This attitude was reflected, if less offensively, in Carnarvon's reply to Monck's request for help: "Whatever may be the issue of the pending events the danger of successful aggression will not have passed away until the whole question of provincial defence is placed on a satisfactory footing." [36]

Yet this critical response did not presage a rejection of the appeal for additional troops, for they were ordered to Canada in September. The reasons for this apparent contradiction in the Imperial government's thought and actions were given by Disraeli, heir apparent to Lord Derby. First and probably foremost, the government was responding to the instinct of political survival. The fragility of its domestic position—there was no comforting majority in Parliament—might be too easily strained by a Fenian raid into Canada or any Irish insurrection which might well accompany or follow it. However, the danger of the government's being overturned was not the only consideration. It was also agreed that it would be unfair to permit the Canadians to be crushed by Fenians at a

[35] G. E. Buckle and W. F. Monypenny, *Life of Benjamin Disraeli* (London, 1916), IV, 276, Disraeli to Derby, September 30, 1866.
[36] Carnarvon to Monck, September 12, 1866, CO, 537/97.

time when they were beginning to show signs of a greater willingness to assume the burdens of their own defence. Finally, the Imperial government conceded that there was no hope of getting anything resembling sense or moderation out of the Americans until the fall elections were over.[37]

Having decided to send troops, it was a perverse sense of humor which persuaded the British government to dispatch the 61st Regiment. Members of this regiment were already suspected of being tainted with Fenianism, as Monck was informed by British Army Headquarters once they were on their way. This information drew from the Governor the understandably sarcastic retort that the reason for selecting them was no doubt "because it was supposed that the Canadians were too strong and that it was intended to handicap them in their contest with the Fenians." Ironically, they served their purpose. The news that reinforcements were on their way not only calmed the fears of the Canadians but in Monck's opinion also frightened off the Fenians. Consequently, when the troops reached North America the crisis had passed, and the Governor quickly ordered them on to the West Indies.[38]

If the exigencies of domestic politics in Britain, the United States, and to some extent Canada shaped the British government's response to this new Fenian crisis, they also helped to shape the attitude of both the American and the British governments to the long-heralded revival of the Civil War claims.

The United States naturally assumed the initiative, and on August 27, Seward sent a long dispatch to Adams which the American Minister was ordered to present to Lord Stanley. From the outset it was clear that the Secretary of State in-

[37] Buckle and Monypenny, *Disraeli*, IV, 276, Disraeli to Derby, September 30, 1866.
[38] Monck to Carnarvon, October 5, 1866, Carnarvon Papers.

tended to capitalize, as far as he could, upon the recent activity in Congress, particularly the Banks bill. In fact, he cited this as evidence of the dissatisfaction of the American people who had decided "in a spirit of self-defence, if not retaliation, in the absence of any other remedy, to conform their principles and policy in conducting their intercourse with the offending state, to that of the party from which the injury proceeds." Although a rather simplistic interpretation of the background of the neutrality bill, as the British well knew, the measure undoubtedly drew much of its support from the American desire to be revenged on Britain. To this extent, Seward's use of it to exert additional pressure upon the British was perfectly sound, but he overstepped the bounds of opportunism in the rest of his argumentative dispatch. He utilized the British policy of abstaining from official protests against Fenian activities to contrast the British attitude toward Confederate activities during the Civil War with the American government's response to Fenianism: "Thus we have seen ruinous and warlike expeditions against the United States practically allowed and tolerated by Her Majesty's Government, notwithstanding remonstrances; and we have seen similar unlawful attempts in this country against Great Britain disallowed and defeated by direct and unprompted action of the Government of the United States." [39] To have held this statement up to the investigation it deserved would, of course, have compelled the British government to sacrifice their policy of cooperation and informal correspondence.

If the British were unlikely to be impressed by or receptive to much of Seward's reasoning, inevitably the question of his motive arises. What did he expect to gain from this dispatch? The answer, no doubt, is that he hoped to make diplomatic

[39] Seward to Adams, August 27, 1866, NA/M77/80.

and political capital out of it. His utilization of Banks's madness re-emphasized the point Bruce had made earlier to the British government, and Lawrence Oliphant had made in the Commons after a conversation with Adams long before that: the re-establishment of amicable Anglo-American relations was the only lasting solution for Fenianism. If this could not be achieved until the problem of the Civil War claims had been resolved, the Banks bill illustrated the need for immediate progress toward a settlement, that is, unless the British were prepared to risk a further deterioration in relations. However, Seward's dispatch was as much an exercise in domestic politics as it was in diplomacy. His argumentative tone, crude opportunism, and the attachment of an eye-catching list of claims that covered in excess of twenty pages when published later in the *Diplomatic Correspondence of the United States*,[40] all suggested an exercise in domestic diplomacy. Written for publication, the dispatch evidently sought to prove to the American people that the Johnson administration was "sound" on the subject of the claims. It was not going to be "soft" with the British.

Certainly Charles Francis Adams was in no doubt about Seward's intentions. Commenting upon the dispatch in his diary, he observed that it "was obviously designed more for the emergency at home than for any hope of result here." This conclusion must have eased his decision to make slight alterations to it before he forwarded it to Stanley. "All I have done to it," he commented, "was to polish and prune the redundance, perhaps softening the tone in one or two places without impairing the meaning. Rapidly as he writes and is obliged to think and act," he concluded condescendingly, Seward "has never had time to study the refinement which

[40] Department of State, *Papers Relating to the Foreign Affairs of the United States*, 1866 (Washington, 1867), pp. 177–203.

gives so much grace and dignity to the Diplomatic style of Europe." [41]

When he visited the Foreign Office on September 19 to present the modified dispatch, Adams was not confident of success. He considered the Tory government's position too weak to risk discussing such a controversial subject. Yet the issue was by this time not quite so sensitive as it had been. Some politicians like Oliphant had long advocated some form of compromise with the United States. This sentiment was also growing in the nation. Even the London *Times* was slowly reaching the conclusion that Lord Russell had erred in refusing to discuss the question earlier and that the difficulties could be settled through arbitration.[42] Finally, the government was being urged to make concessions by its Minister in Washington. Therefore, Lord Stanley carefully refrained from extinguishing all hope in his conversation with Adams. Although he made no comment when the American Minister stressed that "the main point was to reopen the matter because the state of popular feeling in America was such, as shown by the proceedings in Congress, as to lead to an application of the repeal of the neutrality laws if there was no other recourse," Adams emerged from the interview with the impression that the Foreign Secretary "would himself become inclined to some form of negotiation, which is perhaps all that Mr. Seward would stand in need for." [43]

That Lord Stanley was prepared to open some form of negotiation was subsequently confirmed, but unfortunately it was not "all that Mr. Seward would stand in need for." The concession came neither early enough nor was it complete enough when it did come to satisfy Seward's political and diplomatic requirements.

[41] Adams, Diary, September 13, 15, 1866.   [42] January 4, 1867.
[43] Adams, Diary, September 19, 1866.

The fact that the British reply was delayed until December suggests that the home government was not quite as concerned about the plight of the Johnson administration as their Minister in Washington. Stanley had warned Adams that his reply to such an important question would have to be discussed and approved in Cabinet, and as the principal members of the government were then dispersed all over the country this could not be done before the end of October. Yet when Adams returned from a European vacation on November 22, the Foreign Secretary was still not ready, and it was not until the end of the month that his reply was sent to Bruce to be forwarded to Seward.

When Adams saw a copy of the British note he observed that it was "sharp in retort." [44] Without sacrificing the British policy of quiet diplomacy, Stanley successfully refuted Seward's contrast of the respective governments' attitudes toward Confederate and Fenian activities. He pointed out that the former had been secret whereas the latter were "open and avowed." "The Government of the United States needed, therefore," he commented with some asperity, "no research on the part of its own officials, nor even denunciation by British Authorities, to establish against the Fenian agitators a palpable case of infringement of the laws of the United States." [45] For all the sharpness of this riposte, however, Stanley's reply indicated that the British were willing to negotiate the problem of the claims.

If British procrastination denied the Johnson administration whatever immediate domestic political advantage Seward had sought to secure for it with his dispatch, the Secretary of State's diplomatic ambitions foundered upon his rock-like insistence that the British Proclamation of Neutrality be arbi-

[44] *Ibid.*, November 25.
[45] Stanley to Bruce, November 30, 1866, FO, 5/1340.

trated along with the American claims. This point the British refused to yield, because to have done so would have been tantamount to an abnegation of national sovereignty. Thus, Seward's "soundness" upon this aspect of Anglo-American relations cost both governments any chance of rapid progress to their betterment. The resultant impasse was captured some time later in a *Punch* cartoon. Portraying a rather stout and sturdy Mrs. Brittania interrupting two squabbling children, one of whose toy boats lies broken on the floor, the caption reads:

MRS. BRITTANIA—Hoity-Toity! What's all this fuss about?
JOHNNY BULL—It's cousin Columbia, Ma, And she says I broke her ships, and I didn't and I want to be friends—and she's a cross thing—and wants to have it all her own way.[46]

If a concession on the Proclamation of Neutrality was never probable, even evidence of British willingness to arbitrate the claims, had it been given in time to be used by the administration in the fall elections, could scarcely have worked the electoral miracle Andrew Johnson needed. His administration faced a catastrophe, something its ability to posture as the defender of American interests whose firmness had brought the British lion to heel might have mitigated but never overcome.

Ironically, the Fenians emitted one of the few rays of political hope during the fall. Their divisions were magnified and multiplied by election strategy. Roberts clashed with Sweeny at a Fenian Congress held in Troy, New York, in September, over the decision to commit their wing of the Brotherhood to the support of the Radicals.[47] Meanwhile, both men were being denounced by James Stephens. Desper-

[46] London *Punch*, LIV (February 1, 1868), 51.
[47] London *Times*, September 25, 1866.

ately anxious to obtain physical and financial support for another rebellion in Ireland, he sought to convince Irish-Americans that all activity against Canada was doomed to failure. Insisting in speech after speech that President Johnson had had no alternative but to intervene in June, he defended the American government and berated Roberts and Sweeny for their refusal to face up to this fact of international life.[48]

If the Johnson administration could look confidently to the followers of Stephens for succor, yet another sympathetic group entered the arena to pick the carcass of the Irish-American electorate. Calling itself the Central Executive Committee of Irish Citizens and sitting in Washington, it published an address warning citizens of the same national origin against what it described as the hypocritical sympathy of the Radicals. Fastening upon both Banks bills—to relax the neutrality laws and provide for the incorporation of British North America into the United States—it argued that these exposed the Radicals in their true colors: in brief, that they treacherously planned to use the Fenians to conquer the Canadian Colonies and then annex them to the United States, thus depriving "the Fenians of all the advantages they propose to derive from them as a basis of operations in favor of Ireland." [49]

Comforting as this stand must have been for the beleaguered President, the new organization soon revealed that its stand was not inspired by any blind devotion to the presidential person or policies. During an interview with Johnson on September 18, members of the Committee drew his attention to their estimate of the number of Irish-American voters—three quarters of a million—and by implication at least offered them to the government. In return, they demanded firmness in

[48] *New York Tribune,* August 29, 1866.
[49] Bruce to Stanley, September 8, 1866, FO, 5/1339.

the nation's relations with Britain, particularly on the sensitive issues of the *Alabama* and naturalization, and, of more immediate importance, a greater share of the spoils of office for their fellow Irish-Americans. However, demands founded upon unguaranteed promises—the Committee provided no evidence of their ability to "deliver" the votes—have rarely impressed professional politicians. Consequently, the Committee secured from Johnson no more than the customary expression of sympathy for the Irish cause, while Seward refused to remove any men from office so they could be replaced by Irishmen.[50]

All hope of substantial Irish-American support, which the activities of Stephens and the Irish Executive Committee no doubt raised within the administration, appeared forlorn once the election results were tabulated. The government lost the opening round, its candidates going down to defeat in Maine and Vermont. This setback the correspondent of the London *Times* generously attributed to the Fenians, whose attitude he considered ominous for the government in the subsequent elections.

The cause which operated in Maine and Vermont must also have great effect in every other state. I refer to the Fenian vote which almost bodily changed from Democracy to Radicals. Two thousand five hundred Fenians in Vermont and three thousand five hundred in Maine were able by changing sides to work this great result, and as such are to be the Fenian tactics throughout the country the President's weakness can readily be seen.[51]

If this interpretation of these early results was somewhat oversimplified, the subsequent conduct of the Johnson admin-

[50] Antisell (chairman of the Irish Executive Committee) to Johnson, September 20, 1865, Johnson Papers; Dixon to F. Seward, September 17, 1866, Seward Papers.
[51] September 27, 1866.

istration and its supporters does suggest that they believed the Fenians had played their part in the defeat. Thus, in an effort to hold the Irish to their traditional party allegiance, all the remaining prosecutions still pending against Fenians, including Roberts, were abandoned, but if the correspondent of the London *Times* was correct in his assessment, even this failed to stem the tide. The October elections brought further defeats for the government. For this "the Fenian vote is to a large extent responsible," the correspondent insisted, "it having been generally noticed that ardent Fenians who had all their lives been Democrats at this election voted with the Radicals." [52] Now, in the midst of political disaster, the administration resorted to desperate measures in a frantic attempt to save the New York elections held on November 6.

Prodded by the Fenians on one side and their own supporters on the other, Johnson and his colleagues agreed to return the munitions seized earlier in the year. First the Fenians, allegedly on the advice of the Radicals, appointed a delegation to visit the President and press for the return of their weapons.[53] They were followed by Samuel J. Tilden, a power in the Democratic Party in New York, an early and prominent member of the National Johnson Club and Chairman of the State Committee of the President's hastily formed National Union Party. Apparently unconcerned by the dilemma confronting Johnson—perhaps he failed to recognize it—of choosing between the United States' international obligations and domestic political expediency, Tilden endorsed the suggestion of a local politician in upstate New York that the guns be returned. "There is no policy in holding this property as a mere pecuniary fine," he wrote to the President, "and the opponents of the administration are using much demagogical

[52] October 27.   [53] *Ibid.*, September 27.

acts to take from it the votes of the Irish, that no pretext should be given them which clear duty does not compel." [54] Four days later, on September 24, the Cabinet agreed to the return of the weapons after a face-saving but easily circumvented bond, for double their value, had been provided by the Fenians.[55] This news was released in the middle of October, little more than two weeks before polling day in New York.

It was also in an effort to placate the numerous Irish-American residents of New York that the government agreed to remove District-Attorney William A. Dart. His vigor in helping to frustrate the O'Neill expedition and then in attempting to uphold the law by indicting some of the participants had made him anathema to Irish nationalists. Under their pressure his removal had been promised by Thurlow Weed in August, but a squabble over his replacement, between Weed and the local Democratic politicos delayed the announcement until the eve of the New York elections.[56] While the delay proved fortunate in this instance, the general consequences of the uneasy cooperation of the Democrats with the Johnson Republicans, which this incident illustrated were certain to be detrimental to the President's cause. Thus distrusting their Republican allies, particularly Weed, the New York Democrats impeded the full exercise of the power of patronage lest it work to their disadvantage after the 1866 election.[57]

Demeaning as some of the President's concessions to Irish-American opinion undoubtedly were, their futility made them

[54] Tilden to Johnson, September 21, 1866, Johnson Papers.

[55] T. C. Pease and J. G. Randall, eds., *Diary of Orville Hickman Browning*, II (Springfield, Ill., 1933), 95, September 25, 1866.

[56] S. E. Church to Weed, November 15, 1866, Weed Papers; *New York Tribune*, November 3; London *Times*, November 19, 1866.

[57] S. L. M. Barlow to Tilden, September 15, 1866; Tilden to McCullough (Secretary of the Treasury) September 17, 1866, Samuel J. Tilden Papers, New York Public Library.

appear even worse. The omnipresent correspondent of the London *Times* had reached the conclusion by October 16 that Johnson's position in New York was hopeless "in spite of Fenian conciliation." [58] If the reports Tilden received from professional politicians at the local level were more optimistic, some chairmen of county committees conceded that the Fenian vote was still "shaky." [59] Thus, New York members of the Brotherhood made no secret of their hostility; indeed, they had met in August and agreed not to participate in receptions for Johnson during what proved to be his disastrous "swing around the circle." [60] Of course, the subsequent wooing of the Fenians had been designed to conquer this hostility; yet the antagonism between them and the government grew. For this the Radicals could claim some credit; they immediately organized a counterattack to offset the administration's concessions.

In the two weeks prior to the New York elections, the *New York Tribune* subjected Johnson and his Fenian policies to damaging criticism. On October 24, prominently positioned on its front page the newspaper published an inflammatory letter, ostensibly from an Irish-American correspondent, in which the President was assaulted for his legalistic attitude toward the Irish famine of 1846–1847. Recalling how a famine relief bill had been introduced into Congress to appropriate money with which flour and corn could be purchased for the starving Irish, the correspondent also recalled how Congressman Andrew Johnson had opposed the measure in the House of Representatives with the argument that it was unconstitutional. The anonymous author then concluded, "I

[58] October 30, 1866.

[59] R. P. Flower to Tilden, October 22, 1866; Church to Tilden, October 31, 1866, Tilden Papers.

[60] London *Times*, September 15, 1866.

would ask them [Irish-Americans] before daring in the face of such remonstrances to deposit a vote for Andrew Johnson's supporters to recall Andrew Johnson's vote against their relatives and friends."

A natural sequel to this assault was an attack on Johnson's more recent Fenian policy. All the earlier charges on this score were now revived. Never a supporter of the raid, the *Tribune* castigated the President for fomenting it. He had encouraged the Fenians, the newspaper charged, by permitting them to purchase arms from the government, by receiving their delegations at the executive mansion, and by his expressions of "sympathy for all oppressed nations and his particular interest in unhappy Ireland." Then, once the raiders had established themselves on British soil, he had crushed them.[61] As Election Day drew closer, the Radical journal hammered home the message of presidential culpability. "We held, and still hold, that the President of the United States was to blame," it proclaimed on October 31. "A weak policy is always wrong at both ends and bad in the middle; and thus the President has failed to satisfy Irishmen, Americans and Canadians."

A focal point of Irish-American and Canadian dissatisfaction was the Fenian prisoners. On the one hand, the Radicals sought to capitalize on Irish-American sentiment by charging the administration with duplicity and desperately attempting to saddle it with the responsibility for the plight of the men held in Canada. On the other, the Canadian public's desire to punish these terrorists, which was strengthened by the conduct of the United States government, in particular its wholesale abandonment of prosecutions, promised to provide the Radicals with more ammunition.

[61] October 29, 1866.

Monck had delayed the trials, as he said he would, until the current session of Congress was completed. Then, on July 30, as the American politicians left their national capital for the hustings, he wrote to Carnarvon: "I think all angry feeling with respect to them [the prisoners] has disappeared and I shall have no difficulty in dealing with them as I see fit." [62] This confident prediction was written, unwittingly of course, on the eve of another Fenian alarm, which did little to endear the earlier terrorists to the colonists. The government's subsequent if understandable delay in bringing them to trial soon provoked criticism "as it was very generally held that immediate punishment was desirable." [63] However, when Monck at last ceased to "rest on his oars" in October and the trials began, popular opinion in Canada should have been satisfied with the results. Several prisoners were convicted and sentenced to death. This turn of events was a political windfall for the opponents of the Johnson administration and another disaster for the American President and his supporters. Engaged in a desperate struggle to win the New York elections, nothing could have been quite so ill-timed as the newspaper report on October 26 that a Fenian, Robert Lynch, had been sentenced to be executed on December 12, unless it was the report the following day that a Roman Catholic priest, Father McMahon, had been sentenced to the same punishment for the same crime. [64]

The immediate reaction of the government's political organizers and supporters was expressed by Thurlow Weed. In a note to Seward, written appropriately enough from the New York committee rooms of the National Union Party, he commented:

[62] Monck to Carnarvon, July 30, 1866, Carnarvon Papers.
[63] *New York Times*, September 9, 1866.
[64] *Ibid.*, October 26, 27.

You see that Lynch the Fenian has been convicted. This will raise fresh excitement. I hope that our Government will feel that it is proper to move promptly and earnestly in favor of clemency. The prompt and efficient action of the Government to avert the expedition saved Canada many lives and much treasure. You have, therefore, a right to ask for this man's life. Things are improving in this State. We are now hopeful. But without immediate action in the case indicated, all would be lost. The importance of this question cannot be over-estimated.[65]

This viewpoint James Dixon echoed in his correspondence with the President.[66]

Seward's response to this unforeseen and unwelcome development was to do as Weed suggested but in a manner entirely his own. He composed another dispatch designed more for the emergency at home than for that in Canada. Offensively reminiscent of his earlier note to Bruce on June 11, the Secretary of State first cast doubt upon the quality of Canadian justice. "The Government of the United States," he informed the British Minister, "is required by the highest considerations of national dignity, duty and honour to inquire into the legality, justice and regularity of the judicial proceedings which have taken place . . . and we shall expect to make known to Her Majesty's Government . . . such opinions as the President shall adopt." Of course, to do all these things he required transcripts of the trial proceedings. He also suggested that the British government might wish to review Canadian justice. A review, Seward observed, might well be undertaken "with a regard . . . to the maintenance of good relations between the two countries. Such relations are always difficult and delicate in States that are adjacent to each other without being separated by impassable barriers." Then, he followed this thinly

[65] Weed to Seward, October 26, 1866, Seward Papers.
[66] Howard K. Beale, *The Critical Year* (New York, 1930) p. 304.

veiled threat with a final and characteristically sarcastic flourish which was sure to appeal to American readers: "This suggestion is made with freedom and earnestness because the same opinions were proposed to us in our recent civil war by all the countries and publicists of Europe, and by none of them with a greater frankness and kindness than by the statesmen of Great Britain." [67]

Sir Frederick Bruce did not permit Seward's note or any of the other concessions to domestic political expediency to disturb his diplomatic composure. He remained unperturbed despite the frantic efforts at Fenian conciliation. News of the return of the Fenian arms he dismissed as evidence of a conspiracy between Roberts and Santa Anna, the perennial Mexican dictator and exile, to restore the latter to power.[68] Similarly, he refused to grow excited over Seward's dispatch. The speed with which it was released to the press, almost before the ink had had time to dry, and an interview with the Secretary of State convinced him that "party interests require that a show should be made of taking these men formally under protection, and that a course should be pursued which will enable the Government to claim credit for any clemency that may be shown them." [69]

In fact, there was never any doubt in the minds of the Governor of Canada or the British government about the necessity of clemency. Monck had no intention of permitting the condemned men to be executed, but he decided not to commute their sentences until he had received instructions from London. Yet, commutation to a period of imprisonment to be settled later could scarcely have embarrassed an Imperial government which had consistently advocated leniency, and

[67] Seward to Bruce, October 27, 1866, NA/M99/43.
[68] Bruce to Stanley, October 16, 1866, FO, 5/1340.
[69] *Ibid.*, October 30.

these were the instructions Monck soon received from London. By that time, however, the unhappy Johnson administration had paid the price of the Governor's caution.

Reports of the death sentences brought an immediate response from the Foreign Office. "It appears to Lord Stanley very desirable," a minute sent to the Colonial Office read, "that the Governor-General of Canada should be recommended"—and here the Foreign Secretary personally deleted the words "if possible"—"to deal mercifully with the Fenians as to all events to spare their lives."[70] Two days later, on November 12, Carnarvon telegraphed Monck: "Spare the lives of the convicts in question, but do not settle commutation of their sentences till you hear again. Apprize British Minister at Washington."[71] For Johnson and his colleagues this decision, made almost a week after the New York elections, was the final irony. No matter how satisfying the tone and content of Seward's note to Bruce had been to American opinion, the Radicals had easily dismissed it as simply "making just amends to an abused public opinion" by recommending "a merciful and forgiving policy" upon the British government.[72] In effect, the government had encouraged the Fenians to attack the British colony; therefore, the very least it could do was attempt to protect its dupes. However, as Irish-Americans were reminded as they went to the polls on November 6 by Radical agents stationed outside, Fenians were still under sentence of death in Canada.[73]

The significance of this factor in the election results is difficult to assess; nevertheless, the President and his supporters went down to another defeat, and for this they held the

[70] Foreign Office minute, November 10, 1866, FO, 5/1340.
[71] Carnarvon to Monck, November 12, 1866, Carnarvon Papers.
[72] *New York Tribune*, October 31, 1866.
[73] *New York Times*, November 9, 1866.

Fenians responsible. Mayor John Hoffman of New York, the defeated gubernatorial candidate of the Democratic Party, wrote to Tilden, "It looks as if the Radicals have succeeded in capturing by their false statements a large number of Fenian voters and that accounts for our losses." [74] This interpretation of the results was endorsed by Sandford E. Church, an upstate politico. "My apprehensions and yours have been realized," he wrote to Tilden. "We were beaten by the Fenian vote— We had the state by 25,000 majority if we had received our accustomed Irish strength. The defection was not uniform entirely but extended throughout the state to a greater or less extent." [75] Whether the Fenian vote was that decisive may be questioned, but it is certain that the "Fenian agitation . . . exerted a strong influence on the campaign," and "in the interior of the State, wherever the Irish population was numerous, and where the Democrats had not been able to meet the Radical arguments, the Democratic vote fell off, with a proportionate increase in the Radicals' strength." [76]

If the fall elections were a disaster for the conservative forces that uneasily coalesced around Andrew Johnson, the triumph of the "English-haters" could have brought little cheer to the British government. Indeed, it was the knowledge that the "pestiferous" Congress would reassemble in December, perhaps more "pestiferous" than ever in the wake of its success, and an awareness of the temptation the President might experience in the wake of his defeat to insert some rousing passage on the subject of the prisoners into his annual message, that persuaded Bruce to take precautionary meas-

[74] Hoffman to Tilden, November 7, 1866, Tilden Papers.
[75] Church to Tilden, November 10, *ibid.*
[76] Homer Adolph Stebbins, *Political History of New York State, 1865–1869*, Columbia University Studies, LX, no. 1 (New York, 1913), pp. 121–122.

ures. While the message was being composed, he informed
Seward that the final decision on the condemned men had
been left with the Imperial government which would "certainly be animated by a desire so to deal with it as to secure
peace and harmony between populations living in such
immediate proximity and separated by a frontier so easily
traversed." [77] Perhaps as a result of this note in which Bruce
matched Seward's sarcasm with irony, reference to the plight
of the prisoners in the President's annual message was confined to a few lines. The attention of Congress and the nation
was drawn to the government's endeavors on behalf of the
convicted men, and the hope was expressed "that this would
induce in their cases an exercise of clemency and judicious
amnesty." [78] But to claim credit in the aftermath of the elections for the clemency about to be extended to the condemned Fenians was at best a hollow administration triumph.
As for the formal notification of the commutation of the
sentences on Lynch and McMahon, this was forwarded by
Bruce shortly before Congress reassembled—a timely announcement.

While the British Minister maneuvered skillfully in Washington to save his government from unnecessary embarrassment at the hands of a victorious Congress or the defeated
President, in London the Congressional election results may
well have given members of that government reason to reas-
sess British policy toward Fenianism in the United States.
Almost from the day of Bruce's arrival at the American capital, British policy had been conceived as part of a wider

[77] Bruce to Seward, November 15, 1866, Department of State,
Notes from Foreign Legations: Great Britain.

[78] James D. Richardson, *A Compilation of the Messages and Papers
of the Presidents, 1789–1897* (Washington, 1896–1897), VIII, 3655,
December 3, 1866.

strategy to ease the domestic course of the President, a course disputed with increasing bitterness by Congress. Naturally, neither Bruce nor his government was motivated by a spirit of international altruism: their course was dictated by enlightened self-interest. Thus for a short time it appeared possible that the implementation of presidential Reconstruction would permit Britain to escape lightly, if not scot free, from the consequences of her conduct during the Civil War.

By 1865 some Englishmen had grown concerned that the tension that had developed in Anglo-American relations during the war would erupt into violence once the domestic conflict was resolved. Consequently, presidential Reconstruction was attractive because it promised the speedy return of Southern Congressmen—men unlikely to be driven by an antagonism toward Britain which sprang from her allegedly pro-Confederate bias during the war. Presumably, they would oppose any attempt to press claims such as those arising out of the activities of the *Alabama* to the point of a rupture. Of course, all these hopes were to founder on the opposition of Congress, and as this became increasingly evident, the British were compelled to look elsewhere for reassurance. Convinced that Johnson was honest and Seward pacific, Bruce considered it senseless to jeopardize their domestic influence on the eve of crucial elections by embarrassing them over the Fenians. To do this, perhaps in the form of an official and public demand for control of Fenian activities, was possibly to provide the administration's enemies, now labeled "English-haters," with additional propaganda, certainly if concessions were made to the British. Alternatively and more likely, the government would respond to such a demand by publicly adjusting its position to the harsher and more popular stand of its opponents. As a result, the British had confined themselves to "unofficial" correspondence, seeking to persuade the Johnson administration to frustrate the Fenians discreetly. But the President and his advisors were perhaps too discreet, while the Fenians were too bold to permit this problem to be so easily evaded. The upshot was the June raid which ultimately played its part in the defeat of the President in the fall elections and the repudiation of his domestic policies.

Significant as the results were, the fact that the elections were over was bound to influence British policy. Once the Irish-American vote had been cast, there appeared the possibility that Fenianism would cease to be as powerful a magnet as it had recently been for politicians. Although the new session of Congress was quickly marked by the reintroduction on December 10 of a bill "to repeal the Neutrality Laws," [79] by the end of the month the decline of the Brotherhood was being confidently reported. Attributing this to the strong defensive posture of Canada, the barrenness of the Fenian treasury, and the destruction of the members' morale, the correspondent of the London *Times* concluded, "The American politicians, too, no longer take any interest in cajoling the Fenian vote, and this fruitful incentive to excitement is wanting." [80] Of course, few reflective Englishmen deluded themselves with the hope that this specter would never return to haunt them. The *Times* warned "that so long as party feeling runs so high in the States as it does now, and the Irish vote retains its power it is impossible to be certain that unprincipled partisans may not revive" proposals similar to the Banks bills.[81] Nonetheless, for the British government the long and the short of the election aftermath were that without unnecessarily embarrassing an administration that was certainly less odious to them than its opponents, and one with which they would have to deal until it left office, which few as yet had

[79] London *Times*, December 24, 1866.   [80] January 8, 1867.
[81] January 29.

any reason to believe would be before March 4, 1869, they could afford to take a firmer line on Fenianism. The elections were over, and with the passage of time the danger of a rupture over the claims had diminished.

The mood of the British government was reflected in its attitude toward the convicted prisoners in Canada, for "delay and lenity" had originally been conceived largely as an adjustment to the political situation in the United States. Now, whereas Monck suggested that their sentences be commuted to five years' imprisonment, the Imperial government settled upon twenty years' penal servitude. "You will see that the term of imprisonment or Penal Servitude is a far longer one than you seem to contemplate in your telegraphic message," Carnarvon wrote to Monck. "But looking at the atrocious nature of the offence I do not think that a less penalty would have been adequate or at least understood." [82] This stiffening of the British position was further emphasized by their response to Seward's note of October 27, a document the London *Times* considered "very difficult to describe in moderate language." [83] Nor was this sense of outrage confined to the press. Queen Victoria thought that "the United States Government had advanced a pretension, and even asserted a right of interference as regards the administration of justice in Canada, in the case of Fenian convicts, which, her Majesty thinks, can hardly be yielded to without loss of dignity on the part of England, and without establishing a most dangerous precedent." The Queen's anger was also vented on her Ministers, who had failed to show her their answer "though it had been freely canvassed in the newspapers." [84]

[82] Carnarvon to Monck, November 23, 1866, Carnarvon Papers.

[83] January 29, 1867.

[84] Buckle, *Letters of Queen Victoria*, I, 373, Grey to Carnarvon, November 15, 1866.

Replying to the Queen the following day, November 16, Lord Derby sought to reassure her that "there have been no unworthy concessions to unwarrantable demands, and that no official despatches have been sent out without being previously submitted for your Majesty's approval." Admitting that Seward's note was "not characterized by the usual courtesy of diplomatic language," which Derby attributed to the "exigencies of his position," he agreed that the British could fasten upon this to pick a quarrel but said that a quarrel was not in the nation's interests. With respect to the Secretary of State's interference in the cases of Lynch and McMahon, the Prime Minister reminded the Queen that they had been tried as Americans; thus Seward had a right to intercede on their behalf. As for the decision to commute the death sentences, that could not be "attributed to his interference," Derby continued, because it had been ordered by telegraph before Seward's note arrived. Finally, Queen Victoria was assured by her Minister that in future she would be kept informed "of every measure of the least importance on which the Cabinet may have come to a definite conclusion." [85]

In his reply to Seward's note, Lord Stanley, Derby's son and the Foreign Secretary, responding perhaps to the Queen's evident concern, sharply rebuffed any imputation against the quality of Canadian justice and the apparent suggestion that the United States might elect to sit in judgment upon judicial proceedings in the Province. More significant, however, was Stanley's warning that his government was nearing the end of its patience with the Fenians. Although it had decided to deal leniently with the prisoners, "if leniency fails in its effect and fresh disturbances are attempted," Seward was informed, the British government "may be compelled with whatever reluc-

[85] *Ibid.*, p. 374, Derby to Queen Victoria, November 16.

tance to adopt a different course." [86] Evidently the British were shifting a full measure of the responsibility for the treatment of Fenian raiders to the government of the United States. They expected the Johnson administration, no longer facing a crucial election, to exhibit more vigor in frustrating Fenian plans before they were implemented.

[86] Stanley to Bruce, December 7, 1866, FO, 5/1340.

7

Turning Point

December, 1866, is not only a convenient but also an appropriate date at which to re-evaluate the influence of Fenianism
on Anglo-American relations. Until this time, the activity and
significance of the Brotherhood had been essentially North
American. To be sure, revolution had been planned in Ireland, but little had been achieved there. Racked by dissension
and indecision, the Fenians had easily been foiled by the
British authorities. Even their hopes of capitalizing on the
long-standing Anglo-American controversy over expatriation
and naturalization, which the British had of necessity revived
in frustrating them, had been dashed. In North America,
however, particularly in the United States, where everything
was shaped in the image of the struggle between the President
and Congress over Reconstruction, the Fenians had exercised
some influence. While the lines of the American political
battle were being drawn, the Fenians had gathered menac-
ingly along the Canadian border, and then during the preliminary skirmishing they raided the British colony. Immaterial
but not totally irrelevant to the problem of Ireland, these
events had a double significance for North America. First, and
completely unforeseen, they strengthened the cause of Confederation in British America. Second, they injected the

Fenian issue into the fall elections, although the uniformly crucial importance ascribed to it by the correspondent of the London *Times* was a gross oversimplification of the outcome.

If the elections confirmed the victory of Congress, they also emancipated the British government from the diplomatic pressures exerted as a result of the domestic American struggle. The subsequent stiffening of its attitude was induced by the new North American situation. In effect, the British—the opinion was shared even by die-hard opponents of Derby's government—believed that the government of the United States should be called upon to restrain aspiring filibusters. In the words of an acknowledged admirer of the United States and sympathizer with the Irish, John Bright, the Fenians ought to be curbed "with a stronger hand." [1] Yet the restraint of Fenians in North America was by this time largely unnecessary. Although threats were still going to be made against Canada, some of which would be taken seriously, no action materialized until 1870. In the meantime, however, insurrections were attempted in Ireland and acts of terror committed in England. In all of these incidents, Irish-Americans played a conspicuous role. Thus, the end of 1866 marked a turning point in Fenian activity and its significance. From this time, by focusing attention on the British Isles, the Brotherhood at last convinced some powerful English statesmen, notably Gladstone, of the pressing need for remedial measures in Ireland. The Fenians helped to work a change in the traditional English attitude toward Ireland, an attitude Bright summarized when he wrote to Horace Greeley in November, 1866, "Ireland is our humiliation and our ruling class prefer occa-

[1] "Bright-Sumner Letters," *Proceedings of the Massachusetts Historical Society*, XLVI (October, 1912), 152, Bright to Sumner, December 14, 1866.

sional riot and civil war to remedial legislation." [2] Beyond this, these Irish-American revolutionaries finally compelled the British government to confront and resolve the problems raised by the naturalization of native-born British subjects in the United States. In short, the Fenians were to achieve some measure of success. They failed to emancipate Ireland from British rule, but they did help to alleviate the conditions under which her population struggled to eke out an existence. They also played an important role in the liberation of emigrated Irishmen from the legal tentacles of British suzerainty.

Of course, remarkable if not supernatural powers of foresight would have been required to foretell correctly in December, 1866 the turn Fenianism was about to take. Indeed, for some optimists this moment appeared to mark not so much a turning point as the end of the road. The *New York Times* gave expression to this sentiment on December 23: "We should think that by this time the most sincere and devoted Fenians must be convinced of the utter folly and hopelessness of the whole scheme of Irish liberation." Certainly there was a reassuring lack of activity among the supporters of "President" Roberts. They were hamstrung by an empty treasury and, on their own admission, by the American neutrality laws which, for all the political bombast they had evoked, remained unrepealed and unmodified. But if all was quiet on the North American front, what of Ireland?

The other wing of the Fenian Brotherhood, led by James Stephens since the Campobello affair, had not been inactive. During the Congressional elections this Irish nationalist had conducted his own campaign, promoting action in Ireland and attempting to raise the money with which to finance it. Mean-

[2] Bright to Greeley, November 28, 1866, Horace Greeley Papers, New York Public Library.

while, his deputy, Thomas Kelly, made an ill-considered attempt to intimidate President Johnson. He threatened the hostile intervention of himself and some of his colleagues in the New York elections unless the government adopted a far more belligerent posture over the treatment of naturalized Americans in Ireland.[3] If this menace failed to produce any noticeable change in government policy, it did illustrate the strength of the belief, now transformed into an article of Fenian faith, that Irish independence would result from an Anglo-American war. To exacerbate the naturalization problem appeared to be one way of precipitating this confrontation. Another was to incite rebellion and then seek American recognition of the belligerent rights of the rebels—a course expected to appeal to the American public.[4]

Reports from the United States testifying to Stephens' success in persuading groups of Irish-Americans to visit the "old country," and his own melodramatic statements about returning personally to unleash the forces of retribution, caused momentary concern in Britain. Evidence of growing restlessness in Ireland was followed by a more systematic detention of suspicious visitors, the arrival of military reinforcements from England, and elaborate precautions to ensure that Stephens would be arrested before he set foot in the island. As the London *Punch* professed to believe, this was "physic for the Fenians." [5] More perceptive, however, were the comments of the special Irish correspondent of the *New York Tribune*. He challenged the entire basis of the British response to the unrest, namely, that the seizure of Stephens would quell the discontent. Even if the Fenian leader were removed from the scene, he observed:

[3] Oulahan to Johnson, October 6, 1866, Johnson Papers.
[4] Bruce to Stanley, October 30, 1866, FO, 5/1340.
[5] LI (December 8, 1866), 233.

You may depend upon it that Fenianism would still survive in the country and that it will survive in any event until British policy toward Ireland shall have undergone a radical change. . . . The social and political influence of the American Nation on the Irish people inspires and sustains them in the effort to obtain their political rights, and forbids them to despair of ultimate success.[6]

The subsequent events, in which Stephens had no part, vindicated his judgment.

Unfortunately, the British government and public, still obtuse where Ireland was concerned, grew overconfident when Stephens not only failed to appear in Britain but also was reported to have been deposed from his position as Head Centre. This confidence no doubt explains the imperturbability with which the British greeted reports from the United States suggesting that the Johnson administration, far from curbing them "with a stronger hand," was actually encouraging the Fenians. Thus, in his annual message to Congress, though temperate on the subject of the Fenian prisoners in Canada, the President ostensibly invited Congress to amend the neutrality laws. "So long as those laws remain upon our statute books," he commented, "they should be faithfully executed, and if they operate harshly, unjustly, or oppressively Congress alone can apply the remedy by their modification or repeal."[7] Alternatively, this passage could be interpreted as a public disavowal by the administration of the responsibility for moving against the Fenians. It was also possible that these comments were inspired by a natural desire to call the bluff of Congress, whose members had been so hearty in their support of measures designed to catch the eye

[6] January 18, 1867.
[7] Richardson, *Compilation of the Messages and Papers of the Presidents, 1787–1897*, VIII, 3656, December 3, 1866.

and ballot of Irish-Americans. Finally, the message might provide the British with further incentive to meet American demands for a settlement of outstanding problems before popular resentment in the United States expressed itself in some radical measure which the President was obviously threatening not to impede.

If Johnson's comments on the neutrality laws were open to a variety of interpretations, not all of which were mutually exclusive, his nominaion of a Fenian to fill a consular vacancy at Londonderry was less ambiguous. And when, under polite British prodding, he refused to withdraw it,[8] the possibility loomed large that the British would be compelled to resort to a refusal of exequatur. This they were anxious to avoid, their new-found confidence notwithstanding, because it might attract unwelcome publicity. In this instance, as in that of the neutrality laws, the British soon discovered that they were not totally bereft of allies in Washington. Inspired undoubtedly by antagonism for the President rather than sympathy or friendship for Britain, the Senate refused to confirm the nomination. Meanwhile Charles Sumner and his Foreign Relations Committee agreed to bury any plan to repeal the neutrality laws.[9]

To disregard the provocative conduct of the Johnson administration was at best a negative expression of British confidence. More positive was the passage in the Queen's Speech, opening a new session of Parliament in February, 1867, in which the Tory government disclaimed any intention to seek a renewal of the Habeas Corpus Suspension Act. Charles Francis Adams was quick to grasp the diplomatic significance

[8] Adams, Diary, January 22, 1867; Seward to Adams, February 25, 1867, NA/M77/80.

[9] E. L. Pierce, *Memoir and Letters of Charles Sumner* (London, 1893), IV, 291, Sumner to Bemis, December 12, 1866.

of this news. It "will tend to simplify our relations with the Government on this delicate question of citizenship," he confidently predicted.[10] Shortly afterwards, on February 8, when the American Minister called at the Foreign Office to discuss with Stanley the plight of a convicted Fenian, the Foreign Secretary almost exuded confidence. Not only did he promise to see what could be done in this specific case, but he suggested that as the Fenian agitation appeared to be dying out "it might soon be practicable to dispose of all these cases with lenity." [11] However, this return to normality was rudely impeded by the Fenians, whose sudden revival came as an even greater blow to the British just because, as Stanley had plainly intimated, *"Most people had come to the conclusion that Fenianism was on its last legs*—that it had done its best and worst—and that, as a disturbing element in the body politic, the British Government had no reason to apprehend any more serious trouble from its influence." [12]

The incidents that now occurred hardly warranted in themselves the description of "serious trouble." What was alarming was the proof they afforded that Fenianism was not extinct, that it was still capable of eruptions, and would presumably remain active until the British approached in a statesmanlike manner the widespread Irish discontent the Fenians so inadequately represented.

The first of a sudden rash of Fenian escapades centered on Chester Castle. There some nine thousand stand of arms, enough to equip a Fenian army, were guarded by a skeleton force of six men. Although a tempting and easy target, it was missed by the Fenians. Losing the advantage of surprise— they were betrayed by the inevitable informant—they pusil-

[10] Adams to Seward, February 6, 1867, NA/M30/89.
[11] Adams, Diary, February 8, 1867.
[12] *New York Tribune*, February 18, 1867.

lanimously surrendered the initiative. They stood inert while the mayor of this beautiful and historic city on the northeastern border of Wales desperately attempted to match their numbers with local patriots enrolled as special police constables. Finally, when a company of regular troops arrived from nearby Manchester and the news spread that a full regiment had been entrained in London, the Fenians meekly dispersed. The following day, February 12, sixty-seven of them were arrested as they disembarked in Ireland from the Holyhead steamer.[13]

Even as these events were being reported in the English press, the Fenians struck again. On February 13 a pathetically mismanaged insurrection was raised in County Kerry, Ireland. A police courier was shot and telegraph wires were cut— causing a five-hour delay for messages by the Atlantic cable —before the rebels were dispersed.[14] Less than three weeks later, on March 5, a more general but no better organized rising occurred in Cork. Railway lines were uprooted and once again telegraph wires were cut; during the ensuing rupture of communications, isolated police barracks were attacked. With the approach of British troops, the rebels retired hastily into the local mountains where, without tents or blankets to protect them from the ravages of spring rain, hail, and snow, a heavy toll was soon taken of their morale and numbers.[15]

Such forlorn efforts to overthrow British rule invited facetious comment, even in the United States. "We cannot be far wrong in saying," commented the *New York Tribune* in the

[13] *The Annual Register: A Review of Events at Home and Abroad, 1867*, part 2 (London, 1868), pp. 23–27.

[14] Adams, Diary, February 15, 1867.

[15] *House Exec. Doc.*, no. 157, p. 68, Eastman (U.S. consul at Cork) to Seward, March 28, 1867.

aftermath of a traditional March 17 in New York, "that more blood was shed in one street in New York on St. Patrick's Day than has been expended during all the Fenian insurrections of which any account has yet reached us." [16] Similar if more pointed observations were offered by the *New York Times;* indeed both newspapers, for all their political differences, reached much the same conclusion. They agreed that the Derby government would be well advised, despite these pathetic failures, to institute Irish reforms. Only remedial measures, not further punishment, could relieve the condition of Ireland. Specifically naming the abolition of the State Church and reform of the tenantry system, the *Times* was moved to conclude that unless the British made these concessions, they deserved to be "tormented by the Fenians night and day." [17]

Unfortunately, although influential opinion in Britain concurred in the assessment that the incidents were "contemptible in point of numbers—more contemptible still in organization," [18] it failed to draw the same liberal conclusions as the Americans. There was no loud and insistent demand for reform. Instead, the events of February and March simply convinced many Englishmen that the government's proposed relaxation of the emergency measures had been precipitate. The London *Times* observed after the Kerry episode:

It may be difficult to speak gravely of a popular insurrection, but whatever may be its proper designation, it has been serious enough to rekindle alarms which were happily beginning to subside and to prove that the time has not yet come when the ordinary operation of the law can be restored. The suspension of the Habeas Corpus Act is a weapon in the hands of the Government the value of which is keenly appreciated by the enemies

[16] March 25, 1867.   [17] March 9, 1867.
[18] London *Times*, February 18, 1867.

of law and order. To them alone is it formidable and it must be retained for the protection of the public peace.[19]

If the breaking of the British government's promise to restore habeas corpus in Ireland was one result of the Fenian activities, there were others. Fresh life was briefly infused into the movement in the United States, and, even more important, the interest of American politicians was reawakened. Mass meetings were called to celebrate the news from Britain with, it was hoped, monetary contributions. While the meeting called in the wake of the first and grossly exaggerated reports from Chester and Kerry was cancelled as the result of a snowstorm, ten thousand people did brave a steady downpour of rain on March 13 to assemble in Union Square to mark the early news from Cork.[20] Meanwhile, in the midst of all this excitement and activity, Roberts called his supporters into convention at Utica, New York, allegedly to perfect a new plan of operations against Canada. Unhappily, they chose to congregate in the shadow of a lunatic asylum.[21] Yet for all the misfortunes that had befallen the Fenians in Britain and the United States, British diplomats were not unconcerned by the turn of events. There could be no hiding from the fact that not only had the Fenians been chased through the "fastness of Ireland" but that they were also about to be pursued by "Congressional demagogues through the swamps and fens of American politics." [22]

The pursuit was led, understandably enough, by Representatives Robinson and Fernando Wood whose districts were in New York. Robinson called upon the Johnson administration to report all documents "relating to the arrest, imprisonment

[19] February 19.
[20] Edwards (British vice-consul at New York) to Stanley, March 14, 1867, FO, 5/1341.
[21] *New York Times*, February 17, 1867.   [22] *Ibid.*, March 12.

and treatment of American citizens in Great Britain, or its provinces," to the House. This Seward politely declined to do on grounds of "national interest." [23] However, he did release the information on the trials of American citizens in Canada which Nathaniel Banks called for. Congress now learned that, for all the drama the initial convictions of Lynch and McMahon had produced, only twenty-five of the remaining ninety-five prisoners had been convicted and of these not one had forfeited his life.[24] If there were few martyrs to champion, there was still Fernando Wood's rather empty expression of sympathy with the Irish people to support.[25] More radical proposals which threatened the serious business to which Congress was then addressing itself—the curtailment of presidential authority—quickly provoked powerful opposition. Thus when Ignatius Donnelly, reviving the by no means unpopular idea that American policy toward the Fenians should be identical to that pursued by the British in their relations with the Confederacy, proposed that the necessary legislation be brought forward enabling the President to extend at his discretion belligerent rights to Irish rebels, Thaddeus Stevens was in the vanguard of the opposition.[26]

One uneasy observer of all these developments was Sir Frederick Bruce. Sure that the Congressional resolutions, whether they passed or not, helped to keep Fenianism alive in North America, he was also apprehensive lest "some of the demagogues for electioneering purposes" attempt to tamper with the neutrality laws again. If they did, he looked to his friend Charles Sumner to provide the main bulwark of sanity, and not without reason, because "the Government even if it

[23] *House Exec. Doc.*, no. 10, 40th Cong., 1st sess., March 21, 1867.
[24] *Ibid.*, no. 9.
[25] *Congressional Globe*, 40th Cong., 1st sess., p. 41, March 8, 1867.
[26] *Ibid.*, p. 67, March 11, 1867.

had the will has not the power to prevent them." Yet powerless as the administration of Andrew Johnson was in Congress,
strategy as much as expediency dictated that the British government should demand little of it. Any attempt by the President to stifle the political champions of the Fenians, Bruce
argued in a dispatch to Lord Stanley, would be an open
invitation to more violent resolutions from the Republican
majority in Congress. While they were unwilling to provoke
a rupture with Great Britain, perhaps because foreign as well
as domestic emergencies tend to favor the expansion of executive powers they were then seeking to correct, evidence of
presidential opposition would encourage them to believe that
they could further alienate the Irish-Americans from Johnson
without fear of diplomatic embarrassment. Therefore, to
Bruce's mind, if the administration was to exercise an effective
moderating influence, it would only be achieved if the President gave the impression of being determined not to be outbid
for Irish-American support.

Here was one explanation, albeit somewhat belated, not
only of those comments on the neutrality laws in Johnson's
second annual message to Congress, but also of his nomination
of a Fenian to a consular post in Ireland. In effect, the British
were the victims of an elaborate game of political brag, a role
they could scarcely have relished. Naturally, this abruptly terminated any plans to implement the earlier decision to press
the American government to curb the Fenians "with a
stronger hand." Yet this was not a major diplomatic setback,
for it was in Ireland that the Fenians were now active, and the
only way the Johnson administration could have curbed them
was to prohibit or restrict foreign travel by American citizens.
As this was never likely, the British lost little by changing
their policy, particularly if as a result they strengthened the
hand of the President, thus enabling him to moderate the

excitement the activity of Congress generated within Fenian ranks. Bruce did not doubt that all moderating influences should be assiduously weaned, for he thought it "useless to disguise the fact that the discontent in Ireland combined with the hostile character of the Irish element" in the United States constituted "a serious and increasing danger" to peaceful Anglo-American relations. Indeed, although he believed that the Fenian movement was waning in the United States, he warned Stanley that "were the Irish capable of adopting hostility to Great Britain as their device and of pursuing objects which would appeal rather to American interests than American sympathies, their influence in this country would become far more dangerous." It was for this reason that the British Minister looked with increasing concern upon developments in Ireland. For it was not at all improbable that Fenian activities there would raise issues that would appeal to American interests and sympathies.[27]

Another interested and concerned observer of Fenianism in Ireland, and the response of his countrymen to it, was William H. Seward. His interest had not been lessened as a result of the Congressional elections. On the contrary, they had emancipated him as well as the British from the pressures and restraints imposed by the struggle over Reconstruction. The influence of this domestic battle on Seward's diplomacy had been evident from his use of the Fenians in August, 1866, ostensibly to impress upon the British the necessity for a quick settlement of the American claims. From both the tone and content of his dispatch on that occasion, it was readily apparent that his concern was as much domestic advantage as diplomatic success. The fact that the British government subsequently expressed a willingness to arbitrate some of the diffi-

[27] Bruce to Stanley, March 19, 1867, FO, 5/1341.

culties no doubt owed more by way of inspiration to the dramatic events in Europe than the urgings of Seward. However, not even the danger of continued international embarrassment, as Europe was being reordered, could persuade the British to concede all the demands of the United States. Naturally Seward did not accept this rebuff as final, and he redoubled his efforts, utilizing the Fenians in a more single-minded manner.

In a long dispatch to Charles Francis Adams on March 28, the American Secretary of State accepted as the basis of his argument the existence of chronic sedition in Ireland and the likelihood that at some future date the insurgents would proclaim an organized insurrection with a show of delegated authority. In short, they would be in a position to make a not unreasonable request for American recognition of their status as belligerents. Such a request, he warned, would attract widespread sympathy in the United States, where the spirit of compassion sprang from "habitual jealousy of British proximity across our northern border and especially for the reason that this nation indulges a profound sense that it sustained great injury from the sympathy extended in Great Britain to rebels during our civil war." Here, if as yet indistinctly formulated, was the link between annexation and settlement of the war claims which many American politicians were soon to advocate, much to the irritation of the British. Yet much as Seward, whose own expansionist predilections were soon to be well publicized by the purchase of Alaska, would have liked to negotiate the acquisition of Canada, this was not, as his dispatch indicated, to be pressed insistently. Later, on the basis of a report submitted by one of his special agents to Canada, E. H. Derby, and of a petition from Victoria on Vancouver Island requesting the annexation of British Columbia, he did suggest to Bruce that the *Alabama* claims be "set off" against British Columbia, but the British Minister declined to forward the proposal to his government.²⁸ But Seward did not find it difficult to accept this response, for he was content, like many other continentalists, to wait for the growth of those intimate social and economic ties—the inevitable gravitation of interests—which were popularly believed to be the prelude to the peaceful absorption of the rest of North America by the United States.

If Seward was not disposed to insist on the discussion of a settlement of the claims that would embrace the cession of parts of British North America, it did not mean that he was unimpressed with the necessity of reaching some settlement. "The country has hoped and expected," he informed Adams, "that in some way our complaint against Great Britain in that respect would be satisfactorily adjusted. It has been content to wait until now for that consummation." To illustrate his nation's rapidly expiring patience, Seward pointed once again to Congress. If he could be believed, the next proposal to amend the neutrality laws might well pass the Senate as well as the House of Representatives. All of which served to give added weight to his warning: "If delays are continued it may perhaps pass beyond the reach of settlement by friendly correspondence."

Having made this ominous prediction, Seward suddenly exhibited a curious timidity. In the rest of his dispatch to Adams he admitted that he might have misunderstood the situation in Ireland; he accepted that the British government might be preoccupied with the Reform Bill then being debated in Parliament; and he stressed that it was "not the President's desire to do anything which would be or even

²⁸ Van Deusen, *William Henry Seward*, p. 548; James Morton Callahan, *American Foreign Policy in Canadian Relations* (New York, 1937), p. 306.

seem to be unfriendly to Great Britain." Then he concluded
by leaving the fate of his dispatch, the decision whether it or
any part of it should be forwarded to Lord Stanley, to the
Minister's discretion. "Will you take the matter in hand and
act in regard to it as shall seem best," he inquired meekly,
"giving me at least the results of your reflections?" [29]

Amazed as he was by this sudden and unexpected deference
to his judgment, Adams refused to be startled out of his
diplomatic wits. Thus, when he called at the Foreign Office
on April 13 he expected to make little headway. His pessi-
mism sprang from the conviction that it was now too late.
Not wanting confidence in his own abilities, Adams was sure
that he "could have managed it successfully" had Seward
consulted him earlier. Yet he also fancied he understood the
grotesquely uncomfortable and restrictive position from
which the Secretary of State attempted to conduct the international relations of the United States—"trussed in a strait
waistcoat with a factious Senate and delirious representative
chamber on one side, and a not over flexible chief on the
other." [30] If the American Minister approached his interview
with Lord Stanley without any hope of success, it was significant that during their conversation Adams declined to utilize
the one weapon that Seward evidently hoped would bring the
British to his terms.

In refusing to press the Fenians or the "wretched claptraps"
they inspired in Congress into diplomatic service, Adams was
holding to his belief that the agitation of the Irish issue in the
United States "has the effect of undermining the foundation
of our claim to complain in the present instance." "It must be
obvious to you," he wrote to Seward, as if to reprove him for
succumbing so readily to the temptation of misguided oppor-

[29] Seward to Adams, March 28, 1867, NA/M77/80.
[30] Adams, Diary, April 11, 1867.

tunism, "that the adoption of the propositions pressed in Congress must have the necessary effect of wrecking our chances of getting any valuable result at all from arbitration. For if we follow the suit of England when the respective positions come to be reversed I do not perceive how we do not come to justify her conduct." [31]

Adams was equally consistent in his attitude toward the Irish-Americans inevitably detained by the British authorities during the Fenian excitement. Although the American consul at Cork, writing to Seward in the aftermath of the March fiasco, insisted that he "did not know or believe there was one American engaged in the whole affair . . . and should certainly feel ashamed of them if there was, it has turned out such a ridiculous and abortive failure," [32] the British had long been convinced of American involvement. "It would be idle to affect ignorance," the London *Times* commented angrily after the sorry affair in County Kerry, "that this conspiracy is supported by a powerful organization which politicians and legislators think it worthwhile to propitiate in America. Officers, money, arms and ammunition have been sent from beyond the seas during the last eighteen months." [33] In fact, the Irish Directory, composed largely of Irish-Americans—including Thomas Kelly, who had managed to slip into Britain—had been formed in England for the purpose of coordinating acts of Fenian valor which it was thought would in one way or another resuscitate the movement. Branches of the Directory had sprouted in many of the larger cities—Manchester, Leeds, Birmingham, and Liverpool—which had drawn the unskilled Irish, and it had been at Liverpool that

[31] Adams to Seward, April 15, 1867, Adams Papers.
[32] *House Exec. Doc.*, no. 157, p. 68, Eastman to Seward, March 28, 1867. [33] February 16, 1867.

the raid on Chester Castle had been conceived. Naturally, this extensive Irish-American participation led to arrests, sometimes merely on the suspicion this national status excited.

Adams' reluctance to intercede on behalf of such men sprang in part from a deepening dislike of the Fenians which may well have reflected a more general distaste for the Irish. Certainly he shared the concern for the future of American institutions which the mass immigration of "ignorant" Irish helped to plant in the minds of conservatives. As for the Fenians, Adams was determined never to be a party, in any sense, to an organization that in his opinion had such "a poor, grovelling, small adventurer aspect, as if the men engaged in it were trying to turn a penny out of the honest impulses of the unintelligent classes." [34] Yet, this was what to some extent he became, much to his disgust and dismay, when he was hoodwinked, with the connivance of the Governor of New York, into obtaining a pass for the commander designate of the Fenian insurgents to tour the British arsenal at Woolwich. Adams could not tolerate his highly prized rectitude being jeopardized in this manner, particularly when it was manifestly absent from the character of those who placed it in danger. It soon came to light that many of the imprisoned Irish-Americans who now turned to the American Legation for assistance were among those released by the British government the previous year on condition they did not return to Ireland. This proved to Adams' satisfaction their total absence of any regard for the truth or sense of obligation. Consequently, the American Minister more than satisfied his own very strong sense of duty by suggesting to West, now consul at Dublin, that he express to the Irish authorities the hope that

[34] Adams, Diary, April 29, 1867.

no innocent American would be subjected to conditions of liberation that might be considered humiliating.[35]

Once American citizens were placed on trial and sentenced to death, Adams was subjected to heavier pressure to bestir himself. With the frustration of his ambitious plan to use the Fenians to greater diplomatic effect still fresh in his mind, Seward instructed the Minister to protest all doubtful convictions and recommend clemency in all cases. "The sanguinary sentences of the Court," he wrote pointedly, "shock the public sense throughout the United States. Executions conforming to them would leave a painful impression in a country where traditional sympathy with the revolution in Ireland is increased by convictions of national injustice, and therefore is now not only profound but almost universal." [36] Adams, who thought the trials had been fair, was still loath to intervene, however. He discovered in Seward's note all the marks of a concession to domestic opinion, for many of the prisoners and at least one of the condemned men had served with distinction during the Civil War; so he simply dismissed it as a document intended for American rather than British consumption. This conveniently rationalized his decision to ignore the Secretary's instructions in this particular instance, but the reasons for Adams' reticence were more profound. To those he had enumerated earlier he now added another, a dark suspicion of Seward. During May he began to fear that Seward was preparing for a collision with England, and he was determined not to be a party to a development he considered inimical to the best interests of the United States.[37] Less alarmist but for a time equally suspicious was Sir Frederick Bruce.

[35] Adams to West, April 11, 1867, Adams Papers.
[36] Seward to Adams, May 15, 1867, NA/M77/80.
[37] Adams, Diary, May, 18, 22, 1867.

Having once placed so much confidence in Seward's peaceful approach to Anglo-American relations, Bruce suddenly denounced him in a dispatch to Lord Stanley on April 8 as anti-British and untrustworthy. Unlike his American counterpart in London, however, the British Minister was always sure that Seward would carefully avoid any step that might saddle him with the responsibility for a war with Great Britain.[38] If the Secretary of State's caution was a source of some comfort to the British, time brought its traditional benefits. Given time in which to observe and think, Bruce eventually reached the more reassuring conclusion that the American's conduct was simply a variant of his usual posture. In brief, the administration's desire to conciliate the Irish-American electorate, presumably in the forthcoming state elections, would drive it to take any step, "so long as it does not go beyond correspondence and diplomatic intervention."[39]

Whatever his incentive—and his own sympathy with Irish national aspirations should not be entirely discounted—Seward redoubled his efforts on behalf of the doomed men. Not content to rely exclusively on Adams to secure a commutation of the capital sentences, he called on Bruce on May 20—the British Minister was unwell and confined to his residence—to emphasize the political delicacy of this problem.[40] Six days later, when American newspapers reported that Lord Derby was alleged to have remarked that Colonel Thomas Burke, a man whose plight excited considerable sympathy and comment in the United States because of a distinguished career in the Union armies, would hang on May 29, Seward quickly transferred the resultant domestic pressure from the administration to Bruce. The British Minister responded immediately, cabling Stanley: "Seward in name of President earnestly rec-

[38] Bruce to Stanley, April 8, 1867, FO, 5/1341.
[39] *Ibid.*, May 20.   [40] *Ibid.*

ommends no execution."[41] He then supported this telegram, of necessity terse, with a dispatch in which he rationalized any concession to the Americans in terms of imperial interest. With the Fenians reportedly preparing once again for a raid into Canada, this was not the time to provide them with a martyr. Not only would this bolster their zeal, perhaps to the point of committing new acts of terror, it would also evoke an outburst of American public sympathy which would in turn inhibit, if it did not prevent, any positive action by the American government in the event of an emergency.[42] How heavily these considerations would have weighed with the British government is open to conjecture, however, for unknown to Bruce the decision to commute the sentences of death had already been taken in London.

Adams had reluctantly bestirred himself on behalf of the doomed men, of whom Burke was one, on May 25 when it was widely rumored in the British capital that the Cabinet had decided to exact the full penalty. This news should not have been entirely unexpected, because the same government had given notice in December, 1866, that a revival of Fenian activity might exhaust its patience with convicted terrorists. Once he was confronted with imminent executions, Adams decided to approach Lord Stanley, albeit with evident embarrassment, for he found himself uncomfortably placed between his instructions to intercede on one side and his desire to avoid wounding the susceptibilities of the British on the other. To this predicament the American Minister brought all his diplomatic tact and native caution. Thus, in his note to the Foreign Secretary, he not only conceded the fairness of the trials but explicitly disclaimed any intention of creating the impression that he was interfering with the course of British justice as a

[41] Bruce to Stanley, May 27, 1867, FO, 5/1341.   [42] *Ibid.*, May 28.

matter of right. This was in marked contrast, of course, to Seward's earlier intervention on behalf of the Fenians condemned to death in Canada. Distant if not totally isolated from the domestic pressures to which the Secretary of State had then been responding, Adams founded his intercession "upon the peculiar relations into which the two countries are thrown by the fact of the distribution between them now almost in equal numbers of the people" of Ireland.[43] He made his point, and his conciliatory approach brought a very friendly reply from Stanley announcing the commutation of all capital sentences to penal servitude for life.[44]

Denied martyrs, Fenian activity in the United States continued to languish—the threat against Canada proved illusory —while most of the prisoners in Ireland contented themselves with the task of obtaining their release, on condition they returned to the United States, rather than the pursuit of a noble death. Yet even as the Fenian movement appeared to be becalmed on both sides of the Atlantic, in midsummer 1867, a tempest was stirring. The storm warning was hoisted on July 10 when the House of Representatives, once more at the suggestion of Banks, passed a resolution requesting the President to report to the Committee on Foreign Affairs any evidence of the arrest, trial, conviction, and sentencing of any American citizen in Britain for words spoken or acts committed in the United States. Although Seward could find no evidence to support this inflammatory suggestion,[45] a group of Irish-Americans were already busily at work correcting the deficiency.

In May, having purchased a small ocean-going vessel, a

[43] Adams to Stanley, May 25, *ibid.*
[44] Stanley to Adams, May 26, *ibid.*
[45] *House Miscellaneous Document*, no. 46, 40th Cong., 1st sess., July 19, 1867.

band of Fenians loaded it with munitions and set sail for Ireland. The ship, which during the voyage they renamed *Erin's Hope*, successfully navigated the perils of an Atlantic crossing only to run aground, in a metaphorical sense, off the Irish coast. Unable to land at Sligo and liberate Connaught as they had planned, the members of this Fenian expeditionary force fell to quarreling among themselves about their course of action. Erin's hope notwithstanding, they meekly decided to return to the United States. At this juncture, however, they were overruled by the captain, who insisted on putting them ashore. Unfortunately, he selected a place well within sight of a coast guard station, and within twenty-four hours of disembarkation, twenty-eight of the thirty-one liberators had been arrested.[46] Among them was John Warren, who was soon to prove remarkably adept at portraying himself as a man whose only crime had been to speak in the United States in praise of principles traditionally held dear by all Americans.

Once the news of the detention without trial of these men spread—Ireland was still under the Habeas Corpus Suspension Act—loud and critical comment was inevitable in the United States. At least two of the detainees, Warren and Nagle, had served with distinction during the Civil War, and Seward was soon being lobbied on their behalf by patriotic organizations.[47] Meanwhile, Congressional champions had also begun to stir. This, together with the fact that Congress had already called for a report on the detention of American citizens in Ireland, helped to convince Bruce that it would be expedient to release these people before the report appeared.[48] The British Minister's anxiety to outflank Congress, however, was more than matched by that of Seward. With state elections in the offing

[46] *House Exec. Doc.*, no. 157, p. 278.
[47] Seward to Adams, August 7, 1867, NA/M77/80.
[48] Bruce to Stanley, August 26, 1867, FO, 5/1342.

and with "a large number of highly respectable and influential citizens" showing interest in the plight of the detainees,[49] it was not long before the Secretary of State reached the conclusion that "a time has arrived when some explanations seem to the people of the United States necessary."[50]

The most effective means of relieving the pressures which quickly mounted was to secure the release of the prisoners, particularly of Warren and Nagle, whose plight aroused the greatest interest and comment. Consequently, when Fernando Wood addressed a public letter to the President, in which he violently denounced the British, and then followed it with a private note urging him to publish an equally inflammatory reply which Wood thought would aid the Democratic Party in the forthcoming elections, Seward drew Bruce's attention to both missives and insinuated that Johnson might be disposed to follow this advice. However, if the men were released, the Secretary promised to endeavor "to have the President's reply so worded as not to encourage agitation on this subject." Bruce took a hint which even the most obtuse of men could not have missed, and cabled Stanley urging the release of Warren and Nagle.[51] Simultaneously, Seward instructed Adams by cable to press the same course on the Foreign Secretary.[52]

But once again, the Secretary of State had to contend with the reluctance of his representative in London to urge this solution energetically upon the British. Adams was still inhibited by the knowledge that some of these men had been released the previous year on condition they did not return to Ireland; therefore he considered it embarrassing and futile to

[49] Seward to Adams, September 14, 1867, NA/M77/80.
[50] *Ibid.*, October 3.
[51] Bruce to Stanley, August 26, 1867, FO, 5/1342.
[52] Seward to Adams, August 22, 1867, NA/M77/80.

ask the British government to accept the parole of men unwilling to honor it. Additional inhibitions sprang from the confusion over Warren's exact national status—whether he was a native or naturalized American—and the conviction that he and his colleagues were more interested in arousing American public opinion, as the first step toward precipitating the Anglo-American conflict from which they expected to realize their Irish ambitions, than securing their own freedom.[53] Adams had always opposed the subversion of the interests of his nation for the benefit of Ireland.

The activities of Warren must surely have illustrated for the Minister the extent to which Irish nationalists were prepared to use the United States as a pawn in their contest with Britain. This Fenian occupied himself by composing incendiary letters in which he modestly and inaccurately described himself as a man imprisoned in Ireland "for giving expression to opinions in America favourable to the spread of republicanism and self government." These were then smuggled out of prison and carried to the United States where they were published. There they aroused American passions, which Banks had somewhat prematurely sought to tap, and when they were republished in Ireland by the Dublin *Weekly News* they inflamed the British authorities as well.[54] In effect, Warren successfully incensed opinion on both sides of the Atlantic; he had hit upon another way of playing both ends against the middle.

If an appreciation of this Fenian's sinister purpose helped to restrain Adams from extending a helping hand—although to have secured his release and return to the United States might have nullified his abrasiveness—there was another powerful restraint working upon the Minister. He was still holding fast

[53] Adams to Seward, August 23, 27, September 3, 1867, NA/M30/90.
[54] Adams to Seward, September 3, 1867, NA/M30/90.

to his belief that the United States should abide by her own professed standards of international conduct. "I shall persevere in my efforts to be of use to all citizens of the United States," he informed Seward, "but our own indignation is too fresh yet in America against people from here who yielded assistance to our insurgents for me to entertain great sympathy with similar attacks made from our side against the public peace of this kingdom." [55]

More concerned, however, with the exigencies of domestic politics than international consistency, Seward was in no mood to debate the subject. "Urge prompt release of Nagle and Warren," he cabled Adams on September 11. "Affair is embarrassing." [56] Under constant pressure from Seward, exerted in a steady stream of cables and dispatches, Adams, having made it clear to the British government that he was only acting under severe pressure from home, wrote to Lord Stanley to express the hope that as these men had never had an opportunity to commit a crime within "Her Majesty's jurisdiction, which would fairly subject them to the probability of condemnation if tried in a Court of Justice . . . the confinement and severe treatment to which they have already been subjected may be regarded as sufficient penalty for anything they might even be suspected to have intended to do, and entitle them to a release at an early date." [57]

Whether Adams' cautious intervention or the increasingly strident demands of Seward would have persuaded the British to discharge the men is open to surmise. Thus on September 20 the Secretary telegraphed the American Minister, "The President has expected that courtesy and conciliation would induce a compliance with a request which was inspired by good will to Great Britain. A definitive reply has now become

[55] *Ibid.*   [56] Seward to Adams, September 11, 1867, NA/M77/80.
[57] Adams to Stanley, September 13, 1867, FO, 5/1342.

absolutely necessary." [58] No sooner had Seward sent out this telegram than news of a tragic Fenian incident reached the United States, an incident that did far more than either Seward or Adams to mold the British government's attitude toward Warren, Nagle, and their associates.

The events that culminated in tragedy on September 18, 1867, were set in motion in August, when Thomas Kelly called a meeting of Fenians in Manchester for the purpose of reorganizing the Brotherhood in Britain. [59] It passed off quietly enough, and all went well until September 11, when Kelly, having established his headquarters in the northern industrial city, was arrested along with a colleague, Michael Deasy, on suspicion of loitering with intent to commit a robbery. Although both men provided the police with false identities, they were betrayed by their Irish-American accents, and a week later they were remanded on warrants in their true names. As they were being transported from the courts back to prison in a police wagon, they were rescued. Unfortunately, during the melee a policeman, Sergeant Brett, was accidentally killed. Locked inside the well of the wagon from which he supervised the prisoners, each in his or her own cubicle, he was shot through the head by one of the liberators who attempted to smash the door lock with a bullet just as the policeman peered out.

However unpremeditated, this tragedy shocked and angered British public opinion. The London *Punch* captured the prevailing temper with a bitter cartoon in which Fenians and trade unionists, then also struggling for concessions, were portrayed as servants of a demanding mistress, Murder. [60] This

---

[58] Seward to Adams, September 20, 1867, NA/M77/80.
[59] P. S. O'Hegarty, *A History of Ireland under the Union, 1801–1922* (London, 1952), p. 455.
[60] LIII (October 12, 1867), 148–149.

sense of outrage naturally killed any hope that the Fenians imprisoned in Ireland would simply be released. "The news did not increase Her Majesty's desire to yield anything in favour of the Fenians to the interposition of Mr. Adams," the Home Secretary, Gathorne Hardy, wrote to a colleague from Court. "Clearly his interference is a very sore subject here." [61] While her attitude may not have shaped that of the Derby government, it was never probable that her ministers would run the risk of antagonizing the widespread and influential opinion to which Queen Victoria gave expression. Therefore, when Adams called at the Foreign Office on September 23 to discuss the possibility of Warren and Nagle being discharged, he was pointedly informed that demands that these men be placed on trial were reasonable.[62] Evidently, all talk of release was now viewed as unreasonable by the British government.

If Seward's efforts to prize these men loose from the British were doomed from the moment of Brett's death, he realized he had suffered a major setback in this quest even before the news from Manchester reached him. On September 19, Sir Frederick Bruce, while traveling north for a vacation, fell ill and died suddenly in Boston. By the time of his death Bruce appears to have lost some of the influence he had once exerted over British policy toward the United States. Perhaps his value as a conciliator decreased as the danger of a violent Anglo-American confrontation receded and every indication pointed to British compensation for American war claims ultimately being made. Nonetheless, his death cost Seward a valuable ally. Always anxious to promote the least abrasive solution to problems, particularly those posed by the Fenians, he had consistently supported the Secretary of State's at-

[61] Hardy to Ferguson, September 18, 1867, HO, 45/7799.
[62] Adams, Diary, September 23, 1867.

tempts to secure the release of men detained without trial in Ireland.

This double blow, the deaths of Bruce and Brett, forced Seward to change his tack. As it was now futile to continue to press for the discharge of Warren and Nagle, the Secretary of State pressed instead for their early trial. Naturally, with elections both present and imminent in the United States, this had to be done with a vigor that would appeal to the electorate, particularly the large Irish-American section. Therefore, indulging his penchant for offensively worded dispatches, Seward wrote to Adams, "I observe with regret, though not altogether with surprise, that recent disturbances in Manchester are supposed to have created new obstacles to the liberation of United States citizens who are held under arbitrary arrest in Ireland." This merely served as preparation for an ill-disguised fanning of the charges then being leveled at the British by Warren. He continued:

It will be very much regretted if these new embarrassments shall be such as to induce Her Majesty's Government to lend color to the complaint which has been made against them, that they propose to hold indefinitely in custody, without trial or process, citizens of the United States who have neither committed nor attempted to commit any offence in Ireland, and who are only alleged to have exercised a freedom of speech in the United States which is tolerated by our laws.[63]

When he subsequently received word from Adams that Warren and Nagle were committed for trial, Seward welcomed it as a diplomatic triumph, for want of a more substantial achievement. "I learn with satisfaction," he replied, "that Her Majesty's Government have so far changed its position in

[63] Seward to Adams, October 3, 1867, NA/M77/80.

244 Fenians and Anglo-American Relations

regard to citizens of the United States arbitrarily under a suspension of habeas corpus in Ireland as to concede them a prompt, and as I hope the result may prove a fair trial." [64] This last gratuitous jibe readily lent itself to the interpretation that Seward would regard any verdict other than acquittal somewhat short of fair. If any doubts lingered about the target at which he had taken aim in this correspondence with Adams— the British had indicated their intention to try the prisoners as early as September 23—they should have been dispelled by the announcement of the government's decision to return a further fifteen tons of Fenian munitions seized during 1866. This news drew from Adderly, the undersecretary at the Colonial Office, the bitter comment: "What a cursed constitution under which such tricks are played." [65]

As it happened, the long-awaited trials of Warren and Nagle which opened in Dublin on October 25 were quickly, if briefly, overshadowed by dramatic developments in Manchester. There, three days later, the Crown opened its case against five of the twenty-six people arrested for complicity in the rescue of Kelly and Deasy, and hence the murder of the policeman. On November 2 this group were all convicted and sentenced to death. [66]

To this moment, Charles Francis Adams had been little more than an unsympathetic observer of their predicament. His own experiences with Fenians, their violent activities in Ireland, and his concern for law and order no doubt influenced his judgment when he commented in the privacy of his diary: "This matter of killing policemen seems to be getting habitual with these people. It would appear that Irishmen

[64] *Ibid.*, October 31.
[65] Adderly to Stanley, October 14, 1867, CO, 537/99.
[66] London *Times*, November 3, 1867.

cannot comprehend the value of clemency." [67] His disposition did not improve when two of the condemned men, Condon and O'Brien, alias Gould and Shore, claimed American citizenship and denounced him for not interceding on their behalf. Certainly their abuse and claims failed to stir him. The "charges were of so purely a criminal nature and sustained by such strong evidence," he reported to Seward on November 5, "that it did not seem to me to be a proper case to attempt to interfere with the usual course of law." [68] Eleven days later, having received in the interim another appeal from Condon, who unlike O'Brien had no record of Fenian activity, Adams indicated that American intervention was not only uncalled for but futile. "It is useless to approach the Government with any plea in mitigation of the sentence," he informed Seward,[69] and there was no shortage of evidence to support this attitude. The London *Times* was giving expression to an aroused British opinion.

If the murder of a policeman is treated as a comparatively venial offence because he was assassinated in a public capacity, policemen cannot be expected to protect the public against the "American citizens," as they call themselves, who seem to be multiplying both in Ireland and in this country. There is a spirit abroad in the midst of us which nothing but a terrible example will subdue.[70]

For all his personal reservations and the abundant evidence that his intervention would be unpalatable to the British, Adams did write to Lord Stanley on behalf of Condon when a report from the American consul at Manchester supported this hapless individual's assertions that he had played an insig-

---

[67] Adams, Diary, November 2, 1867.
[68] Adams to Seward, November 5, 1867, NA/M30/90.
[69] *Ibid.*, November 16.　　　[70] November 4, 1867.

nificant role in the tragic affray.[71] However, that was as far as Adams would unbend. He adamantly refused to do anything for O'Brien, even to the extent of ignoring instructions from Seward. Conscious of the difficult position of the British government, which was confronted with Irish demonstrations demanding relief and a public showing signs of panic in the wake of Fenian activities, Adams realized that it could ill afford to give the appearance of "giving way to an extraneous influence of which already a great deal of jealousy has been manifested." He was convinced that further interference would do "more harm then good," [72] for it might provoke the British into a sharp rebuff which would do little to improve Anglo-American relations and even less for the prisoners, probably destroying "all chances of success for either of them." [73] Consequently, he continued to ignore instructions from Washington to intercede for both men. He saved Condon, but on November 23, O'Brien, along with two other men—the fourth had been pardoned when additional evidence vindicated his protestations of innocence—was executed in Manchester.

The Manchester "martyrs" were immediately accorded a prominent place in the folklore of Fenianism. "The cause wanted nothing so much as a martyr," the *New York Tribune* observed. "Now it has three." [74] A few days later it concluded that "the British Government has infused new life into their ranks, and from them a rallying cry." [75] Yet the significance of the tragic events in Manchester for Anglo-American relations was not the emotional stimulus they gave to the Fenian movement, important as that may have been. It

[71] Adams to Stanley, November 20, 1867, FO, 5/1342.
[72] Adams to Seward, November 22, 1867, NA/M30/90.
[73] Adams, Diary, November 20, 1867.
[74] November 25, 1867.   [75] November 29.

was the murder rather than the judicial homicides which influenced the subsequent course of those relations. The death of Sergeant Brett had served to illustrate for many Englishmen the alarming spread of Fenian activity in England, and this naturally aroused a louder cry for the punishment of captured terrorists. The principal object of British anger was the Irish-American. "If there be one class of Fenian conspirators rather than another which deserves no mercy at the hands of the Government," the London *Times* thundered, "it is the class of American filibusters who have long infected Dublin and are beginning to infect our own great cities." [76]

In this climate of opinion few governments, least of all that of the Earl of Derby, which was not built on the soundest of political foundations, could have released Fenians in Ireland or England at the behest of the United States. Instead, in the aftermath of September 18 in Manchester, it committed itself to the prosecution of Warren and Nagle. This decision, however, was fraught with danger because Warren was a naturalized American and a native-born British subject. Whereas the crime of murder cut across nationality—the citizenship of Condon and O'Brien was immaterial to their trial—the national status of Warren became an integral part of his defence and prosecution. Therefore, the Manchester affair played its part in reviving the unresolved Anglo-American problem of expatriation. No doubt this is the explanation of Seward's comment to Adams when, in turning from the forlorn task of saving the lives of the condemned men in Manchester, he wrote: "The proceedings in the case of Colonel Warren at Dublin are the subject of even more serious concern." [77]

[76] November 5, 1867.
[77] Seward to Adams, November 21, 1867, NA/M77/80.

8

The Naturalization Treaty of 1870

Fenian activity in Ireland had always threatened to bring to the boil the long-simmering Anglo-American dispute over expatriation. Only pragmatic concessions had prevented eruption in 1865 and 1866. But as the nations had not surrendered their diametrically opposed doctrines, the day of reckoning had merely been postponed, and there was every indication of its being nigh when the Irish-Americans resumed operations in 1867. The British were all too easily persuaded to continue the suspension of habeas corpus, which greatly facilitated, as it was intended to do, the detention of men who claimed American nationality. Inevitably these men appealed to the diplomatic officials of the United States for assistance, but the British were initially disposed to treat with scant respect intervention on behalf of detainees who could not prove their claims of American citizenship.[1]

In an effort to overcome this difficulty, Seward proposed that both governments accept passports as the requisite evidence. In this suggestion, however, Lord Stanley quickly

---

[1] Ford (chargé d'affaires) to Stanley, October 5, 1867, FO, 5/1342.

detected a fatal flaw. To accept the passport of a naturalized American as conclusive proof of his national status was to concede the principle of expatriation. Therefore, in a deliberately evasive reply, he announced that the services of the American officials would not be denied to anyone who claimed to be an American. In effect, the passport proposal was cautiously skirted because, as Adams informed Seward, "it is feared it may revive the old question of the right of expatriation which we had succeeded in putting in abeyance." [2] Just two days later, on October 25, the trial of John Warren opened in Dublin, and this immediately dispelled any hope that the issue would remain in abeyance.

As direct force had failed to overthrow British rule in Ireland, John Warren, a skillful agent provocateur, sedulously sought to incite the Anglo-American conflict from which the brethren confidently expected an independent Erin to emerge. What Kelly had failed to secure through political blackmail—namely, a more belligerent American posture over the treatment of naturalized Americans in Britain—Warren sought to provoke. Having laid the groundwork with his inflammatory assertions that he had been arrested in Ireland for enunciating American principles in the United States, he now grasped his opportunity to parade as an innocent victim of the British government's arrogant disregard of American law. As soon as his trial opened, he invoked an ancient principle of English law, *de medietate linguae*, to demand a jury of which at least half were fellow Americans. Irritating as this misinterpretation of the law undoubtedly was to the British, for it merely accorded aliens the right to be tried by a mixed jury of aliens (not necessarily of the same nationality as the defendant) and British subjects, the real provocation was

---

[2] Adams to Seward, October 23, 1867, NA/M30/90.

Warren's founding of it upon his naturalization as an American citizen. When this brought the inevitable response from the presiding judge, namely dismissal of the demand and an emphatic restatement of the doctrine of inalienable allegiance, Warren instructed his counsel to withdraw from the case and melodramatically proclaimed: "I now place it in the hands of the United States which has now become the principal." [3]

Ill disposed as he was to heed any call from Warren, Charles Francis Adams was nonetheless forced to concede privately that his government would become a party to the dispute, and he looked no further than to domestic political advantage for the incentive. The judge's formal statement of the British doctrine of allegiance, and the subsequent distinction drawn between Warren and Nagle—the latter, a native-born American, had also demanded a mixed jury and for this reason his trial had been postponed—was bound to attract attention in Washington. "I have not much confidence in their independence of the Irish influence," he cynically observed of his government, "although the President ought to understand by this time how small his chances of public life have become." [4] However, in an effort to moderate the enthusiasm with which his superiors were sure to approach this issue, Adams, consistent to the last, reminded Seward of an embarrassing contradiction in American law and practice. Indeed, this was a weakness the evidently uneasy British had gratefully fastened upon. On November 5 the London *Times*, sensing trouble over Warren, discussed the problem of expatriation at some length before concluding, "Very few propositions of international law are better established or more familiar than the axiom that a natural born subject cannot transfer his allegiance from one sovereign to another at

[3] London *Times*, November 5, 1867.
[4] Adams, Diary, November 1, 1867.

pleasure." The newspaper did not fail to point out that British law "is here identical with that of the United States." Enclosing a copy of this editorial with his dispatch to Seward, Adams observed, "It is much to be regretted that on this point there should always have been some conflict between established policy of the Executive Department and the ruling of the Federal Judiciary." [5]

This conflict certainly made Seward pause before launching a diplomatic offensive. "I content myself for the present," he replied to Adams, "with informing you that the pretensions of the Irish Court cannot be allowed by this Government. I shall have occasion soon to address you more fully on this subject." [6] Meanwhile, the President's annual message to Congress was utilized to impress upon the nation's legislators the administration's predicament. Drawing their attention to the conflict between executive practice and the decisions of American jurists, which the British unfeelingly cited to support their contention of indefeasible allegiance, Johnson appealed to them to "declare the national will unmistakeably upon this important question." [7]

There was little chance that this issue could be postponed until Congress acted. Demands for action were soon heard. Naturally the Fenians were in the vanguard, only too willing to capitalize on the developments in Britain "to elevate themselves into greater importance and strengthen their political influence" in the United States.[8] Their "Senate" quickly convened and resolved to organize a campaign to procure the intervention of the government and Congress on behalf of

[5] Adams to Seward, November 5, 1867, NA/M30/90.
[6] Seward to Adams, November 21, 1867, NA/M77/80.
[7] Richardson, *Compilation of the Messages and Papers of the Presidents, 1787–1897*, VIII, 3778, December 3, 1867.
[8] Archibald to Stanley, November 22, 1867, FO, 5/1342.

naturalized Americans. At a mass meeting held in New York's Cooper Institute on November 26 the appropriate resolutions were adopted and a committee of seven appointed to convey them to the government. Among the conspicuous participants at such gatherings were politicians from both parties, and Congress soon reverberated with their oratory. To dismiss their activities as a cynical serving of their "own self-interest and those of their respective parties," as British observers and Adams were inclined to do, was somewhat uncharitable.[9] Undoubtedly, the thought of political advantage was never absent from their minds, yet that fact should not discredit entirely their proclaimed interest in the plight of Americans, particularly naturalized ones, abroad. The political representatives of a nation whose population embraced so many immigrants, not all of whom were Irish, had to be profoundly moved by their treatment at the hands of foreign governments: dignity and national honor would tolerate nothing less. The plight of the Irish-Americans was rendered doubly sensitive because they also stirred the traditional American sympathy for subject peoples struggling for liberty. Thus when Andrew Johnson, confronted by Fenian delegations, gave voice to this sentiment, although it was the politically expedient response, it may also have been genuine. Similarly, although Seward's concern for Ireland had usually been expressed to gatherings of Irish-Americans, this does not prove that he never meant exactly what he said. Convictions and sympathies are no less deeply held because they prove to be expedient.

Charles Francis Adams soon became the principal target of the invective of those Fenians and politicians who, no matter what their purpose, whether it was to uphold a principle or

[9] *Ibid.*, November 27.

secure political advantage, sought protection for Americans in Britain. In Congress, Robinson, an Irish-American Representative from New York, led the attack, denouncing the Minister for failing to intercede with sufficient vigor on behalf of the imprisoned men. Not content simply to berate him, Robinson also called for his impeachment,[10] but this proposal was soon lost in the shadow cast by the report of the House Judiciary Committee recommending the impeachment of the President.

It was never likely that denunciation or even the threat of impeachment would shake Adams from his course. As in 1866, he found himself the victim of his own reticence, which sprang from his determination not to jeopardize his nation's claims against Britain by championing Fenians or permitting them to use the United States as a pawn in their struggle against Britain. The fact that others were not as discerning would never have distracted him. Of course, his interpretation of national interest was conveniently buttressed by a personal distaste for the men involved, and he soon grew bored with his office as his time was increasingly taken up with efforts to reclaim Irishmen from the punishment he thought most of them richly deserved. Therefore he wrote to Seward in November of 1867 asking, admittedly not for the first time, to be relieved of his duties.[11] What part, if any, his frustration of Seward's efforts to use the Fenians to squeeze further concessions from the British over the *Alabama*, or his unwillingness to defend naturalized or even native Americans with the vigor that American political exigencies if nothing else required, played in the decision to accept his resignation this time is open to conjecture. Adams could not have been denied any-

[10] *Congressional Globe*, 40th Cong., 1st sess., p. 786, November 21, 1867.

[11] Adams to Seward, November 21, 1867, Adams Papers.

way. Still, his independence could scarcely have pleased Seward when it resulted in heavier domestic pressure being exerted upon him because he was "believed by the Fenians to approve of Mr. Adams' conduct." [12] Perhaps it was in an effort to correct this impression that he also made the Minister the butt for criticism. On December 9, Seward wrote to Adams damning him with faint praise for his efforts to help the men condemned and then executed in Manchester, men whose crime, he suggested significanctly, had been political rather than criminal. [13] However, by the time these tidings reached London, another Fenian tragedy had merely served to strengthen Adams' faith in his own conduct.

On December 13, in a tragically naive attempt to liberate an associate imprisoned at Clerkenwell, London, a group of Fenians foolishly placed a barrel of gunpowder against the outer wall of the prison, lit the fuse, and retired a safe distance. The subsequent explosion produced a yawning breech, some sixty feet in length, but it also killed three people and injured many others living in the neighboring houses. Meanwhile, the Fenian prisoner was safely locked in his cell. [14]

Adams viewed this tragedy as vindication of his conservative attitude toward the prisoners and a crushing repudiation of Seward's concept of Irish patriotism, which, to his mind, seemed to embrace the murder of policemen and the blowing up of innocent people. [15] In a pointed reply to the Secretary's dispatch, he wrote of the Fenians: "It would seem as impossible to place them within the category of a meritorious political movement alluded to in your Despatch, as it would have been with us to shield the assassins of President Lincoln and

[12] Archibald to Stanley, November 22, 1867, FO, 5/1342.
[13] Seward to Adams, December 9, 1867, NA/M77/80.
[14] London *Times*, December 14, 1867.
[15] Adams, Diary, December 24, 1867.

yourself under the same plea." [16] But the Clerkenwell disaster did more than confirm Adams in his policy; it also re-aroused all the fear and anger the Manchester murder had first excited in England. The London *Punch* gave pictorial expression to this sentiment with a bitter cartoon in which a vicious Irishman was portrayed sitting on a barrel of gunpowder, armed with a pistol, holding an ember, and surrounded by inquisitive children. [17]

This venomous atmosphere was not dispelled by reports that a band of assassins had already departed the United States for England, where, or so it was rumored, they planned to murder the Queen, Lords Derby and Stanley, Benjamin Disraeli, and a host of other personages in British public life. To deal with this threat, which did not appear at all imaginary in the wake of the Clerkenwell explosion, the Home Secretary remained at his desk throughout December coordinating the government's precautionary measures. While ships of the Royal Navy stood off the Irish coast waiting to intercept any vessel suspected of carrying the assassins, thousands of special constables were called out to guard public buildings. [18] Concerned also for the safety of innocent members of the Irish communities to be found in many of the larger English cities, the government, in a season conspicuously devoid of traditional good will, forbade any demonstrations mourning the Manchester "martyrs" or Irish liberty. [19] With English public opinion already dangerously strained, these might well have brought down upon the Irish in England the indiscriminate terrors of mob violence. Instead it was the government which

---

[16] Adams to Seward, December 24, 1867, NA/M30/91.

[17] LIII (December 28, 1867), 263.

[18] Hardy to Buckingham, December 26; Stanley to Disraeli, December 20, 1867, Duke of Buckingham Papers, British Museum.

[19] Adams to Seward, December 14, 1867, NA/M30/91.

soon found itself under attack as the public tension found expression in mounting criticism of its "feebleness and lenity" in the treatment of Fenians.[20]

As the closest American observer of these developments, Adams quickly sought to impress upon his government the temporary inadvisability of further intervention on behalf of the Fenian prisoners. Consequently, he was understandably dismayed when shortly thereafter he received a dispatch in which it was suggested that he should advise the British, "as an act of wisdom," to dismiss the prosecution of Nagle and discharge some of the other Fenians who had been tried, convicted, and sentenced to periods of penal servitude.[21] Not only did Adams regard as unwarranted Seward's assertion that the punishment of these men had been exceptionally severe, but he considered the characteristically offensive tone of the note "so dictatorial and assuming" that he was "a little embarrassed about using it." In fact, all his recently suppressed doubts about the Secretary's motives were briefly revived. "I get Despatches from Washington," he wrote in his diary, "which rather indicate a disposition to pick a quarrel with this country."[22]

In this instance, however, the root of the matter, as Adams should have recognized, was a time lag in communication rather than Seward's deliberately provocative language. Dated December 14, his note had been written and sent out before the first reports of the Clerkenwell tragedy reached the United States. Indeed, the vessel carrying it must have been almost within sight of the British coast before Adams penned his own dispatch warning against further interference on behalf of the prisoners. Equally significant was the fact that for all the

[20] *Ibid.*, December 24.
[21] Seward to Adams, December 14, 1867, NA/M77/80.
[22] Adams, Diary, January 4, 1868.

offensiveness of his advice, now exaggerated by the latest Fenian crime, Seward had taken the precaution of leaving to the Minister's discretion the time and form of its presentation to the British. In short, he was seeking to secure the maximum political benefit from the publication of his dispatch in the United States but at the same time minimize its diplomatic liability. Adams, as Seward must surely have realized he would, eagerly grasped the latitude offered to him. Thus, he waited until January 20, by which time the English public temper had cooled, before presenting the contents of Seward's note to Lord Stanley, and then in an informal and general way describing Seward's remarks as an expression of opinion rather than a formal communication which required an answer. This approach greatly reduced the danger of Stanley's asking for a copy or even requesting to see it. "Thus I have tried to get rid of the most awkward commission laid upon me," a much relieved Adams commented after the interview. "Luckily the communication was left to my discretion, and copies of the paragraphs were authorized to be given only in case Lord Stanley asked for them." It was a more relaxed diplomat who now concluded tolerantly, "Mr. Seward is sometimes the master of the art of giving offence without knowing it." [23] For Adams this was an uncharacteristically naive observation.

If Adams was able to postpone and temper the discussion of the plight of the Fenian prisoners, evasion of the wider issue they had revived was more difficult. The question of expatriation remained unresolved and it quickly excited comment. And had the British arrogantly held to their traditional position, which the *London Court Journal* crudely summarized when it proclaimed, "We are not going to oblige Americans

[23] *Ibid.*, January 20.

by calling ourselves Americans at their bidding or letting our fellow countrymen be so called," the two countries might well have found themselves "in a conflict of pretensions" from which neither could "recede with honor," thus forcing "a bloody issue." [24] Happily, more moderate opinion prevailed.

On December 11, shortly after the publication in England of the first reports of President Johnson's annual message to Congress in which he had discussed the problem of naturalization, the London *Times* published a letter to the editor from a prominent lawyer, Vernon Harcourt, written over the pseudonym of "Historicus." In it he presented strong arguments, based on classical legal authorities and precedent, for a revision of the doctrine of perpetual allegiance, a doctrine which, as Harcourt pointed out, "had its origin in a system which is obsolete, and found its application in a condition of society which has passed away—Feudal Tenure." To those who argued that to change the law now was to handicap the government in its dealings with the Fenians, he replied, "The more clearly such men are recognized as American Citizens the more directly responsible would be the American government for their conduct abroad."

For those too obtuse to grasp Harcourt's meaning, the influential *Times* drew the obvious conclusions in an accompanying editorial. "We admit," it commented, "that, on grounds of policy not to say commonsense the argument for revision is irresistible. We see, then, no good reason why the British Government should decline any friendly overtures that may be made by the United States with a view to its amendment." [25] Charles Francis Adams, who believed expatriation to be "one of the most threatening problems to the

[24] *New York Tribune,* December 2, 1867.
[25] December 11, 1867.

peace of the two countries," [26] was anxious to take advantage of this sentiment. "The mode in which this difficult matter is treated by both writers," he wrote to Seward, "affords encouragement to the belief that something may be done to harmonize the rule as well here as at home into one system. In my opinion nothing is more desirable in order to remove amicably the cause for future collisions on this subject." [27]

Seward, however, was far less enthusiastic at the prospect of an immediate settlement of the problem. Indeed, he exhibited an uncharacteristic but by no means purposeless lethargy. The articles from the London *Times* which Adams had forwarded to him were dismissed as "acceptable indications of a disposition in a certain quarter to relieve the two governments of the embarrassments which have arisen from the unnecessary and indiscreet assertion in Great Britain of a principle which has become practically obsolete." Seward had not forgotten the contradiction that still existed in American law and practice. Until Congress moved to correct this, he informed Adams, the President would not feel free to express his official position on the naturalization issue. [28]

Yet it would be incorrect to assume that the Secretary of State had at last been infected with Adams' concern for international consistency. His reticence was much more ambitiously conceived. Thus while working from the same premise as the Member of Parliament who explained to Adams that although the path to a settlement of the *Alabama* was blocked, a solution to the naturalization problem was easy because it was in Britain's interest to amend the existing law, [29] Seward reached a quite different conclusion. He saw in the British

[26] Adams, Diary, December 11, 1867.
[27] Adams to Seward, December 11, 1867, NA/M30/91.
[28] Seward to Adams, December 27, 1867, NA/M77/80.
[29] Adams, Diary, January 8, 1868.

anxiety to settle the latter problem the instrument with which to clear the path to the *Alabama*. Here, or so it evidently appeared to him, was another opportunity to utilize the Fenians, albeit indirectly, to extract the concessions he wanted from the British. Presumably even Adams would not balk at a diplomatic exchange—a naturalization settlement in return for the negotiation of the war claims on American terms. Seward skillfully laid the groundwork for just such a solution when he replied to Adams on December 27, 1867.

As it was fundamental to his policy that the British should be impressed with the advisability of a settlement, he made no effort to minimize the seriousness of the expatriation issue or the dangers of a collision over it. "At the same time," he continued, "I think it necessary to say that in view of the failure hitherto to obtain a satisfactory settlement of our complaint against Great Britain which occurred during the late rebellion in the United States," and the severity practiced upon naturalized Americans by British courts, "I do not think that a situation exists in the United States favourable to the initiation of negotiations by this Department limited to the single purpose of obtaining a revision of the law concerning expatriation." [30]

Having briefed Adams on how to respond to British overtures, Seward sat back to await developments. One he undoubtedly did not expect was Congressional legislation. There was little disposition within either House to do the bidding of a President many members were anxious to impeach, or to clarify a situation when continued confusion provided such excellent material in a presidential election year. Here was an issue more intelligible to the general public than the *Alabama*, and one on which there was every likelihood of a complete

[30] Seward to Adams, December 27, 1867, NA/M77/80.

unity of sentiment.[31] Therefore, as Seward may well have expected, Congress passed more resolutions of support for the condemned men instead of a naturalization law. Meanwhile, the Fenians also moved in a predictable way. More mass meetings were organized to protest the conduct of the British and Adams, and to demand the Minister's recall.

Seward eagerly adapted this activity to his purpose of increasing the pressure on the British government. Despite reports of the tragedy at Clerkenwell "it is plainly to be observed," he wrote to Adams on January 13, 1868, "that the sympathies of the people of the United States are every day more profoundly moved and more generally moved on behalf of Ireland." Then, describing the British claims to indefeasible allegiance and what he termed their illegitimate behavior during the Civil War as the principal obstacles to amicable relations, he concluded, "Perhaps after this popular protest shall have earnest expression in both Houses of Congress, British statesmen may perceive that a restoration of cordial and friendly relations and sympathies between the two countries is impossible while the causes of irritation to which I have referred are allowed to endure." [32] As if taking his cue from the Secretary, Nathaniel P. Banks reported out of his committee just two weeks later a bill "Concerning the Rights of American Citizens in Foreign States." The most startling feature of this measure was a politically eye-catching reprisal clause which provided that for every American detained abroad "upon the allegation that naturalization in the United States does not operate to dissolve his allegiance, the President shall be, and hereby is, empowered to order and detain in custody any subject or citizen of such foreign government who may

[31] Sumner to Bright, January 7, 1868, Bright Papers.
[32] Seward to Adams, January 13, 1868, NA/M77/80.

be found within the jurisdiction of the United States." [33] Radical as this solution was, it did not lack public support. "The vigorous measures authorized by the Committee must be fearlessly carried out," the *New York Tribune* announced, "and whether Great Britain be brought to acknowledge the soundness of our theory or not, it must be distinctly understood that we shall not submit to the exercise of hers." [34] However, if Seward hoped that the British would be driven to negotiate on his terms by the thought of their nationals being rounded up in the United States with the same alacrity Irish-Americans were detained in Ireland, or that they would be unnerved by wild talk of war in some American newspapers if the *Alabama* and naturalization issues were not solved quickly,[35] he was soon disappointed.

The activities he had harnessed in support of his policy aroused more irritation than alarm in Britain. The British were naturally antagonized by the libel, repeated with tiresome regularity by American politicians, Seward included,[36] that Irish-Americans had been imprisoned for words spoken and acts committed in the United States. Similarly, self-righteous American indignation over the doctrine of inalienable allegiance was difficult to ignore. Certainly it was too difficult for Harcourt who gave vent to an opinion shared by members of the government when, on the basis of existing American law, he concluded in another letter to the editor of the London *Times* that "of all countries there is none which is bound to address itself to the difficult discussion with more modesty and moderation than the United States." [37]

[33] *Congressional Globe*, 40th Cong., 2d sess., p. 783, January 27, 1868.
[34] January 28, 1868.   [35] *Ibid.*, February 7.
[36] *House Exec. Doc.*, no. 157, p. 293, Seward to Stanbery, December 21, 1867.   [37] January 10, 1868.

Meanwhile, in his conversations with Adams, Lord Stanley offered scant hope that he could be panicked into the omnibus settlement of Anglo-American problems which Seward had contemplated. Thus, when the American Minister called at the Foreign Office on February 15 to discuss this proposal, he discovered that the British were still inclined to negotiate only those problems they considered it in their national interests to settle at this time. He was informed that they were quite prepared to seek a solution to the naturalization issue; in fact he learned that Stanley had already authorized the new British Minister to the United States, Edward Thornton, to engage in any consultation "that might have for its object the arrangement of all existing differences on this head." But that was as far as the British were at this time prepared to go, for the Foreign Secretary then went on to express his doubts "whether it would be found more easy to come to an understanding by accumulating all the different topics . . . in one heap than treating them separately." [38]

Normally Seward would have responded vigorously in an effort to overcome this cautious British opposition, but not in March, 1868. Instead, his diplomacy underwent a radical if not fundamental change. The extent of the revolution that had occurred in the Secretary's view of the relationship between the naturalization issue and the other outstanding Anglo-American problems was clear from a dispatch he wrote to Adams on March 7. Describing naturalization as the issue "which more urgently needs removal than any other" for it will "admit of no delay compatible with the preservation of harmony between our two countries," he then added, "While that uneasiness shall remain unrelieved it would seem almost hopeless to attempt an adjustment of the other differences." [39]

[38] Adams to Seward, February 18, 1868, NA/M30/91.
[39] Seward to Adams, March 7, 1868, NA/M77/80.

In short, a naturalization settlement had suddenly become a prerequisite rather than the *quid pro quo* in the negotiation of the *Alabama* claims.

Meanwhile, Seward was also pressing the gospel of haste upon Thornton, and the British Minister was quickly converted to the cause of a speedy settlement. Believing that this "would tend considerably to weaken the hold which Fenianism has upon the minds of a part of the population of this country," that it would give the British government even stronger grounds "for insisting upon the United States Authorities not conniving at the organization in this country of any expedition against our possessions, and that above all it would open the road to negotiations upon the San Juan question and the joint settlement of the Alabama and British claims," [40] Thornton cabled to London the bases of an agreement proposed by Seward, along with his endorsement of them. Five in number, they provided that naturalization and residence for five years were sufficient to change nationality, that naturalized citizens returning to their native country might be tried for offences committed before emigration, that extradition remain as it was, that a naturalized citizen who returned to his native country for a period in excess of two years forfeited the protection of his adopted country, and that a naturalized citizen should be treated in his native country in precisely the same manner as a native citizen of his adopted country. [41]

When he received Thornton's telegram, Stanley forwarded the proposals to Gathorne Hardy at the Home Office, asking him for an opinion as to the expediency of authorizing negotiations. The Foreign Secretary also sought the approval of the Law Officers, and this he could not obtain. They quickly

[40] Thornton to Stanley, March 30, 1868, FO, 5/1343.
[41] *Ibid.*, March 7, 1868, FO, 5/1356.

discovered those ambiguities that alternately offend and gratify precise legal minds, and when Stanley and Hardy attempted for political reasons to reconcile them to the American proposals, closer investigation uncovered even more numerous objections.[42] Consequently, on March 20 a telegram was sent to the Minister in Washington informing him that there were "no objections in principle to a change in the law of naturalization which shall suit American views, but legal details require careful consideration and public enquiry will be necessary before any Treaty can be signed."[43] Although another rebuff for Seward, rendered doubly embarrassing by Thornton's enthusiasm wherein he had exceeded his instructions and led Seward to believe that he would be authorized to sign a draft treaty, the British did their best to cushion the blow. Stanley constantly re-emphasized two points, the concession of which he evidently hoped would appease the Secretary of State: first, that "the obstacles to immediate action which we see are of a legal not a political character," and second, that the British government "disclaim the idea of desiring to maintain and enforce the doctrine of indefeasible allegiance, and are quite willing to adopt the principle of expatriation."[44]

Yet even this sweeping concession of principle, which Stanley also announced in the House of Commons on March 20, failed to mollify Seward. Instead, he continued to press for an immediate and formal settlement along the lines he had already outlined. This behavior, the fact that the Secretary now attached so much importance to the naturalization question and so little apparently to the *Alabama*, puzzled the British. The only explanation of this diplomatic *volte-face* that

---

[42] Stanley to Thornton, March 21, 1868, *ibid.*
[43] *Ibid.*, March 20.   [44] *Ibid.*, March 21.

Thornton could provide was Seward's own: the signing of a naturalization treaty with Prussia (North German Confederation) had opened his eyes to the possibility of a similar settlement with Britain, if it was completed quickly and without publicity.[45] Plausible as this was, Stanley remained unconvinced, and when Adams called at the Foreign Office on March 31 to forward Seward's latest demands for instant progress, he was asked for an explanation. Answering first in his official capacity, the American Minister suggested that the Secretary was merely responding to the domestic pressure for a settlement. Then, speaking unofficially, he went on to express the belief that as Seward expected an early termination to his services as Secretary of State, he was desperate to complete something with the British before leaving office.[46]

A naturalization treaty upholding the American doctrine of expatriation would have been no mean parting triumph. The issue had bedeviled Anglo-American relations for too long to be casually dismissed. Thus, while Seward did not confine his discussions of this problem to Britain (following the Prussian settlement, he opened and subsequently closed successfully negotiations with several nations [47]), they were of first importance for both historical and contemporary reasons. Therefore he was particularly anxious that they should not become mired down in a bog of legal technicalities. "Mr. Seward still urges that England and the United States come to a simple Treaty engagement on the great principles of expatriation and naturalization," Thornton reported on April 13, "and that the discussion and negotiation of further details should be deferred to a later period when experiences may have thrown

[45] Thornton to Stanley, March 10, 1868, FO, 5/1343.
[46] Adams, Diary, March 31, 1868.
[47] Sanford (U.S. Minister to Belgium) to Seward, July 3, 1868, Seward Papers.

more light upon the subject." [48] However, this was the American's last serious effort to secure a formal agreement from the British until late in May. During the interim the immediate future of the Johnson administration was being decided.

When Charles Francis Adams raised the possibility of an early end to Seward's seven-year tenure in the State Department, he was not speaking of death from natural political causes. Although 1868 was a presidential election year and whoever won was unlikely to reappoint Seward, the certainty of losing office on March 4, 1869, still almost a full year away, hardly justified the frantic pressure upon the British. This, like Adams' comment, was inspired by the determined effort of the Republican majority in Congress to impeach Andrew Johnson. Still doggedly refusing to concede total victory to his Congressional enemies, the President challenged their Tenure of Office Act by removing the abrasive Edwin Stanton from his position as Secretary of War. Unhappily, this merely rallied to the cause of impeachment the supporters it had earlier lacked in sufficient number. Thus, the months of March, April, and May witnessed a mounting political crisis as Johnson was first impeached by Congress and then tried before the Senate. Twice during this period Seward placed his resignation in the hands of the President with the request that it be accepted in the event of a conviction. [49] Here was the danger of an abrupt termination to his services.

While the fate of the Johnson administration was hanging in the balance, the British government quietly pursued its course. A mark of its continuing desire to conciliate American opinion was the gradual release, on the condition that they returned immediately to the United States, of Fenians detained without trial during the crises of the previous year.

[48] Thornton to Stanley, April 13, 1868, FO, 5/1356.
[49] Large Diary, May 15, 1868, Johnson Papers.

Moreover, with the unavowed help of Adams,[50] confessions and apologies were secured from Nagle and some of his fellow passengers on the *Erin's Hope*, admitting that they had traveled to Ireland to incite rebellion. These documents, which won release and deportation for the penitents,[51] also provided the British with unimpeachable evidence against Warren. His protestations of innocence were now refuted by his own colleagues.

These developments relieved Adams of considerable anxiety on the eve of his own departure from Britain. The steady release of prisoners and the refuting of Warren's inflammatory charges encouraged the retiring American Minister to believe that one more ground for Anglo-American antagonism was slowly being removed.[52] Perhaps he derived particular satisfaction from this turn of events, for he had always sought to prevent the Fenians jeopardizing peaceful relations between the two nations, a fact that had not escaped the attention of others. Consequently, while his name evoked cheers in the British Parliament, it was jeered at Fenian rallies in the United States.

Another ground for antagonism, primarily associated with the Fenians, which showed signs of being slowly removed, was the naturalization question. On May 21, shortly after Adams' departure, the British government announced the establishment of a Royal Commission to investigate the laws of allegiance. Here was the public inquiry upon which the British had insisted as a prerequisite for a settlement. Equally significant for progress toward a solution was President Johnson's escape from impeachment by the slimmest of margins on May 26. The following day, Seward, now unembarrassed by

[50] Adams, Diary, May 5, 1868.
[51] Diary of Benjamin Moran, May 9, 1868, Library of Congress.
[52] Adams, Diary, May 9, 1868.

the possibility of sudden removal from office, returned to the task of extracting a treaty from the British. "I learn from the cable," he wrote to Benjamin Moran, who was serving as chargé d'affaires in London until a successor to Adams arrived, "that a commission of Lord Clarendon and others have been appointed to examine the British naturalization laws. Please sound the Government again upon the question of empowering Mr. Thornton to negotiate with us here on the principle of the North German Treaty." [53] If this communication did not reflect quite the same sense of urgency that his notes in March had, it did indicate that Seward would not be easily deflected from his purpose—a point that was further emphasized by the alacrity with which he grasped every opportunity to bring the British to terms.

One weapon that came readily to hand was the revival of Fenian threats against Canada. The political atmosphere encouraged belligerence, for to the normal excitement and indecisiveness of an election year, particularly one in which the presidency was to be contested, was added the crisis of impeachment. Also, an internal reorganization had apparently provided the Fenians with the leadership needed to utilize this opportunity to the full. William Roberts, a dry goods merchant, resigned as president of the "Canada first" wing of the Brotherhood and was replaced by "General" O'Neill, the man of action. O'Neill was convinced that a raid could be organized with little likelihood of American interference, and he also believed "that if he can only commence active warfare on the frontier, he will draw to his standard Fenians from all sections and thus practically heal the existing feuds." [54] In short, he expected to lead a reunited Brotherhood into Canada. In reality the organization was still hamstrung by bank-

---

[53] Seward to Moran, May 27, 1868, NA/M77/80.
[54] Archibald to Stanley, March 11, 1868, FO, 5/1343.

ruptcy, as many British observers realized, and this proved as destructive to his ambitions as it had to his predecessor's. However, Edward Thornton, lacking the confidence prolonged exposure to Fenian activity brought, turned to Seward for assurances of the American government's determination to frustrate O'Neill's avowed aim.

Throughout the month of April, the British Minister pressed for the written pledge which Seward, during an interview on March 22, had encouraged him to think he could secure. Yet his persistence won nothing more than an unconvincing verbal assurance that the American government "as then constituted" would do its best to prevent a raid being organized and effected, and even this was quietly withdrawn as time passed. The reasons for the Secretary's reneging on his promise to put something in writing are not difficult to discern. Domestically it was inopportune. This was not the time to expose the administration to the charge of being moved by friendship for Britain. The prevalence of anglophobia had been evident from the reception accorded Banks's latest bill in the House of Representatives. It passed on April 20, the reprisal clause still intact, by an overwhelming vote.[55] Therefore, with the Executive on trial and presidential elections in the offing, this was not the moment to multiply the difficulties of the administration or its supporters. Even confidential pledges have on occasion been divulged, and if written they are doubly difficult to disown. However, there was another good reason for Seward's reticence. A more convincing assurance of American activity against the Fenians was diplomatically inexpedient. Indeed, threats against Canada offered the Secretary another lever with which to prize a formal settlement of the naturalization problem from the British.

[55] Pierce, *Memoir and Letters of Charles Sumner*, IV, 346.

He cautiously employed this new tool, to prod rather than to prize, during an interview with Thornton on May 2. Still inhibited by the grave doubt the impeachment trial raised about the administration's future, he did no more than repeat to the British Minister his conviction that "if naturalization and expatriation could be agreed upon between the two countries, one of the pretexts put forward by the Fenians would be removed, and the hands of the United States Government would be strengthened in repelling any hostile acts they might be meditating against Canada." [56] However, when Thornton broached the subject of Fenian activity again at the end of the month, Seward was far more positive in his approach. "Whatever danger there may be of a disturbance of the peace at the frontier at the present time," he replied on May 28, two days after Johnson's escape from his Congressional enemies, "that danger is altogether due to the omission by the British Government to reasonably remove, either by legislation or negotiation, the indefeasible features of British policy on the subject of the rights of naturalized citizens of the United States." Seward was not willing to offer the meager comfort of a verbal assurance of his government's determination to frustrate a Fenian attack. Far from it, for he concluded with the ominous warning: "In asking your attention to this subject once more, I do so with a view to averting from this Government undue responsibility in the event of new fronteir collisions especially liable to occur in a season of high political excitement in both countries." [57]

Whenever Thornton gave him the chance, by reviving the question of Fenian activity, Seward re-emphasized the critical nature of the next few months. He warned that emboldened by the sympathy of the politicians, the expression of which

[56] Thornton to Stanley, May 2, 1868, FO, 5/1343.
[57] Seward to Thornton, May 28, 1868, NA/M99/43.

was inevitable, the Fenians could be expected to take full advantage of the election season. "Naturalized citizens are entitled to protection in all their rights of citizenship as though they were native born," the Republican Party's platform proclaimed, "and no citizen of the United States, native or naturalized, must be liable to arrest and imprisonment by a foreign power for acts done or words spoken in this country; and if so arrested and imprisoned, it is the duty of the Government to interfere on his behalf." [58] The Democrats naturally followed suit at their convention. These yanks on the Lion's tail might be interpreted by the Fenians as encouragement to attack Canada. In reminding Thornton of this, Seward also prescribed his remedy for such a potentially dangerous complication to the lingering ailments of Anglo-American relations: a speedy solution to the naturalization problem. The "delay which attends the proceedings of the British Government is a cause of serious embarrassment to the United States," he wrote. "Indeed it may soon prove injurious to the peace on the Canadian border." [59] But the threat of another Fenian raid did not prove to be as persuasive a diplomatic weapon as Seward evidently hoped it would.

The British had always found in the Brotherhood's bankruptcy one reason for ignoring threats against Canada, but far more encouraging was the evidence that now came to light of the American government's unavowed determination to prevent a raid. Canadian telegraph operators intercepted orders to the American military commanders along the border instructing them to prevent any violation of international law, [60] while Thornton gleaned much the same information from private sources in the American capital. Although Seward

---

[58] *New York Tribune*, May 23, 1868.
[59] Seward to Thornton, June 9, 1868, FO, 5/1356.
[60] Monck to Buckingham, June 11, 1868, Buckingham Papers.

consistently refused to confirm these reports—had he done otherwise he would have undermined his own policy—the British Minister could still report to Lord Stanley on June 15 that he had learned from "other quarters that the Secretary of War receives daily telegrams from officers employed by him on the frontier and that, besides these, a special officer, General Sharp, is employed by the State Department to watch the movements of the Fenians in the direction of St. Albans, whence there seems the greatest possibility of an expedition being despatched." [61]

With the British all too obviously unmoved by the possibility of fresh disturbances along the border, Seward was reduced to pressing Congress into diplomatic service once again. He was spurred on by a Congressional resolution which called upon the administration to secure the release of Warren and a fellow passenger on the *Erin's Hope*, Costello. This implied criticism of his conduct brought yet another dispatch written primarily with an eye to domestic consumption. Thus quickly moving to counter any accusation that he had been remiss in his duty to protect American citizens abroad, Seward referred to the records of the American Legation in London which, he proclaimed, were full of "remonstrances and expostulation" on this very subject. Similarly, he drew the attention of all interested persons to the frequency with which he had urged a settlement of the naturalization problem on the British. As this was a diplomatic dispatch, Seward presumably felt obliged to exhibit some purpose other than an apologia for his conduct. Consequently, he made a public attempt to bring the British to terms. By way of incentive he pointed to the progress through Congress of Banks's bill "Concerning the Rights of American Citizens." "I further call your attention,"

[61] Thornton to Stanley, June 15, 1868, FO, 5/1343.

he wrote to Moran on June 22, "to the fact that the Bill which has passed the House of Representatives is now engaging the Senate, the effect of which Bill, if it shall become law, will be to require the President to make reprisal in cases of judicial denial in Great Britain to a naturalized American of the rights which are conceded there to native American citizens." [62]

The British government, however, still refused to be drawn or pulled into discussions. Although the publication of Seward's note served to irritate some Englishmen, it failed to ruffle Lord Stanley. When Moran called at the Foreign Office on July 9 to discuss this latest move, the Foreign Secretary "made no remarks upon the spirit of the despatch, but said Mr. Seward was simply carrying out the wishes of Congress and could not do otherwise." [63] Such equanimity was not founded entirely upon Lord Stanley's English character. The British still looked to Charles Sumner as a bulwark of Congressional sanity, and their faith was shared, they believed, by many of the Representatives who had voted for the Banks bill in the House. Such confidence was not misplaced, for while the measure passed the House in April, it did not emerge from Sumner's committee until July 18. It only emerged then because he was alarmed lest further delay prejudice his party's chance of success in the forthcoming elections. Once the bill came before the Senate for debate, Sumner led the successful assault upon the reprisal clause. "Your Lordship will perceive that the most objectionable provisions of the Bill . . . have been eliminated," Thornton reported on July 27, "and as far as England is concerned I do not see that any disagreeable discussion should properly arise out of the inclosed Bill as it now stands." [64]

[62] Seward to Moran, June 22, 1868, NA/M77/80.
[63] Moran, Diary, July 9, 1868.
[64] Thornton to Stanley, July 27, 1868, FO, 5/1344.

Yet even as they resisted Seward's efforts to expedite a settlement, the British sought to be conciliatory. Thus, although he refused to open negotiations before the Royal Commission's report was ready, for that would be "putting the cart before the horse," and while he warned Moran that even if the report were ready, it would be impossible to push the legislation necessary to implement its provisions through the present session of Parliament, Stanley repeated his assurance that the British government had conceded the principle of defeasibility contended for by the American government. He also held out the probability of his government's submitting some plan to the United States for consideration before the end of the year, several months before Seward left office.[65]

When he forwarded this news to Washington, Moran did his best to smooth its reception. The Royal Commission had met for the first time on June 10, and the American chargé d'affaires was kept informed of its deliberations by one of the members, W. E. Forster. From Forster he learned that naturalization would be placed on a basis entirely acceptable to the United States.[66] Consequently, it was on the best possible authority that he in turn informed Seward that he had "good reason for stating that the Commissioners anticipate no difficulty in arriving at a satisfactory conclusion on the points in which the United States is concerned."[67] For all this, there was no way of hiding the fact that further delays were inevitable, and as this was not the news the Secretary of State wanted to receive, Moran prudently refrained from hurrying it to him over the transatlantic cable. Instead, he forwarded it in the regular diplomatic bag, leaving Seward to deduce from the delay that his urgings had been unsuccessful.[68]

[65] Moran, Diary, June 15, 1868.   [66] *Ibid.*, June 11.
[67] Moran to Seward, June 16, 1868, NA/M30/91.
[68] Moran, Diary, June 16, 1868.

Although frustrated at every turn, the American still re-fused to concede to the British the initiative in setting the pace for a settlement. He continued to grasp every opportunity to press for expedition. In June, President Johnson nominated Senator Reverdy Johnson to fill the vacancy Adams' resignation had created at the American Legation in London. This reward had been earned during the impeachment trial when Senator Johnson's home was used for regular conferences between fellow senators who favored acquittal and representatives of the President. Yet the selection was also an astute one because, as a faithful member of Sumner's Senate Foreign Relations Committee, President Johnson's nominee did not provoke the struggle over confirmation which might otherwise have been unavoidable. Once safely appointed, the new Minister received his instructions from Seward, and first on his list of priorities was naturalization. "You will address yourself to this as the most important question requiring attention on your arrival in London," Johnson was informed. "You will frankly state to Lord Stanley that, unless this difficulty shall be removed, it is believed by the President that any attempt to settle any of the existing controversies between the two countries would be unavailing and therefore inexpedient." [69] In short, Seward was holding fast with one hand to his policy that a naturalization settlement was the prerequisite for all others. With the other, even as Johnson was familiarizing himself with his new environment, the Secretary was playing an interesting variation on another familiar theme.

Thornton, without losing his confidence in the American authorities, had nonetheless grown concerned over renewed Fenian threats against Canada. As he explained to Edmund

---

[69] Baker, *Works of William H. Seward*, IV, 480.

Hammond, the permanent undersecretary at the Foreign Office:

The Fenians are still alive, and I really believe that they mean still to make an attempt on Canada. This Government under the circumstances of the Presidential elections, under which they become peculiarly timid as to hurting the feelings of the Irish, will do nothing as long as they can avoid it, but I am almost convinced that whenever anything serious shall be attempted they will step in and endeavour to prevent the Fenians from crossing the frontier, if they are not too late. But their extreme timidity with regard to the feelings of these Irish deprives them of the right of calling themselves statesmen.[70]

However, when he called upon Seward to discuss the situation, the American was unusually reassuring. Although Seward expressed the personal opinion that the Fenians did not possess sufficient funds to launch a raid, he promised that "an efficient watch would be kept and insinuated, without saying, that if anything serious were discovered the United States Authorities would interfere." [71] Of course Seward made it quite clear during a subsequent conversation that he expected the British government to reciprocate such friendliness by expediting a naturalization settlement.[72] In effect, as his earlier refusal to give assurances had failed to increase the British momentum in this direction, Seward now admitted his vigilance and sought to obtain a settlement as the reward. When, in the absence of any news of progress from England, it appeared likely that this new attitude had been no more successful than the old, the Secretary of State gave vent to his impatience and resentment. By September 23, anxious—or so

[70] Thornton to Hammond, August 10, 1868, Edmund Hammond Papers, Public Record Office.
[71] Thornton to Stanley, August 18, 1868, CO, 537/99.
[72] Seward to Johnson, August 27, 1868, NA/M77/80.

he informed his Minister—to eradicate this problem from the list that would confront the new American government as yet not elected and the reconstructed government which appeared to be the probable outcome of the forthcoming British elections, he was demanding a settlement before Congress met in December. Perhaps more indicative of the state of his temper was his warning that further procrastination would merely serve to increase distrust of Britain in the United States, an observation that was accompanied by an unfavorable comparison of the conduct of Great Britain with that of the North German Confederation on this question.[73]

As it happened, this rather intemperate dispatch was unnecessary, for by now the British were prepared to reward the Secretary of State's persistence. Yet it is doubtful that they were inspired by a desire to accommodate him. More significant for them, no doubt, was Reverdy Johnson's transparent ambition to crown his brief term as Minister with the most sought after and elusive of American diplomatic triumphs, an *Alabama* settlement, and his restatement of Seward's instructions that he was not authorized to discuss the *Alabama* until the naturalization matter "had been disposed of." [74] Of course Johnson's ambition was only a pale reflection of that of the Secretary. For the British, the thought of negotiating a settlement of the war claims with men whose judgment might be clouded by an ambition which time could thwart must have encouraged them to remove the obstacle, and this they did with their decision that they should "place on record their desire to come to an agreement with the United States on this subject and have accordingly, in communication with the proper Law Advisers of the Crown, framed a Protocol." Here was a compromise that satisfied the needs of two gov-

[73] *Ibid.*, September 23.
[74] Stanley to Thornton, September 19, 1868, FO, 5/1356.

ernments anxious to press on with other business. It formally conceded the points Seward had long contended for, in particular that people naturalized under American law should be held by Great Britain to be American and treated accordingly. However, it was signed by Lord Stanley only with the reservation that it would not take effect until provision could be made "by Parliament, on the report of the Royal Commission, for such revision of the existing laws as the adoption of the principles embodied in it involves." [75]

With the naturalization issue conveniently swept aside, Seward authorized Reverdy Johnson to go ahead with the negotiation of the other outstanding grievances. In January, 1869, the Minister signed an ill-fated convention with Lord Clarendon, who had returned to the Foreign Office following the success of the Liberals, now led by Gladstone, in the British elections. Johnson, under Seward's direction, conceded too much when he simply agreed to the adjudication of all individual claims on both sides since the last convention in 1853. This was hardly the *Alabama* settlement most Americans had visualized, and it had already been overwhelmingly repudiated by the press when the Senate delivered the *coup de grace*.

Meanwhile, the final settlement, by formal convention, of the naturalization problem also dragged on. The Senate found that the "pressure of other business" prevented it from advising and consenting to the negotiation of a convention on the basis of the Protocol until the administration of Andrew Johnson had left office. Perhaps no ordinary stroke of fate saw it take the decision to advise and consent on April 13, 1869, the very day it struck down the Johnson-Clarendon Convention. The claims and the naturalization problem were still in

[75] *Ibid.*, October 9, 1868.

harness. When the Grant administration's replacement for
Reverdy Johnson, the diplomat-historian John L. Motley,
carried the news of the Senate's decision on the Protocol to
the Foreign Office, he learned that the British now found that
the pressure of other business prevented them from pressing
on. Ironically, one obstruction to the implementation by Parliament of the proposals of the Royal Commission, which had
presented its report on February 27, 1869, was the Irish Land
Bill, which, along with the Irish Disestablishment Act, might
be considered the first fruit of Fenianism. Certainly Fenian
activity in Britain during 1867 and 1868 had drawn Gladstone's attention to the Irish problem, and it was as a convert
to remedial measures that he entered office with the statement
that his mission was to save Ireland. As a result, it was May 12,
1870, before the necessary naturalization legislation was enacted, and May 13 before a convention was signed by Motley
and Clarendon, bringing to an end this traditional Anglo-
American dispute.

If the Motley-Clarendon Convention, or Naturalization
Treaty, did no more than confirm the provisions of the Protocol, it re-emphasized the vital role the Fenians had played in
the final settlement. Although they had never intended to
remove problems that marred Anglo-American relations, they
had nonetheless provided the incentive for a solution. Here,
then, was another fruit of Fenianism, but a highly distasteful
one to the Brotherhood, for their inability to provoke an
Anglo-American confrontation over this issue was yet another serious blow to their hopes of liberating Ireland. Indeed,
with the failure of this, their most subtle policy, and their
manifest failure to organize an insurrection with a show of
delegated authority in Ireland, which would have enabled
them to appeal to the United States for recognition of their
status as belligerents and thus tap the bitter American memo-

ries of the Civil War, they were reduced to one last gamble: another assault on Canada. If they could conquer a portion of the Dominion, perhaps they could use it to ransom Irish independence, or even establish a government in exile there and turn to the United States for recognition. In short, they might yet provoke an Anglo-American rupture.

9

"The Last Throw in a Desperate Game"

Although the signing of the Naturalization Protocol provided the struggling Fenian Brotherhood with an additional incentive to invade Canada, for some time thereafter it remained dormant as a filibustering force. Nevertheless, the Brotherhood continued to exercise the diplomatic talents of the United States and Great Britain. After all, Irish-Americans convicted for their part in the raid on Canada in 1866 or for their efforts to raise rebellion in Ireland still occupied British prison cells, a fact their colleagues in the United States were anxious the American public and government should not forget.

The imagined plight of these men still evoked a sympathetic public response, as a mass meeting held in the Cooper Institute on February 16, 1869, indicated. In fact, most of the men imprisoned at Chatham in England were treated leniently. The usual rigors of prison life were somewhat moderated. The prisoners were provided with shelter while they performed their tasks—not infrequently they were employed tying bundles of firewood—and were allowed the luxury of conversation.[1] Still, their surroundings could have been more congenial, their occupation more interesting, and their pay more than threepence per week. Moreover, the image of a dark and dank British dungeon made good copy in the United States.

Seward had never needed to be prodded into activity on their behalf, for he had never lost sight of the political desirability of securing the release of these unfortunate men. In September, while the presidential election was still in full swing, he had made it plain to Reverdy Johnson that a relaxation of the British government's "judicial severity" would have a favorable effect on American opinion.[2] Although this brought no immediate response from the British, they were moving cautiously toward the re-establishment of some semblance of normality in Ireland. To this end, the Gladstone Cabinet agreed, early in the new year, to grant a limited Fenian amnesty and not to seek a renewal of the suspension of habeas corpus.

The release of a carefully selected group of prisoners promised not only to check the demand voiced by a growing number of Irish, in England as well as in Ireland, for a general amnesty—something the Lord-Lieutenant and the Attorney-General of Ireland considered too great a risk—but also to conciliate the powerful Roman Catholic clergy in the island. They were seeking to regain some of the influence they had lost as a result of their opposition to Fenianism "by throwing themselves heartily with the movement for the amnesty."[3] It was with these results in mind, then, that the Secretary of State for Ireland informed the Commons on

[1] Moran, Diary, November 3, 1868.
[2] Seward to Johnson, September 14, 1868, NA/M77/80.
[3] Spencer to Gladstone, March 30, 1869, Gladstone Papers.

February 22, 1869, that forty-nine Fenian prisoners would be liberated in the near future—news that neither Parliament nor public welcomed universally.[4]

While their decision to discharge those "who can, with reference to public safety, be set at liberty"[5] had not been prompted by American pressure, the British were quite prepared to seize this opportunity to make some concession to American opinion. Thus Clarendon telegraphed to Thornton the information that Warren and Costello would be among those released.[6] Warren, an inveterate *agent provocateur*, celebrated his discharge with a series of violently anti-British tirades in Ireland. This, as he no doubt intended, ended any prospect of immediate release for those still imprisoned. As long as Irish-Americans were incarcerated in British prisons, there remained a chance that their plight could advance the Fenian cause.

If the jail door had been closed again in Britain, at least for the time being, the cause of those incarcerated in Canada might still be championed to good effect. Of these, Robert Lynch and Father McMahon attracted considerable attention in the United States. Congress had passed resolutions requesting the President to intercede with the British on their behalf, and these formal expressions of concern no doubt encouraged Seward's spasmodic but unsuccessful attempts to secure their discharge. The urgings were more insistent and consistent when the Johnson administration gave way to that of General Grant, for now the Fenians had a highly placed friend in the person of Vice-President Schuyler Colfax. The suggestion by the new Secretary of State, Hamilton Fish, soon after he entered the State Department, that it would be expedient for

[4] Granville to Rogers, April 10, 1869, CO, 537/100.
[5] Clarendon to Johnson, March 3, 1869, FO, 5/1345.
[6] Clarendon to Thornton, February 19, *ibid.*

the British to release these two men was endorsed by Edward Thornton when he forwarded it to London. The Minister's belief in the new American government's determination "to discountenance the schemes of the Fenians against Canada" convinced him that "it might conduce to a better feeling in the country against Fenian projects" if a similar clemency to that extended to prisoners in England "could be shown towards some at least of the convicts" in Canada.[7]

For Earl Granville, the Colonial Secretary, to whom these representations were referred by the Foreign Office, the problem was more complex than the conciliation of American opinion. Unsure of the American government's purpose in requesting the release of Lynch and McMahon—was it simply hunting popularity among Irish-Americans or deliberately seeking to raise some grievance against Britain for domestic and international advantage?—Granville, who seems to have arbitrarily excluded the possibility of genuine concern for the prisoners' welfare, was worried by the danger, more apparent than real, that to release Fenians at the request of the United States was to encourage rather than to dissuade such filibusters. But it was the likely response of the Canadian government that really restrained the Colonial Secretary. It seemed peculiarly inopportune for the British government to recommend the release of Fenians at a time when British regulars were being withdrawn from the Dominion over the protests of the Canadian government. "It would be galling," Granville commented to a member of his staff, "if at the time we [are] exhorting them to defend themselves against the Fenians, we were to express an opinion that they should let free men who had invaded their soil and killed their countrymen."[8] As a result, the Gladstone Cabinet prudently agreed to leave this de-

[7] Thornton to Clarendon, April 5, *ibid.*
[8] Granville to Rogers, April 4, 1869, CO, 537/100.

cision entirely to the Canadians, who subsequently decided that "the answer to Lynch's case will be a respectful refusal, and in McMahon's the deferring the consideration of the release so that its eventual concession may be attributed rather to Canadian than United States influence." [9] Thus, the Catholic priest had to wait until July when the release of a Protestant clergyman provided the Canadian government with an opportunity to liberate him simultaneously as a mark of their respect for the Canadian Catholic clergy.

Important as these developments were to the prisoners, their plight had ceased to be anything more than the most prosaic of Anglo-American problems since the signing of the Naturalization Protocol. More exciting were the consequences of attempts by Presidents Johnson and Grant to compensate political supporters, who also happened to be prominent Fenians, with diplomatic appointments in Britain.

On December 5, 1868, the British Minister reported to his government Johnson's nomination of a leading Fenian, John Savage, to a consular vacancy at Leeds. Thornton could hold out no hope of a withdrawal in the face of British protests. This did not mean that the President was deliberately seeking to provoke the British but rather that he was anxious to make some show of rewarding Savage for his efforts to hold Irish-Americans to their traditional political allegiance. A vote for the Democratic party in 1866 and 1868 had also been a vote for the President's view of Reconstruction. It was the misfortune of Savage and the British that Leeds happened to be the only available vacancy. Of course, neither President nor Secretary of State expected the British government to accept this man, but if the nomination was intended merely as a gesture, it was important that the responsibility for its failure be borne by

[9] Young to Granville, June 3, 1869, FO, 5/1346.

others. In short, its emptiness should not be blatant, for if the President was virtually powerless to reward his supporters, he could at least impress them with his sincere efforts on their behalf. But to make the British his scapegoats was "hardly fair," or so Thornton complained to Seward. "By taking a step which could not be acceptable to England," he continued," the United States government was forcing Her Majesty's Government to do what might be equally disagreeable to the people of the United States." [10]

Disagreeable or not, the British government, interpreting the nomination as a studied insult, began to amass evidence against Savage in preparation for a formal refusal of exequatur. However, as in the case of Johnson's earlier consular aberration, an unwelcome public repudiation of the nominee by the British was avoided with the help of the United States Senate. The fussy Reverdy Johnson had foreseen the probability of his former colleagues' declining to confirm the nomination, yet he had still pressed the President to withdraw it voluntarily. With the naturalization problem removed by the Protocol, he was negotiating the *Alabama* and other remaining problems, and he was anxious to maintain the best possible climate of opinion in London. This could be achieved only by withdrawal rather than rejection of Savage, he argued, but to no avail. [11]

Meanwhile, British anxiety should have been eased by the knowledge that Congress had already decided to withhold confirmation of Johnson's appointments. Although impeachment had failed, that body had no intention of permitting the President to reward his supporters with office. Yet this assurance of rejection failed to satisfy Thornton. He drew the attention of a member of the Senate Committee on Appoint-

[10] Thornton to Stanley, December 5, 1868, FO, 5/1344.
[11] Seward to Johnson, January 13, 1869, Seward Papers.

ments to this specific case and reported to Clarendon on February 1, 1869, "I presume that it was in consequence of my observation that, two or three days later, the Committee took up the matter and unanimously made a report to the Senate adverse to the appointment of Mr. John Savage." [12] In the light of the President's unhappy relationship with Congress, however, this conclusion was somewhat naive. Similarly, Thornton's assumption implied a willingness on the part of the Senate to oblige the British, which hardly reflected the temper of that chamber or the American nation at this time.

On January 4, Reverdy Johnson, despite the President's refusal to withdraw the nomination of Savage, had signed a claims convention with Lord Clarendon. This news and the document itself were quickly transmitted to the United States by cable, and Andrew Johnson forwarded a copy to the Senate. The *New York Times* faithfully endorsed the settlement: "It is not too much to say that, upon the whole, the terms of the Protocol are eminently favourable to the United States." [13] However, the newspaper was soon drowned by the rising tide of criticism. Americans looked in vain for a British apology and provision for the "indirect claims." The *New York Tribune* was more representative of American opinion than the *Times* when it proclaimed: "No mere list of ships actually destroyed by English built privateers can cover our claims; the commerce of the United States was swept from the seas by British agencies and that is the measure of British liabilities." [14]

The Senate was not immune to this sentiment; indeed, in this chamber it had received its most dramatic expression. Charles Sumner's speech recommending the rejection of the Johnson-Clarendon Convention included a compilation of in-

[12] Thornton to Clarendon, February 1, 1869, FO, 5/1345.
[13] January 19, 1869.   [14] January 26, 1869.

juries, direct and indirect, for which, by inference at least, only a British cession of Canada could compensate.

In England the repudiation of the Convention and Sumner's tirade evoked indignation and concern. The fact that the Senate had taken three months to render a decision had not been entirely unexpected. On January 15 the London *Times* had correctly forecast that President Johnson's acrimonious relationship with Congress ensured that no action would be taken before he left office. But the influential English newspaper had gone on to warn its readers that this delay "is the utmost that can be conceded." Having denied Johnson and Seward the pleasure of formally closing the *Alabama* account, the Senate was expected by the English to ratify the settlement early in the life of the Grant administration. Instead, that chamber repudiated it, 54 to 1, while Sumner, a man to whom the British had looked for sanity in the past, and who was expected by them to exercise a powerful influence over the foreign relations of the new government since Fish was an unknown quantity, amassed his unreasonable list of grievances. All in all, events had taken a sinister turn in the United States, or so Clarendon believed. "There is not the slightest doubt," he wrote to Queen Victoria, "that if we are engaged in a continental quarrel we should immediately find ourselves at war with the United States." [15]

If the relations of the British government and the new American administration had not opened on the most harmonious of notes, another discord was quickly sounded. Like any other government of the United States, that of Grant was soon engaged in the congenial task of filling appointments. When the diplomatic nominations were published, elements of the American press began to insinuate that several of the

[15] Buckle, *Letters of Queen Victoria*, I, 594–595, Clarendon to Queen Victoria, May 1, 1869.

appointees were tainted with Fenianism. If these reports were intended to unsettle the British, they had a measure of success. Its experiences with the Johnson administration had taught the British government that such suggestions could not be prudently ignored. Yet exhaustive investigations of those appointed to positions in Britain and Canada revealed a strange dichotomy in the Grant administration's conduct. On the one side, William A. Dart, whose enthusiastic frustration and attempted prosecution of Fenians in 1866 had cost him his position as District-Attorney at Buffalo, was nominated to a consulate in Canada. This, the Governor-General observed, was calculated "to inspire confidence and reliance on the peaceful disposition of the United States Authorities in Canada." [16] The other side of the coin was less pleasant, however. The same American government had nominated another notorious Fenian, James Haggerty, as Consul at Glasgow. When he arrived in England somewhat prematurely to take up his appointment, he was immediately recognized by a detective who, unaware of Haggerty's elevation to the ranks of the American diplomatic service, kept him under constant surveillance.[17]

In this instance, as in that of Savage, the appointment had not been expressly intended to antagonize the British. Haggerty had drawn the nomination as a reward for his services as a stump speaker during the presidential election, and it is possible that his Fenian antecedents had been overlooked. Certainly Hamilton Fish was surprised, and Thornton thought genuinely so, by the charge when the British Minister made it. However, surprised or not, the Secretary of State expressed the hope that the British would not refuse a grant of exequatur. He attempted to impress upon Thornton the dan-

[16] Young to Thornton, April 24, 1869, CO, 537/100.
[17] Hammond to Thornton, June 5, 1869, Hammond Papers.

ger of such a step further exciting American opinion and hence further delaying a settlement of all outstanding problems.[18]

The British government, however, still smarting from the repudiation of the Johnson-Clarendon Convention, was in no mood to be bullied into accepting a Fenian as an American consul in Britain. "Her Majesty's Government, I am desired to tell you," Edmund Hammond, the permanent undersecretary at the Foreign Office, wrote to Thornton, "are sorry that an act so hostile and offensive to this country . . . should have been committed by the new Government of the United States." Although indignant, the British were anxious not to precipitate a further deterioration in their uneasy relations with the United States. They wanted to be rid of Haggerty, but in the least troublesome way, and this could best be achieved if the Americans could be persuaded to withdraw his nomination. If persuasion did not accomplish the purpose, a refusal of exequatur would have to be exercised. No matter what the procedure, expediency dictated that the British be conciliatory, and Thornton was instructed to communicate with Fish "in terms expressed so as to be as little unpalatable as possible."[19]

The British Minister in Washington did not need to be cautioned. Not only was he convinced of Fish's innocence in this matter, but he believed that the Secretary of State was "becoming much more friendly and outspoken with me and I am unwilling to check his freedom of speech by any severe expression unless I should be obliged by instructions to do so."[20] These of course he never received, even though conciliation failed to secure the withdrawal of the offensive nomina-

[18] Diary of Hamilton Fish, June 2, 1869, Library of Congress.
[19] Hammond to Thornton, June 5, 1869, Hammond Papers.
[20] Thornton to Hammond, June 22, *ibid.*

tion—a failure Thornton attributed to two factors. First, the administration was unable to overcome the traditional American timidity "about offending any class of voters, even such a despicable set as the Fenians." Second, there existed, the Minister reported with commendable composure, the "fact of Haggerty being a temperance man and having preached in that cause makes General Grant have a certain sympathy for him, for it is well known that General Grant was at one time much addicted to drink but has given it up and now drinks nothing but water." [21] For the British government this meant that there was now no avoiding a refusal of exequatur. On July 31, Clarendon informed John L. Motley, Reverdy Johnson's successor, of the government's decision, but he made the refusal as palatable as possible. He expressed his regret at being compelled to take this extreme step, provided evidence of Haggerty's involvement with the Fenian movement, and concluded by affirming his belief that the American government had been unaware of this association when it nominated him.[22]

British anxiety to avoid a refusal of exequatur had been motivated in large part by the desire not to provide the Fenians with a public issue upon which they might found a revival of their flagging fortunes, at a time when sentiment in the United States was distinctly hostile to Britain. Conversely, an indication of the Brotherhood's revolutionary and diplomatic significance was its ability to capitalize on these advantages, perhaps to the extent or organizing another raid into Canada. Judged by this standard, Fenianism was unquestionably on the wane.

One seemingly insuperable obstacle, even for the dynamic O'Neill, who had "adopted and put into practice more sys-

[21] *Ibid.*, June 29.
[22] Clarendon to Motley, July 31, 1869, FO, 5/1346.

tematic plans and arrangements for efficient action than any of his predecessors,"[23] was a lack of money. In a desperate attempt to raise the revenue needed for new military adventures, he visited some of the larger American cities and addressed fund-raising meetings of Irish-Americans. At the beginning of March, 1869, he called on them to donate one dollar to the cause on St. Patrick's Day, but instead of the four million responses expected by some optimists, there were less than eight thousand. The decline in revenue led to a pruning of the top-heavy Fenian staff in an effort to cut administrative costs, but this failed to halt the drain on the treasury. Between October, 1868, and April, 1869, the Fenian reserves dropped from twenty thousand dollars to less than thirty-eight hundred, news that tempted the new Governor-General of Canada, Sir John Young, to predict: "A raid may be attempted as a last effort—the last throw in a desperate game—but I cannot think it will assume greater proportions than can be safely dealt with by a very small force."[24]

The inability of the Brotherhood to raise funds had a significance that extended beyond the crippling of military adventures. Its failure to extract money from the large Irish-American population suggested a loss of confidence in it as the chosen instrument of Irish liberation. After all, the Brotherhood had failed to capitalize to the full upon the opportunities of the immediate postwar period, and the chances of success did not improve with the passage of time. By 1869 the United States had largely recovered from the inevitable economic and social dislocation that follows protracted warfare, and Fenian recruits were no longer abundant. If, for want of a settlement of the *Alabama* and other claims, anglophobia was still prevalent in many parts of the United States, the domestic political

[23] Archibald to Stanley, November 2, 1868, FO, 5/1344.
[24] Young to Granville, June 3, 1869, CO, 537/100.

confusion that arose out of the contest for control of Reconstruction (the source of much of the Fenians' power and opportunity in 1865 and 1866) had been resolved. The triumph of Congress—a victory General Grant was not disposed to challenge—saw a decline in the political influence of the Brotherhood. This is not to imply that the electoral power of the Irish-Americans had been broken, but simply that the Fenians ceased to be treated with the same circumspection. No doubt their failure to extract money from the Irish population of the United States encouraged the government to believe that more positive measures could be risked without fear of a massive Irish-American electoral retaliation. Thus, without giving unnecessary offense even to the Fenians, the Johnson administration had exhibited a greater willingness during its last months in office to adopt whatever preventive measures seemed appropriate to the occasion. The change in administrations in March, 1869, for all the tension attendant upon the repudiation of the claims convention, did not impede this development.

Never immune to doubt, particularly about Fenian activities, Consul Archibald was the first to cry wolf. By July he was convinced that members of the Brotherhood were about to capitalize on "the prospect of a more active American sympathy in consequence of the disturbed feeling towards England growing out of the *Alabama* claims question," on the possibility that the Irish vote would dissuade the new government from adopting repressive measures, on "the withdrawal from Canada of the regular forces," and on their possession of "about 10 to 12,000 breechloading rifles" to attack the Dominion.[25] While such alarms brought into focus the current dispute between the Canadian and British governments over

[25] Archibald to Clarendon, July 12, 1869, FO, 5/1346.

the stationing of British regulars in Canada, the response of the Grant administration merely served to re-emphasize the declining political power of Fenianism. When Thornton broached the subject, Fish warned him, as Seward had often done in the past, that even if caches of arms were discovered, "it would be useless to seize them unless it could be proved that they were intended for hostile not commercial purposes; for unless this could be done they would have to be restored to their owners." In short, the American required the specific information the British lacked before he could take action under the neutrality laws. This did not mean, however, that the American government intended to remain idle. On the contrary, Fish promised to urge the Attorney-General to instruct the relevant United States marshals "to use the greatest vigilance with regard to Fenian movements, and [urge] the Secretary of War to furnish similar instructions to any military officers who might be in that neighborhood." [26]

If these precautions sounded somewhat haphazard, the same could not be said of the government's subsequent activity. On August 2, Thornton informed Clarendon of the decision of the United States government to employ a group of private detectives to investigate the rumors of Fenian activity. Even more significant, the British Minister was persuaded that the government had artfully ensured also that adequate military forces were encamped conveniently close to the border. Troops had been ordered to the frontier, Thornton reported, "on the pretext of giving them the advantage of a cooler climate during the summer, but really that they might be ready to prevent, if necessary, any hostile expedition which may be attempted by the Fenians against Canada." [27] And when that notorious Fenian, John Warren, visited Washing-

[26] Thornton to Clarendon, July 26, 1869, CO, 537/100.
[27] *Ibid.*, August 2, FO, 5/1347.

ton in search of an assurance of the government's toleration of Fenian ambitions against Canada, Thornton was convinced that the administration, from the President on down, had quenched any such hope.[28]

This news was understandably welcome in London, and Clarendon soon instructed Thornton to express to Fish the British government's appreciation "of this friendly act upon the part of the President of the United States." [29] Further improvement in Anglo-American relations might have followed a British decision to discharge the remaining Fenian prisoners, but, although Gladstone appears to have been willing to set most of them free, he was restrained by his colleagues. Lord Spencer, the Lord-Lieutenant of Ireland, opposed another amnesty on the grounds that the Brotherhood's flagging fortunes would certainly revive should Britain find herself embroiled in the European difficulties then threatening to erupt. He also expressed concern at the danger of further releases, so soon after those in the spring, discouraging loyal men from opposing the Fenians in the event of another attempt at rebellion in Ireland.[30] Consequently, he wrote to Gladstone on October 12, "I can most distinctly state that I consider the release of the Fenian prisoners at this time would be dangerous in its bearings upon public security, and upon the authority of the law." [31]

The Prime Minister was also cautioned by Earl Granville. To him it seemed inexpedient to liberate Fenians at a time when an extremely vocal amnesty movement was active in Britain. "If I were an autocrat," he wrote in reply to a request from Gladstone for advice, "I would release all the Fenians

[28] Thornton to Hammond, August 3, 1869, Hammond Papers.
[29] Clarendon to Thornton, August 21, 1869, CO, 537/100.
[30] Spencer to Gladstone, September 29, 1869, Gladstone Papers.
[31] *Ibid.*, October 12.

notwithstanding the bluster of their friends, but as you are not quite in that position, and have a very difficult task before you, you had better do nothing for them at the present. If your Land Bill passes notwithstanding sufficient opposition to make it popular in Ireland, and you could release them before fresh demands were made, it would probably do much good." [32] In short, this was not the moment to appear to lend credence to the charge that Gladstone's reform measures for Ireland were weak-kneed concessions to Irish pressure. The Prime Minister agreed with Granville and therefore he framed a negative reply to a petition he had received from the amnesty movement for a general release of Fenian prisoners.

Although he had played an important role in this decision, Granville was not unaware of the danger of its causing difficulties in North America. While the American government received the news calmly enough, there was some concern over the likely response of the Fenians. Presented with two means of retaliation, it seemed unlikely that they would decline both. First, they could attempt to make good their earlier threat to assassinate Prince Arthur during his tour of North America. This danger could not be dismissed in the aftermath of the murder of the prominent Irish-Canadian politician D'Arcy McGee by an alleged Fenian, and the attempt upon the life of the Duke of Edinburgh in Australia. As a result, the guard on the Prince was doubled.[33] Second, the possibility of the Fenians' seeking revenge by raiding Canada had also occurred to Granville, as indeed it had to the Canadians.

During the fall of 1869 they claimed to possess evidence to support their fears of an imminent Fenian assault, but their

[32] Agatha Ramm, ed., *The Political Correspondence of Mr. Gladstone and Lord Granville, 1868–1871* (London, 1952), I, 67, Granville to Gladstone, October 13, 1869.

[33] Young to Granville, November 4, 1869, CO, 537/100.

fears were discounted by Archibald, usually the most prominent of alarmists. The result was that Thornton was left
bewildered by conflicting reports. "With regard to the Fenians," he wrote to Hammond on October 26, "I don't know
what to believe." [34] However, Fish helped him to escape from
this quandary. At Thornton's request, he ordered the United
States Marshal for upper New York to investigate the rumors
of Fenian activity there. The subsequent report was turned
over to the British Minister and forwarded by him to Clarendon, not only because it allayed fears of a raid, but also
because it provided tangible evidence, or so he thought, of
"how much readiness is shown by the Secretary of State in
taking measures of precaution against any Fenian attack upon
Canada." [35] Ironically, just as Thornton was holding Fish up
as a model of good faith, Clarendon was beginning to express
intuitive doubts about the man. "I don't think him honest,"
the Foreign Secretary observed to Granville, "but even if he
was so he is evidently afraid of the Senate and Sumner the
misguider of that body." [36] For the suspicious Foreign Secretary, a report he received from Thornton in January, highly
unpleasant as it was, must have appeared as vindication of his
judgment.

During a Cabinet meeting on November 26, Grant had
announced his determination to keep the *Alabama* claims open
until Britain was prepared to relinquish Canada. The sensible
Fish was sure that the British would never cede the Dominion,
except at the request of the Canadians, and certainly not in
settlement for the *Alabama*, which is what Grant obviously
had in mind. [37] Yet he outlined just such a solution to Thorn-

---

[34] Thornton to Hammond, October 26, 1869, Hammond Papers.
[35] Thornton to Clarendon, November 2, 1869, CO, 537/100.
[36] Clarendon to Granville, November 30, 1869, Earl Granville Papers, Public Record Office.
[37] Fish, Diary, November 26, 1869.

ton on December 23 and by so doing gave the impression of taking to their logical diplomatic conclusion the remarks made by Sumner on April 13 during the debate on the Johnson-Clarendon Convention. "Fish and Co.," Clarendon informed Granville, "are now going in for the British Possessions in North America as part payment for claims and a preliminary step for negotiations."[38]

From the most interested party, this impudent American proposal evoked an understandably angry response. In a special memorandum which they forwarded to London, Macdonald and his colleagues in the Canadian government gave vent to feelings they had long been waiting to express.

Mr. Fish's object could not have been to ascertain whether England would abstain from coercing the colonies, but was apparently to elicit some expression of opinion calculated to encourage the disaffected Canadians with whom he maintains a friendly correspondence, and further to ascertain whether in the event of Civil War the Americans might rely on the non-intervention of England in the contest, the consequences of which might be that the loyal Canadian people might be overpowered by the Fenians and Filibusters who are permitted to organize armies in the United States, and to deposit arms on the frontier thereby causing alarm to the peaceable inhabitants of Canada and serious expense to the Government.[39]

This protest did not lose any of its force when the Fenians began to indulge, with ominous intensity, their predilection for activity along the border. Indeed, their activities assumed a peculiar significance for Anglo-American relations when it was agreed in London: "The test of Fish's sincerity will be found in the course that he may take in the event of a Fenian raid on Canada."[40]

[38] Clarendon to Granville, January 24, 1870, Granville Papers.
[39] Young to Granville, January 22, 1870, CO, 537/101.
[40] Hammond to Thornton, March 5, 1870, Hammond Papers.

There existed, however, some debate on the Canadian side as to the exact course the American government should be asked to follow. Aware of the paucity of United States civil and military forces close to the border which would prevent any comprehensive seizure of the munitions the Fenians had cached there, conscious of the probability that it would prove impossible to convince an American court that any arms seized were intended for an illegal purpose, and learning from their own agents that O'Neill would never be able to muster more than three thousand Fenians into service, Young and Macdonald agreed that "it was better to let the raid take place so as to give the raiders a lesson which will not be easily forgotten and will probably 'squash' the Fenian organization altogether." [41] Obviously, the Canadian government had forsaken prevention for cure.

Thornton was informed of this decision by Clarendon. On February 10 he was advised that the American government, in the event of a raid, should simply prevent reinforcements from crossing the border to support the initial band of raiders. Two days later the new Canadian policy was made more explicit. "Canadian government," Clarendon cabled Thornton, "know about the store of arms but would prefer letting the raiders come supposing such an expedition to be meditated at all." [42] But the British Minister ignored these instructions and continued to impress upon Fish the need for adequate preventive measures. To secure these he was not above using the American government's acquisitive interest in Canada. During an interview on February 14, Thornton informed Hammond, "I plainly told him that if they [Fenians] did succeed in crossing the border and committing ravages on the other side it would but tend to encourage the bitterness of the

[41] Young to Granville, February 10, 1870, CO, 537/101.
[42] Clarendon to Thornton, February 12, 1870, FO, 5/1348.

Canadians against the United States, which whatever he might think to the contrary really existed in Canada on account of the expense and loss caused by the previous raid." [43]

Not content simply to ignore the instructions embodying the new Fenian policy, Thornton struggled to convince Macdonald and Young that it was "too clever by half." Admitting, in a letter to the Canadian Prime Minister, the theoretical attractiveness of such a punishing strategy, he challenged its practicality. "However desirable such an arrangement might be," he wrote, "it would probably be difficult exactly to regulate the movement, for even a slight success or reported success gained by the first party might induce thousands of followers to join and the United States Authorities might find it difficult to prevent the latter from crossing the border." Once he had planted the seed of doubt in the minds of the members of the Canadian government, Thornton carefully nurtured it. "If then I were to receive positive intelligence of a raid being meditated, would you think that I should be justified in not immediately communicating it to Mr. Fish in order to prevent it? Or would you rather that I shall delay communication with him until one could see what turn matters might take." [44]

The British Minister's argument and perceptive questions made deep inroads into Canadian confidence, and together with the evidence he forwarded of the American government's determination to prevent a raid brought a change of policy in the Dominion. "I think the advice not to let the raiders come," the Governor-General wrote to Macdonald, "if by an action of the United States Government they can be kept at home, preferable to the bloodshed . . . involved even

[43] Thornton to Hammond, February 15, 1870, Hammond Papers.
[44] Thornton to Macdonald, February, 1870, Macdonald Papers.

in the tiniest foray." [45] Three days later Young was writing to Granville to inform him of the Canadian government's decision to revert to the traditional policy of seeking prevention. The information derived from Thornton, which had played its part in reshaping the Canadian policy, was certainly reassuring. He made much of Fish's response to reports that the Fenians were organizing a four-pronged invasion of Canada. In this instance the Secretary of State requested his colleagues at the Treasury, Navy, and War Departments to instruct commanders of vessels on the Great Lakes and officers commanding military posts close to the frontier to protect the territorial integrity of Canada. For Thornton this was conclusive proof of the Grant administration's good intentions, so conclusive in fact that he was able to ignore a crudely opportunistic attempt by Fish to utilize the Fenians to advance American territorial ambitions upon Canada. During an interview with the British Minister on March 24, the American followed a line of reasoning which Seward, for all his expansionist predilections and desire to secure parts of British North America as settlement of the *Alabama* claims, had never pursued. [46] Fish argued that the severance of all British connections with Canada would remove the incentive for Fenian attacks, and, as a result, another source of Anglo-American friction would be removed. [47] The logic of his argument was irrefutable, of course, if one conceded that amputation was the best curative for a carbuncle on a limb. No doubt Fish placed his trust in the "natural gravitation of interests" to ensure that an amputated Canada would ultimately be grafted onto the torso of the United States.

Refusing to be taken aback by the suggestion of such a

[45] Young to Macdonald, March 28, *ibid.*
[46] Van Deusen, *William Henry Seward*, p. 548.
[47] Fish, Diary, March 24, 1870.

drastic remedy, Thornton blandly informed Fish that although his government was willing and anxious to separate Britain from Canada, this was not a step it could initiate; only the Canadians could do that. For his part, the American could discern "no evidence of this willingness." [48] Meanwhile Thornton also refused to permit this aberration to shake his faith in the Grant administration's determination to prevent another raid. No doubt he interpreted the subsequent events as vindication of his judgment.

Fish was openhanded with information, taking care to show Thornton a report on the disposition of United States Marshals along the border, something the British Minister accepted as "one of the many proofs that the United States Government are really anxious to prevent a violation of the neutrality of their territory." [49] Praiseworthy as this American conduct seemed, it was not motivated by any sentiment of friendship for Britain, nor was the Grant administration inclined to stretch its powers for the convenience of the British. On the contrary, from Grant down it was determined to uphold the law, but to the letter and no further. Thus, when a report recommending the seizure of the Fenian munitions was read in the Cabinet, Grant growled, "The British did not seize or stop the Alabama." [50] The President also gave expression to the widespread resentment of British conduct during the war when he ordered the dismissal of a group of detectives after the date of the rumored invasion of Canada they had been hired to investigate had passed without incident. "The British did not employ detectives to prevent raids from Canada during our war," he remarked.[51] The very employment of these men, however, illustrated the Grant administration's determi-

[48] *Ibid.*
[49] Thornton to Clarendon, April 12, 1870, FO, 5/1348.
[50] Fish, Diary, April 15, 1870.   [51] *Ibid.*, April 25.

nation to be rigidly correct in its attitude. The President and his Cabinet officers agreed to do what the law required. Thus during the discussion in the Cabinet of the proposal that the Fenian munitions cached near the border should be seized, Hamilton Fish advised his colleagues that all they were required to do under law was to warn the British. Inability to prove illegal intent eliminated the necessity of seizure.[52]

No matter how legalistic this response was, it did represent a marked improvement over the procrastination and lethargy that had characterized the Johnson administration's response to Fenian activities during 1866. Yet it is unlikely that one government was more concerned with the enforcement of American law than the other. Therefore, the explanation for the evident disparity in conduct probably lies elsewhere. The dissimilar responses evoked by two similar newspaper reports provides evidence to support the most obvious of answers. Thus the report published in the London *Times* in 1865, thanking Seward for alleged information that helped the British frustrate Fenianism in Ireland provoked a furor, whereas the republication in a Washington newspaper of a Canadian report attributing the Dominion's state of preparedness to information provided by Hamilton Fish was greeted with silence. In 1865 public denunciations of Seward had been followed by denials and evidence of the Johnson administration's concern for Irish-American sensibilities. In 1870 Fish calmly accepted Sir John Young's assurance that the report had been derived from Canadian sources and not from some inspired leak of the information forwarded to the Dominion by Thornton but passed to him by the Americans.[53] This one episode, otherwise quite inconsequential, illustrated the extent

[52] *Ibid.*, April 14.
[53] Thornton to Clarendon, April 12, 1870, CO, 537/101.

to which the political influence of the Irish-Americans was waning. Confirmation of that fact came soon enough.

Although given to dismissing Fenian activity as an elaborate hoax, perpetrated at the expense of the American, Canadian, and British governments and those Irish chambermaids popularly considered to be the principal source of Fenian revenue, Fish continued to respond to reports and rumors of such activity. The United States Marshal at Detroit, a city separated from the Canadian town of Windsor by the somewhat less than formidable obstacle of the Detroit River, was authorized to employ twenty additional men when Irish-American activities took on a sinister character in that locality. When bands of militia known to contain Fenians appeared at Buffalo to exercise, the *Michigan* was stationed at the mouth of the harbor "to prevent any armed body of Fenians from leaving it." [54] Reports from Foster, the United States Marshal in Vermont, which suggested that the Fenians might be gathering for a raid in the Missisquoi Valley area were forwarded, quite properly, to Thornton.[55]

Appreciative as he was of American conduct, the British Minister still found cause for concern. "I must do this Government justice," he wrote to Edmund Hammond on May 3, "to say that I believe they will readily endeavour to prevent the Fenians from annoying us; the question is how far they will be able to enforce their instructions; the frontier is immense in extent; some of the authorities sympathize with the Fenians, as do many of the United States soldiers, if they are not actively Fenians." [56] Thus the presidential proclamation published in American newspapers on May 25 proved to be a most ineffective restraint. It sounded firm enough, warning all American citizens against raiding Canada unless they were

[54] *Ibid.*, April 25.   [55] *Ibid.*, April 18.
[56] Thornton to Hammond, May 3, 1870, Hammond Papers.

prepared "to forfeit all right to the protection of the Government, or its interference on their behalf to rescue them from the consequences of their own acts";[57] but while the decision to issue the proclamation was taken on May 23, it did not appear until the very day O'Neill attempted to lead his cohorts across the border. How much influence it would have exercised had it been published earlier is questionable, however, for even when its existence was known, some sympathetic local authorities continued to permit Fenian munitions to be shipped to the border.[58]

As usual, a more effective restraint on Fenian ardor were the military reinforcements—eleven companies of artillery—dispatched to the border. Their arrival in the wake of the repulse of the Fenian advance by the forces massed on the Canadian side (13,500 men called out by Sir John Young) and the *opéra bouffe* of O'Neill's arrest—Marshal Foster had driven through the Fenian ranks in a carriage and apprehended him single-handed—destroyed what remained of Fenian morale.[59] They withdrew in dispirited confusion to St. Albans, several miles south of the border.

This news brought an immediate response from Clarendon. First, he telegraphed Thornton on May 27, instructing him to express to Fish the British government's satisfaction at the issuance of the proclamation, "at the movement which is said to have been made of United States troops for the purpose of preventing the consequences of that inroad, and at the arrest of the so-called General O'Neill by the Civil Authorities of the United States." [60] Then, once it became clear that the danger to Canada had passed for the time being, the Foreign

---

[57] Fish, Diary, May 24, 1870.
[58] Thornton to Clarendon, May 30, 1870, CO 537/101.
[59] Dakers to Young, May 26, *ibid.*
[60] Clarendon to Thornton, May 27, 1870, CO, 537/101.

Secretary turned to the task of ensuring that there would be no more Fenian filibustering. Not content with the arrest of the leaders, he thought it "very desirable that the United States Authorities should be directed to seize Fenian arms and stores, as the most effectual means not only of suppressing the present movement, but of obstructing similar outbreaks hereafter." [61]

When he called upon Fish, armed with Clarendon's telegraphed instructions, Thornton was quickly "deluged" with evidence of the Grant administration's determination to prevent a third invasion of Canada. He learned that thirty tons of Fenian munitions had been seized and were already being transported to Federal arsenals for safekeeping. He was informed of the arrest of several prominent Fenians in addition to O'Neill, and the Secretary of State expressed the hope that they would be tried and convicted. [62] The following day in fact, May 31, Grant ordered Attorney-General Hoar to prosecute these men if he thought it could be done with any probability of success—a marked improvement over the sequence of events in 1866, when the Johnson administration's overriding concern had been to be rid of these men as quickly as possible and ultimately had entered a nolle prosequi in every case. [63] Fish did not overlook the opportunity to contrast the attitudes of the two administrations. He told Thornton that "he thought Mr. Seward had done wrong on the occasion of the raid of 1866 in paying the return of the Fenians to their homes, and giving them back their arms. He insinuated that on this occasion neither would be done. There might be a difficulty about the arms if it could be proved that they

---

[61] *Ibid.*, May 29, FO, 5/1349.
[62] Thornton to Clarendon, May 30, *ibid.*
[63] Fish, Diary, May 31, 1870.

belonged to innocent owners; but this he thought not likely." [64]

The decision to deny Fenian requests for transportation home at the federal government's expense was Grant's alone. No doubt incensed by their unmilitary conduct in disregarding his proclamation, he decided to punish them and those American residents along the border who by their sympathy had encouraged such insubordination. His weapon was the rejection of free transportation. Dispirited and penniless, anxious to get home but without the means, the Fenians soon grew restless and then unruly. The sympathy of the border residents quickly changed to concern and they began, as Grant intended they should, to "sweat a little." [65] Eventually the Fenians made their own way home, crowding into railroad cars in sufficient force to ensure transportation without payment. [66] After this experience, it seemed unlikely that railroad warehouses would ever again be offered as depositories for Fenian munitions.

All in all, Thornton was satisfied that Fish and the government he represented had passed the "sincerity test." Attributing the failure of the Fenian raid largely (he did not entirely overlook the Canadian effort) to the American measures, and fully cognizant of the meager military forces the American government had at its disposal, he informed Clarendon: "On the whole I feel bound to acknowledge that the United States Government have given proof of entire good faith in the matter and have done all that lay in their power to prevent a hostile invasion of Canada from their territory." [67] Others were less congratulatory, however. In fact they were downright critical of the conduct of the American government.

[64] Thornton to Clarendon, May 30, 1870, FO, 5/1349.
[65] Fish, Diary, May 29, 1870.
[66] Thornton to Clarendon, May 30, 1870, FO, 5/1349.   [67] *Ibid.*

The catalogue of Canadian grievances was best summarized by Lieutenant-General Lindsay, the commander of the British troops in the Dominion, in a private note to Edward Cardwell, Secretary of War in the Gladstone government. Some of his complaints reflected a certain measure of ignorance of American conditions. Thus, the American government was indicted for dispatching so few troops to the frontier at a time when the army command embracing the Northeastern states belied its grandiose designation as the Department of the East. The Annual Report of the Secretary of War in 1870 put the total strength of the regular army at 37,358 men, scattered over forty-two states and territories.[68] Lindsay also criticized the use of the troops that were sent, insofar as they were not allowed to assume the initiative but were ordered to supplement the civil authorities—not a convincing indictment.

The General also did not approve of the American President's decision to refuse the Fenians free transportation away from the border, for he argued that this merely sustained the tension in that area.[69] Of course, Seward's contrary course in 1866 had not escaped criticism in Canada either. Then, the provision of free transportation had been interpreted as further evidence of his government's thinly veiled sympathy for the Fenian cause. Yet the plight of the American government, doomed to be abused in Canada, should not excite too much pity. Its predicament was, at least in large part, of its own making. The Canadians would have required an unusual store of international charity to have responded in any other way to the unprovoked assaults by citizens and residents of a nation with which they were supposedly on terms of amity. They were hardly mollified by the belated public opposition of

[68] *Annual Report of the Secretary of War, 1870* (Washington, 1871), p. 1.
[69] Lindsay to Cardwell, June 3, 1870, FO, 5/1350.

successive American governments to such filibustering. To them the difference between the Grant and Johnson administrations must have been inconsiderable. Grant issued his formal statement of opposition on the day of the raid in 1870, in contrast to Johnson's proclamation which appeared five days after the initial raiding party crossed into Canada in 1866, even though the Canadian government had been agitating for this step for more than a month. Here then was the heart of the Canadian complaint, and Lindsay touched upon it when he criticized the American government for its failure to seize the Fenian leaders and munitions much earlier. It seemed ridiculous if not unthinkable to most Canadians that the Fenians could not have been frustrated long before they attempted to march across the Canadian border.[70]

This attitude was not peculiarly Canadian; it was shared by Lord Clarendon. Thus while elements of the English press were expressing their appreciation of the "singular promptitude" of the United States authorities in suppressing the Fenians, the Foreign Secretary was writing to Thornton:

We have little if anything for which to thank the United States Government though Motley has been receiving congratulations upon the honest and friendly action of the President. He got none from me however and I cannot wonder at the bitter feeling of indignation that animates the Canadians who if the United States Government had behaved decently would have been saved all the troubles, anxiety and expense that they have endured for several years—yet that Government which has allowed the existence of a senate, the creation of an army, the collection of revenue and the public support of the American Authorities for the avowed purpose of the spoilation of a British colony and the slaughter and robbery of British subjects has the impudence to complain of our want of sympathy with them in the war, and

[70] Thornton to Hammond, May 30, 1870, Hammond Papers.

our not taking means for the suppression of opinion! At the moment too that they were encouraging (I use the word advisedly) the Fenians they put forward their sentimental grievance against us with as much unreasoning ferocity as ever.[71]

In this frame of mind Clarendon eagerly grasped the first opportunity to give vent to his irritation. It came soon enough, when Grant sent a special message to Congress as part of his administration's avowed policy of frustrating American-based Cuban revolutionaries. The Foreign Secretary jumped at the chance to instruct Thornton to secure from Fish an explanation of the American government's failure to adopt an identical policy toward the Fenians.[72] Unknown to the British, the Cuban message had been extracted from Grant over the threat of Fish's resignation.[73] Had they known, however, the situation would scarcely have been changed. Presumably they would have inquired of the Secretary of State why he had not been prepared to make a similar stand on behalf of Canada. Perhaps he would have given the same answer he gave to Clarendon's question: Cuban revolutionaries did not vote. The administration, the Secretary of State candidly explained to Thornton, was far more circumspect in its dealings with the Fenians because it did not wish to incur the wrath of Congress or provide the Democratic Party with ammunition.[74] In brief, if Irish-Americans had ceased to exercise the politicians to the extent that they had a few years earlier, if they and those who purported to represent them were no longer treated with quite the same tenderness, they

[71] Clarendon to Thornton, June 4, 1870, Clarendon Papers, Public Record Office. [72] *Ibid.*

[73] Allan Nevins, *Hamilton Fish: The Inner History of the Grant Administration* (New York, 1936) I, 355–359.

[74] Thornton to Clarendon, June 21, 1870, Clarendon Papers, Public Record Office.

could not be disdainfully ignored, for they could still muster a formidable number of voters on the seemingly ever imminent election days in the United States.

With this explanation the British had to be satisfied. Whether Clarendon would have found it satisfactory is open to surmise, for he was dead by the time the news reached England. On June 27, in his seventy-first year, sorely afflicted with gout and debilitated by a prolonged bout of diarrhea, he died. As Foreign Secretary he was succeeded by Lord Granville, a man a correspondent of William H. Seward described as "not too old to learn." He "is liberal, has travelled widely and has not the narrow views of most of his class." [75] In short, he was likely to be more flexible than his predecessor. Without being less impressed with the need to reach a settlement with the United States, Clarendon had been cast in a somewhat less conciliatory mold. He had always been willing to adopt a strident tone with respect to Fenianism, while he had greeted the revival of the *Alabama* correspondence with the United States in 1870 with the comment: "All this correspondence can do nothing but harm, and I have made my answer as short as is consistent with courtesy." [76]

Perhaps this was where the difference lay between the deceased Foreign Secretary and his successor. The younger man, who was returning to an office he had held briefly nineteen years earlier at the tender age of thirty-six, was more anxious to seize the initiative to improve Anglo-American relations. He had, of course, the added incentive of the European crisis of 1870. "I can conceive of no greater object," he wrote to John Bright in November of that year, "than to put

[75] Sanford to Seward, June 27, 1870, Seward Papers.
[76] Sir Herbert Maxwell, *The Life and Letters of George William Frederick, Fourth Earl of Clarendon* (London, 1913), II, 364, Clarendon to Gladstone, March 17, 1870.

our relations on a satisfactory footing with them. Our present position cripples us in every way. Not only would it do so if we wished for war, but it impedes our pacific efforts, making people attribute to fear that which is prompted by a sense of duty." [77] Within a few weeks Sir John Rose had been packed off to Washington on a "private" visit, and there he opened the negotiations that culminated in the Treaty of Washington.

Determined to improve relations, Granville thus penned no denunciations of American perfidy, but this did not mean that he was prepared to surrender those demands Clarendon had considered indispensable to the preservation of peace along the Canadian border. Having come direct from the Colonial Office, Granville understood how important the trial and imprisonment of the Fenian leaders and the confiscation of their munitions were to the Canadians. As a result, there was no weakening of the British resolve to keep the Grant administration up to the mark on these points. On the other hand, there was the substantial Irish-American electorate in the United States, something Grant and his colleagues did not forget.

There was no repetition of the sorry events of 1866, when the Johnson administration, responding belatedly to the dictates of domestic political expediency, had entered a nolle prosequi in every case pending against a Fenian and then returned to the Brotherhood the material seized during the border excitement. Now, in 1870, O'Neill and several leading associates were tried, convicted, and sentenced to terms of imprisonment that ranged from six to twenty-four months. But as the Congressional elections of that year neared, Thorn-

[77] Lord Edmund Fitzmaurice, *The Life of Granville George Leveson Gower, Second Earl of Granville, 1815–1891* (London, 1905), II, 28, Granville to Bright, November 21, 1870.

ton informed Hammond: "Great pressure is being brought to bear upon the President to pardon all the Fenians, and I suspect he will yield to it, though not just yet." [78] Grant yielded on October 12, shortly before Election Day in New York and shortly after the close of the Canadian fishing season. In little doubt about the Canadian reaction to this news, the American government was anxious to ensure that they did not vent their indignation on American fishermen. The fisheries question was a sufficiently contentious issue already. Of course, Fish had attempted to disarm the inevitable British and Canadian criticism of the President's decision to pardon these men some time before October 12. At the end of August when he prepared Thornton for the news, he had attempted to sweeten it with the assurance that on this occasion the Fenians' arms would not be restored to them, that pardons would be accompanied by a proclamation warning against any repetition of the events in May, and that the released men would be kept under constant surveillance. "Mr. Fish begged me," Thornton reported to Granville, "to convey to the Governor-General of Canada his view upon the subject, and express his hope that, if the Fenian prisoners should be pardoned, the Canadian Government would not on that account suppose that the Government of the United States wished to encourage such outrages as had lately been committed against Canada, but would on the contrary believe that there was a determination to prevent them." [79]

The Canadian government, however, was signally unimpressed by these assurances. When Thornton traveled to Canada early in September, he expected to find considerable irritation with the United States over the Fenian raids, but "I was not prepared," he wrote to Hammond, "to meet amongst

[78] Thornton to Hammond, August 9, 1870, Hammond Papers.
[79] Thornton to Granville, August 29, 1870, CO, 537/101.

the members of the Government such an intense feeling of bitterness as they manifest on every point against this [American] Government." [80] Dissatisfied with the length of O'Neill's sentence, Sir John A. Macdonald was even less pleased by the news of this Fenian's imminent pardon, and he and his colleagues decided that the British government "should be made aware that Canada is not a consenting party to the course proposed to be pursued by the pardoning of the Fenian leaders, but on the contrary views it with regret and apprehension." [81] Macdonald placed no faith in the American promise to keep O'Neill and his associates under surveillance, because he reasoned that once pardoned the Fenian leader would be entitled to all the constitutional privileges of a free man, including freedom from police harassment. Indeed, the Canadian Prime Minister's apprehensions were not misplaced, for the following year O'Neill attempted to lead another band of filibusters into Canada, while that promised proclamation, when it appeared, was so carefully worded that it was valueless from the British standpoint. "To Canada," a member of the British government commented, "Mr. Fish says look at my proclamation which shows that the pardon of the Fenians is not meant to encourage them. To the Irish look at my pardon which shows that the proclamation is meant against Cuban filibusters and not you." [82]

Even as the Colonial Office complained of this example of American chicanery, political expediency, which had encouraged the Grant administration so to word the proclamation as not to antagonize Irish-American voters, was persuading the British to release their Fenian prisoners. The general subsidence of Fenian activity, a temporary lull in the agitation for

[80] Thornton to Hammond, September 18, 1870, Hammond Papers.
[81] Young to Kimberley, October 13, 1870, CO, 537/101.
[82] Colonial Office minute, November 2, 1870, CO, 537/101.

amnesty, and the fact that the Americans had recently shown little overt interest in the remaining prisoners provided the Gladstone government with an opportunity to discharge them without giving the impression of doing so under duress. If the opportunity to release them was present, so was the incentive. A Royal Commission established to investigate reports of the ill treatment of Fenian prisoners was almost ready to report, and while it did not support the allegations, it did conclude that the treatment of what were essentially political prisoners as felons was severe and should be amended. Gladstone was anxious to be rid of these prisoners before the Commission's report was published. Consequently, he informed the Queen of the Cabinet's decision to discharge them on condition that they accept transportation to the United States,[83] and on January 15, 1871, the first group embarked for the United States aboard the *Russia*.[84] This vessel was followed later in the year by other Fenian arks.

There remained only the prisoners in Canada. The wily Macdonald soon expressed his readiness to release them if the British government accepted full responsibility for a decision that might very well excite adverse comment in the Dominion. When this offer was declined, the Canadian Prime Minister cautiously went ahead on his own, until by February, 1872, all the Fenian prisoners in the Dominion except one had been discharged. The remaining prisoner had been captured during O'Neill's pathetic attempt to interfere in the Red River Rebellion in 1871. But this so-called Fenian raid on Manitoba was Fenian only insofar as O'Neill led it and some of his sorely inadequate party of filibusters had also been members of the Brotherhood. Indeed, at the time of the raid,

[83] Buckle, *Letters of Queen Victoria*, II, 81–82, Gladstone to Queen Victoria, November 11, 1870.
[84] Moran to Fish, January 15, 1871, NA/M30/104.

the Fenian Brotherhood was slipping out of sight, at least under that name. Irish-American nationalist organizations continued to flourish; some, such as the "Dynamiters," achieved a measure of notoriety, but none ever exercised the influence the Fenians had on Anglo-American relations. Yet by 1871 the very name Fenian excited scorn among Irish-Americans. "I hate that name—Fenianism," the editor of the Boston *Pilot*, a former Fenian organ, wrote, "that meanly sounding word, with its associations of defeat, dissension, and trickery has been a millstone on the neck of our nationality for years past." [85] Though to describe Fenianism as a millstone around the neck of Anglo-American relations between 1865 and 1871 may be melodramatic, it had certainly been an encumbrance.

[85] W. O'Brien and D. Ryan, eds., *Devoy's Post Bag: The Letters of John Devoy, 1871–1928* (Dublin, 1948), p. 54, O'Reilly to Devoy, January 28, 1871.

10

Postscript

By 1871, Fenianism was obviously a spent force, and just as evidently it had failed to effect the national independence of Ireland. Yet it had not been devoid of significance for the island. The belated remedial measures successfully proposed by Gladstone in 1869 and 1870 (the Disestablishment Act and the Land Act) testified to this. The campaign for further liberalization of Irish land practices, in particular the concession of legal safeguards to tenants, continued to attract adherents in England as well as Ireland. Thus in 1881, at the urging of another Gladstone government, Parliament enacted a measure that granted the tenant farmer the so-called three *F*'s—fair rents, fixity of tenure, and free sale. Of course, once these had been conceded, the next step in the land agitation was clear: the demand that the peasantry be given the opportunity to own the soil. Ten years later, in 1891, the passage of the Land Purchase Bill "set in full flow that transference of property which has made Ireland a land of peasant proprietors." [1]

If the cry of "Ireland for the Irish" which the land agitators voiced reflected social and economic aspirations, it was taken up during the 1880's by the advocates of Home Rule. Forsak-

[1] Curtis, *History of Ireland*, p. 381.

ing the Fenian program of national independence, a group of "prominent men of the Protestant and educated classes," led by Isaac Butt, revived the cause of repeal. They sought Irish control of the domestic affairs of the island, leaving to the British Parliament "control over trade, the army and navy, foreign policy and all imperial matters." [2] The cautious pursuit of this goal by the conservative Butt soon cost him the leadership of the British Home Rule Confederation. His successor was Charles Stewart Parnell. Parnell had won the respect of most of his fellow Home Rulers at Westminster by his active participation in the campaign of obstructionism, whereas Butt advocated conciliation of the Commons, and had won the support of the remaining Fenians with his defense of the "Manchester Martyrs" during a debate in June of 1876. Thus, it was around Parnell that those seeking concessions or independence for Ireland coalesced in 1877. Under his leadership "Fenian and parliamentarian, peasant-terrorist and priest, exile and stay-at-home were brought together . . . to shake the United Kingdom to its foundations." It was this coalition that "broke the Anglo-Irish control of the land" and made Ireland the "first order of business in British politics." [3]

As leader of the Confederation, Parnell soon sought to harness Irish-America to the cause of Home Rule. To win friends for the movement and to raise funds to help relieve famine in Ireland at the end of the 1870's, he undertook an exhausting tour of the United States in 1880, traveling more than sixteen thousand miles to address meetings in sixty-two cities and a joint session of Congress. In addition to general American and Irish-American support, Parnell also sought the

[2] *Ibid.*, p. 376.
[3] Thomas N. Brown, *Irish-American Nationalism, 1870–1890* (Philadelphia and New York, 1966), p. 85.

assistance of the revolutionaries enrolled in the Clan-na-Gael. As for the Fenians, while they did not formally disband until 1886, they had long since given way to the Clan as the foremost organization of Irish-American revolutionary nationalists.

The virtual demise of the Fenian Brotherhood following O'Neill's farcical efforts to invade Canada had coincided with an apparent lull in nationalist activities. During the depression years between 1873 and 1878 most Irish-Americans were more concerned with their own plight than that of those who had remained in Ireland. As the rank and file of the American army of unskilled laborers, they were among the first sections of the industrial community to experience the rigors of the depression. Consequently, the most notorious Irish-American society of the 1870's was the Molly Maguires. It gave violent expression to the economic grievances of the Irish anthracite coal miners in Pennsylvania, and the fact that the management of the mines was largely English and Welsh in national origins was no more than a bonus for the membership. But as the decade wore on, and as business began to pick up and re-employed Irish-Americans had more money in their pockets, another revolutionary organization developed.

The Clan-na-Gael had been founded in 1867 and had sought to avoid the errors of Fenianism. It attempted, unsuccessfully as it proved, to escape the factionalism that had plagued the Brotherhood by placing less emphasis on personalities. There was no concession of autocratic powers to a James Stephens or a John O'Mahoney. In addition, the Clan abandoned publicity for secrecy. Indeed, with its "camps," admission to which was by recommendation only,[4] it more closely resembled the Hunters of the 1830's than the Fenians,

---

[4] *Ibid.*, p. 65.

who had erected all the paraphernalia of a government in exile.

The Clan and, until 1886, the remnants of the Fenian Brotherhood were anxious to contribute in a variety of ways to the cause of Home Rule, and, beyond that, Irish independence. By the late 1870's money was once again flowing across the Atlantic, though never in the expected quantities. Meanwhile the more ardent spirits resorted to terrorism. On May 6, 1882, a group of terrorists murdered two British officials, one of them the Chief Secretary for Ireland, in Phoenix Park, Dublin. More indiscriminate were the "Dynamiters." On June 10, 1881, two of them had been caught attempting to blow up Liverpool Town Hall. Less than two years later, charges were detonated in Westminster. The following year a bomb exploded in Victoria Station, and the police then discovered others in several of London's railroad stations. All of these "consisted of American cloth bags, containing American clockwork and dynamite." [5] Then, on January 24, 1885, "two dynamite bombs exploded in Westminster and one in the Tower of London." [6]

Parallel to this campaign of terror the Clan-na-Gael sought, as had the Fenians before them, to capitalize on Britain's external difficulties. Anglo-Russian tension over the struggle for power in the Balkans, as the Turkish Empire grew ever more feeble, saw representatives of the Clan meet with the Russian Ambassador to the United States. Their advances, like those of the Massachusetts Irish Emigrant Aid Society during the Crimean War, were rejected. The Spanish did not prove any more receptive, even when the Clan held out what it thought would be the irresistible bait of Gibraltar.[7] As a result, by 1879 these Irish-American revolutionaries were

[5] Pletcher, *The Awkward Years*, p. 251.　　[6] *Ibid.*, p. 253.
[7] Brown, *Irish-American Nationalism*, pp. 66–67.

forced to pin their hopes on the Zulus of South Africa.[8] Indeed, South Africa was fertile ground for Irish-American hopes. Thus, with the outbreak of the Boer War, a group of "belated Fenians" called on Governor Theodore Roosevelt of New York to verify their belief that a gentleman of Dutch descent would permit, if not encourage, them to organize a raid on Canada. Instead, the Governor threatened to clap them in jail.[9]

Roosevelt's response to the Irish-Americans' proposal was evidence not only of his personal integrity but also of the continuing decline of their political influence. Naturally, this had diminished following the victory of Congress in the struggle over Reconstruction, but the politicians continued to handle them with care in election years. After all, they still constituted a sizable portion of the electorate in several states (13.7 per cent of the population of the state of New York in 1880 were Irish-born, and thousands more had at least one Irish parent [10]), and the period between Reconstruction and the political revolution of 1894–1896 was one in which the two major political parties were delicately balanced. In short, successive American governments throughout the seventies and eighties were reluctant to restrain the nationalists; on the contrary, they were all too often anxious to court them.

In this atmosphere, Anglo-American tension, particularly over the activities of the terrorists, was only to be expected. The British expected the American authorities to exhibit a greater willingness to restrain the "Dynamiters," for even the *New York Tribune* admitted that "these plots were framed in New York; the money was raised here; the agents . . . were

[8] *Ibid.*, p. 87.
[9] Charles S. Campbell, Jr., *Anglo-American Understanding, 1898–1903* (Baltimore, 1957), p. 176.
[10] Pletcher, *The Awkward Years*, p. 239.

not Irish refugees, but Americans." [11] In the aftermath of the explosions in 1883 and 1884 President Arthur issued an order directing Federal marshals "to use special vigilance in preventing the transportation of explosives." [12] However, this directive was unlikely to cause the terrorists any inconvenience, as the American press realized. As for the bill to punish dynamiters severely, introduced by Senator Edmunds after the 1885 incidents, it was killed in committee.[13]

While the British were requesting effective control of the terrorists, without success, the American authorities were demanding in their turn the release of those Irish-Americans detained in Britain merely on the suspicion of complicity in the bombings. This double problem, namely, the restraint and the protection of the nationalists, "might have seriously embroiled Britain and the United States if the British government had insisted on holding the suspects without trial." [14] Instead, they resorted in most instances to the traditional expedient of releasing all those who agreed to return immediately to the United States.[15]

But concessions to Irish-American opinion, which soon included the sacrifice of a settlement of the long-standing Canadian-American fisheries dispute, became less necessary with the stabilization of American politics after 1896. Thus in 1900, another presidential year, the McKinley administration continued to pursue a course harmful to the Boers despite howls of protest from Dutch-, German-, and Irish-Americans.[16] Perhaps the clearest expression of the diminishing political influence of the Irish, however, was the conduct of Woodrow Wilson during the First World War. As the Democratic President of a Republican nation, whose path to the

[11] *Ibid.*, p. 249.   [12] *Ibid.*, p. 251.   [13] *Ibid.*, p. 253.   [14] *Ibid.*
[15] *Ibid.*, p. 243.
[16] Campbell, *Anglo-American Understanding*, pp. 175–179.

White House had been cleared by the temporary splintering of Republican unity in 1912, Wilson might have been expected to give sympathetic consideration to the wishes of such traditional supporters of his party.

The outbreak of war in Europe would normally have seen the Irish inhabitants of a neutral America cheering the enemies of Britain from the sidelines. But in 1914 there was an unusual lack of harmony among this group of onlookers, which was explained by the British concession of Home Rule to the island, twenty-four years after the disgrace and fall of Parnell. However, Home Rule failed to satisfy some radicals in Ireland, while others were irritated by the suspension of its application for the duration of the war, and together they attempted rebellion in April, 1916. Once again the insurgents were quickly suppressed by the British, but in so doing the British revived the Irish-Americans' common bond of anglophobia.[17] Consequently, while some of them had declined to endorse the Clan-na-Gael policy of American aid to Germany in 1914, those attending the Irish Race Convention in New York on March 4–5, 1916, called for impartial American neutrality. Here was the slogan for a far more sophisticated attempt to cripple the British war effort. A German victory, the Irish-Americans reasoned, would further the cause of independence. When the Wilson administration showed little disposition to accede to their demands, they threatened to flex their electoral muscles—all 4,500,000 of them.

At this point Wilson should have sought refuge in reassuring statements if not actions; instead, he publicly rebuked the correspondent who had issued this threat. He wrote: "I would feel deeply mortified to have you or anybody like you vote for me. Since you have access to many disloyal Americans and

[17] Arthur S. Link, *Wilson: The Struggle for Neutrality, 1914–1915* (Princeton, 1960), p. 22.

I have not I will ask you to convey this message to them." [18] In impugning their patriotism, Wilson correctly judged the general temper of the American people. Still, on the eve of a presidential election, and one that promised to be very close, since the Republicans had virtually reunited behind Charles Evans Hughes, it was a remarkably bald statement and one that would have been unthinkable twenty-five years earlier. As it happened, the Irish were soon provided with an opportunity to seek revenge. The Versailles settlement made no provision for the freedom and independence of Ireland, and the Irish-Americans were in the vanguard of the hyphenate elements vehemently opposed to its ratification by the United States. But Ireland ceased to be an issue in Anglo-American relations when in December, 1921, the Irish Free State "was recognized as a Dominion with full powers of self-government and determination, but leaving Great Britain the control of certain harbours for the purposes of defence." [19] Within two decades even these remaining symbols of British authority were removed with the recognition of an independent Eire.

In retrospect, it is obvious that Fenianism was in the mainstream of Irish-American nationalism. The Brotherhood's ambitions and the means by which it sought to realize them were not markedly different from those of a host of other organizations. Yet it was also a phenomenon of the Civil War and Reconstruction. The war helped to stimulate and heighten Irish group consciousness; it facilitated the increase of Fenian sentiment and trained soldiers; in fact, it produced Fenians in the true meaning of that word. The war also saw the birth of an American public opinion unusually tolerant of Irish-Amer-

[18] Ernest R. May, *The World War and American Isolation, 1914-1917* (Chicago, 1966), pp. 344-345.
[19] Curtis, *History of Ireland*, p. 410.

ican nationalism. Thus, while nativism slumbered, some naturalized and native Americans discovered a common enemy in the British. Even under more stable political conditions this widespread anglophobia and the weight of Irish ballots would have encouraged Congress and the Executive to handle the Fenians with care, but with these two branches of government at loggerheads over Reconstruction, the political importance of the Irish vote was greatly exaggerated. Consequently, the belief that the Brotherhood represented the sentiments of the considerable body of Irish-American electors ensured it a brief heyday as all parties to the domestic dispute sought its support. In spite of all these advantages, the Fenians failed to liberate Ireland. Although they were instrumental in persuading the British to adopt remedial measures there, neither attacks on Canada nor action in England and Ireland secured the victory they sought. Unable to effect their own success, they also failed to provoke the Anglo-American rupture many considered necessary for Ireland's salvation.

For those Irish-American nationalists who placed their faith in an Anglo-American war, the aftermath of the Civil War must have appeared full of promise. The Americans emerged from their struggle hostile toward the British and with a long list of grievances, at the top of which they placed the *Alabama*. Inevitably, Fenianism became entangled with the abrasive problem of the war claims. Indeed, Fenian activities and the controversy over naturalization which they revived were viewed by some Americans as the spurs that might hasten the British into a generous settlement of the claims—one that embraced the cession of parts, if not all, of Canada. But the American government did not promote Fenianism as a means of realizing its ambitions, nor did it seek to collect the *Alabama* account or annex Canada by force when diplomacy failed. In short, a sharp line was drawn between the utilization of the nationalists and their deliberate encouragement as an instrument of American policy.

On the other side of the Atlantic, the British, having shunned war with the United States in 1861, when conditions had been far more favorable and the provocation in the wake of the *Trent* affair almost as severe, were in no mood or position to issue a belligerent challenge to the victorious Union over Fenian activities after 1865. Canada remained hostage to peaceful relations with the United States, and the six years following the end of the American war were critical ones in Europe. The attitude of the British government toward American problems was influenced by the political turmoil of Europe, just as the American government's policy was often governed by the exigencies of domestic politics. Nevertheless, the events of the postwar period did re-emphasize what the incidents of the Civil War had already illustrated: Britain and the United States were determined to avoid war with each other.

Selected Bibliography

PRIMARY SOURCES

Manuscripts

Public Documents

ENGLAND

Colonial Office. Ser. 42, Correspondence of the Governor-General of Canada. Public Record Office, London.
——. Ser. 537, Supplementary Correspondence: Canada. Public Record Office, London.
Foreign Office. Ser. 5, vols. 1344–1351, General Correspondence with the United States of America: The Activities of the Fenian Brotherhood, 1864–1871. Public Record Office, London.
——. Ser. 5, vols. 1356–1357, Correspondence Relating to the Naturalization Convention with the United States, 1870. Public Record Office, London.
Home Office. Ser. 45, Registered Papers, vols. 6877 and 7799: Fenians. Public Record Office, London.

IRELAND

Dublin Police Reports, 1865–1867. State Paper Office, Dublin.

UNITED STATES

Department of State. Record Group 59, General Records. National Archives, Washington, D.C., Great Britain: Diplomatic Instructions, Diplomatic Despatches, Notes to Foreign Legations, and Notes from Foreign Legations.

Private Papers

CANADA

Sir Edward M. Archibald Papers, Public Archives of Canada, Ottawa.

George Brown Papers, Public Archives of Canada, Ottawa.

Sir John A. Macdonald Papers, Public Archives of Canada, Ottawa.

Baron Monck Papers, Public Archives of Canada, Ottawa.

ENGLAND

John Bright Papers, British Museum, London.

Duke of Buckingham and Chandos Papers, British Museum, London.

Edward Cardwell Papers, Public Record Office, London.

Earl of Carnarvon Papers, Public Record Office, London.

Earl of Clarendon Papers, Public Record Office, London and Bodleian Library, Oxford.

William E. Gladstone Papers, British Museum, London.

Earl Granville Papers, Public Record Office, London.

Edmund Hammond Papers, Public Record Office, London.

Sir A. H. Layard Papers, British Museum, London.

IRELAND

Samuel Lee Anderson Papers, State Paper Office, Dublin.

Sir Thomas Larcom Papers, National Library of Ireland, Dublin.

UNITED STATES

Charles Francis Adams Diary and Papers, Massachusetts Historical Society, Boston. Microfilm.

S. S. Cox Papers, New York Public Library and Library of Congress, Washington, D.C.

Hamilton Fish Diary, Library of Congress, Washington, D.C.

Horace Greeley Papers, New York Public Library and Library of Congress, Washington, D.C.

Andrew Johnson Papers, Library of Congress, Washington, D.C.
Benjamin Moran Diary, Library of Congress, Washington, D.C.
Henry J. Raymond Papers, New York Public Library.
William H. Seward Papers, University of Rochester, Rochester, N.Y.
Horatio Seymour Papers, Fairchild Collection, New York Historical Society, New York, and New York Public Library.
Samuel J. Tilden Papers, New York Public Library.
Thurlow Weed Papers, University of Rochester, Rochester, New York.
Gideon Welles Papers, New York Public Library and Library of Congress, Washington, D.C.

Published Works

Public Documents

ENGLAND

British Sessional Papers, 1867, vol. XLVIII, *Correspondence Respecting the Recent Fenian Aggression upon Canada.*
British Sessional Papers, 1868–1869, vol. XXV, *Report of the Royal Commission for Inquiring into the Laws of Naturalization and Allegiance.*
Hansard's Parliamentary Debates, 3d ser., CLXXVII–CCVIII, 1865–1871.

UNITED STATES

Congress. *Congressional Globe,* 39th and 40th Congress, 1865–1869.
——. *House Executive Documents:* 40th Congress, 1st session, nos. 9, 10, 1867; 40th Congress, 2d session, nos. 157, 312, 1868.
——. *House Miscellaneous Documents:* 40th Congress 1st session, nos. 25, 46, 1867.
——. *Senate Executive Documents:* 40th Congress, 2d session, no. 42, 1868.

Department of State. *Papers Relating to the Foreign Affairs of the United States,* 1865–1866, parts 1 and 2; 1866–1867, 1867, 1868.

——. *Papers Relating to the Foreign Relations of the United States,* 1870–1873.

——. *Papers Relating to the Treaty of Washington, Geneva Arbitration,* II.

Messages of the Presidents of the United States to the Two Houses of Congress . . . with the Reports of the Heads of Departments: Annual Report of the Secretary of War, 1866, 1868, 1870.

Richardson, James D., comp. *A Compilation of the Messages and Papers of the Presidents, 1789–1897.* 10 vols. Washington, D.C., 1896–1899.

Personal Papers

Baker, G. E. *The Works of William H. Seward.* 5 vols. New York, 1853–1884.

Beale, H. K., ed. *Diary of Edward Bates.* Washington, D.C., 1933.

——. *Diary of Gideon Welles.* 3 vols. New York, 1960.

"Bright-Sumner Letters," *Proceedings of the Massachusetts Historical Society,* XLVI (October, 1912), 96–164.

Buckle, G. E., ed. *Letters of Queen Victoria.* 2d ser. I: 1862–1869; II: 1870–1878. London, 1926.

Doughty, Sir A. G., ed. *Elgin-Grey Papers, 1846–1852.* 4 vols. Ottawa, 1937.

Gooch, G. P., ed. *Later Correspondence of Lord John Russell, 1848–1878.* 2 vols. London, 1925.

Maxwell, Sir Herbert. *The Life and Letters of George William Frederick Fourth Earl of Clarendon.* 2 vols. London, 1913.

Meade, G. G., ed. *Life and Letters of George Gordon Meade.* 2 vols. New York, 1913.

Moore, John B., ed. *The Works of James Buchanan.* 12 vols. New York, 1908–1911.

Nevins, Allan, and M. H. Thomas, eds. *Diary of George Templeton Strong.* 3 vols. New York, 1952.

O'Brien, W., and D. Ryan, eds. *Devoy's Post Bag: The Letters of John Devoy, 1871–1928.* Dublin, 1948.

Pease, T. C., and J. G. Randall, eds. *Diary of Orville Hickman Browning.* 2 vols. Springfield, Ill., 1925–1933.

Pierce, E. L. *Memoir and Letters of Charles Sumner.* 4 vols. London, 1893.

Quaife, M. M., ed. *Diary of James K. Polk during His Presidency, 1845–1849.* Chicago, 1910.

Ramm, Agatha, ed. *The Political Correspondence of Mr. Gladstone and Lord Granville, 1868–1871.* 2 vols. London, 1952.

Walling, R. A. J., ed. *Diaries of John Bright.* London, 1930.

SECONDARY SOURCES

Books

Adams, Ephraim Douglass. *Great Britain and the American Civil War.* 2 vols. London, 1925.

Adams, Henry. *The Education of Henry Adams.* Boston, 1960.

The Annual Register: A Review of Events at Home and Abroad, 1866 (London, 1867); *1870* (London, 1871); *1871* (London, 1872).

Appleton, D., ed. *American Annual Cyclopedia and Register of Important Events, 1865* (New York, 1866); *1867* (New York, 1868).

Armstrong, William M. *E. L. Godkin and American Foreign Policy, 1865–1900.* New York, 1957.

Bailey, T. A. *Diplomatic History of the American People.* 3d ed. New York, 1946.

Beach, T. M. *Twenty-Five Years in the Secret Service: The Recollections of a Spy.* London, 1892.

Beale, H. K. *The Critical Year.* New York, 1930.

Bell, Herbert C. F. *Lord Palmerston.* 2 vols. London, 1936.

Bemis, S. F., ed. *American Secretaries of State and Their Diplomacy.* 10 vols. New York, 1927–1929.

Bigelow, J. *Retrospections on an Active Life.* 6 vols. New York, 1909.

Billington, Ray Allen. *The Protestant Crusade, 1800–1860.* Chicago, 1964.

Brebner, J. B. *North Atlantic Triangle: The Interplay of Canada, the United States, and Great Britain.* New Haven, 1945.

Brock, W. R. *An American Crisis: Congress and Reconstruction 1865–1867.* London, 1963.

Brown, T. N. *Irish-American Nationalism, 1870–1890.* Philadelphia and New York, 1960.

Buckle, G. E., and W. F. Monypenny. *Life of Benjamin Disraeli.* 5 vols. London, 1916.

Callahan, James Morton. *American Foreign Policy in Canadian Relations.* New York, 1937.

Campbell, C. S., Jr. *Anglo-American Understanding, 1898–1903,* Baltimore, 1957.

Cleaves, F. *Meade of Gettysburg.* Norman, Okla., 1960.

Cochran, Thomas C., and William Miller. *The Age of Enterprise: A Social History of Industrial America.* New York, 1961.

Cockburn, Sir A. *Nationality—Or the Law Relating to Subjects and Aliens with a View to Future Legislation.* London, 1869.

Cole, Arthur C. *Era of the Civil War, 1848–1870.* Centennial History of Illinois, III. Springfield, Ill., 1919.

Coleman, C. H. *The Election of 1868.* New York, 1933.

Cox, LaWanda and John H. *Politics, Principle and Prejudice, 1865–1866.* New York, 1963.

Crane, Verner Winslow. *Benjamin Franklin: Englishman and American.* Baltimore, 1936.

Creighton, D. *John A. Macdonald.* 2 vols. Toronto, 1952.

Crilly, F. L. *Fenian Movement: The Manchester Martyrs.* London, 1908.

Curtis, Edmund. *A History of Ireland.* London, 1950.

D'Arcy, William. *The Fenian Movement in the United States, 1858–1886.* Washington, 1947.

Dasent, A. I. *John Thadeus Delane: His Life and Correspondence.* 2 vols. London, 1908.

Deak, F., and P. C. Jessup, eds. *A Collection of Neutrality Laws,*

Regulations and Treaties of Various Countries. 2 vols. Washington, 1939.

Dent, John Charles. *The Last Forty Years: Canada since the Union of 1841.* 2 vols. Toronto, 1881.

Dillon, W. *Life of John Mitchel.* 2 vols. London, 1908.

Duberman, M. B. *Charles Francis Adams, 1807–1886.* Boston, 1961.

Eaton, Clement. *The Growth of Southern Civilization 1790–1860.* New York, 1961.

An Exposé of Fenianism in the United Kingdom and United States. Eglington's Irish Series. London, 1883.

Fenwick, C. G. *A History of the Neutrality Laws of the United States.* Baltimore, 1912.

Filler, Louis. *The Crusade against Slavery, 1830–1860.* New York, 1960.

Fitzmaurice, Lord Edmund. *The Life of Granville George Leveson Gower, Second Earl of Granville, 1815–1891.* 2 vols. London, 1905.

Franklin, F. G. *Legislative History of Naturalization in the United States until 1861.* Chicago, 1906.

Gibson, Florence E. *The Attitudes of the New York Irish toward State and National Affairs, 1848–1892.* New York, 1951.

Hammond, J. L. *Gladstone and the Irish Nation.* London, 1938.

Handlin, Oscar. *Boston's Immigrants: A Study in Acculturation.* Cambridge, Mass., 1959.

Hanham, H. J. *Elections and Party Management.* London, 1959.

Hardinge, Sir A. *Life of Henry Howard Molyneux Herbert, Fourth Earl of Carnarvon.* London, 1925.

Harrington, F. H. *Fighting Politician: Major-General Nathaniel P. Banks.* Philadelphia, 1948.

Hesseltine, W. B. *Ulysses S. Grant, Politician.* New York, 1935.

James Stephens—Origins and Progress of the Fenian Brotherhood. New York, 1866.

Jones, Howard Mumford. *O Strange New World.* London, 1965.

Jones, Maldwyn A. *American Immigration.* Chicago, 1960.

Keenleyside, H. L. *Canada and the United States.* New York, 1952.

King, W. L. *Lincoln's Manager: David Davis.* Cambridge, Mass., 1960.

Lang, A. *Sir Stafford Northcote: First Earl of Iddesleigh.* Edinburgh, 1891.

Leslie, S. *The Irish Issue in Its American Aspect.* New York, 1917.

Link, A. S. *Wilson: The Struggle for Neutrality, 1914–1915.* Princeton, 1960.

Lonn, E. *Foreigners in the Confederacy.* Chapel Hill, N.C., 1940.

——. *Foreigners in the Union Army and Navy.* Baton Rouge, La., 1951.

Macdonald, H. *Canadian Public Opinion and the American Civil War.* New York, 1926.

Macdonald, J. *History of the Irish in Wisconsin in the Nineteenth Century.* Washington, 1954.

Maguire, J. F. *The Irish in America.* Montreal, 1873.

Maurice, F. *History of the Scots Guards, 1642–1914.* 2 vols. London, 1934.

May, E. R. *The World War and American Isolation, 1914–1917.* Chicago, 1966.

McKitrick, E. L. *Andrew Johnson and Reconstruction.* Chicago, 1960.

Merk, Frederick. *Manifest Destiny and Mission in American History: A Reinterpretation.* New York, 1963.

Miers, Earl Schenk. *The Great Rebellion: The Emergence of the American Conscience from Sumter to Appomattox.* New York, 1961.

Miller, John C. *Origins of the American Revolution.* Boston, 1943.

——. *Triumph of Freedom.* Boston, 1948.

Mitchell, Stewart. *Horatio Seymour of New York.* Cambridge, Mass., 1938.

Moore, J. B. *History and Digest of the International Arbitrations* to *Which the United States Has Been a Party*. 6 vols. Washington, 1898.

Morton, W. L. *The Critical Years: The Union of British North America, 1857–1873*. Toronto, 1964.

Nevins, Allan. *Hamilton Fish: The Inner History of the Grant Administration*. 2 vols. New York, 1936.

O'Hegarty, P. S. *A History of Ireland under the Union, 1801–1922*. London, 1952.

O'Leary, J. *Recollections of Fenians and Fenianism*. 2 vols. London, 1896.

Patrick, Rembert W. *The Reconstruction of the Nation*. New York, 1967.

Phelan, J. *The Ardent Exile: Life and Times of Thomas D'Arcy McGee*. Toronto, 1951.

Pletcher, David M. *The Awkward Years: American Foreign Relations under Garfield and Arthur*. Columbia, Mo., 1962.

Pope, Sir J. *Memoirs of Sir John Alexander Macdonald*. London, 1894.

Rhodes, J. F. *History of the United States from the Compromise of 1850*. New York, 1920.

Rowse, A. L. *The Expansion of Elizabethan England*. New York, 1955.

Rutherford, J. *Secret History of the Fenian Conspiracy*. London, 1887.

Schrier, Arnold. *Ireland and the American Emigration, 1850–1890*. Minneapolis, 1958.

Seward, Frederick W. *Reminiscences of a War-Time Statesman and Diplomat, 1830–1915*. New York, 1916.

——. *Seward at Washington*. New York, 1891.

Shannon, W. V. *The American Irish*. New York, 1966.

Shippee, L. B. *Canadian-American Relations, 1849–1874*. New Haven, 1939.

Skelton, I. *Life of Thomas D'Arcy McGee*. Gardenvale, Que., 1925.

Smith, Goldwin. *Treaty of Washington, 1871*. New York, 1941.

Smith, J. M. *Freedom's Fetters: The Alien and Sedition Laws and American Civil Liberties.* Ithaca, N.Y., 1956.

Smith, J. P. *The Republican Expansionists of the Early Reconstruction Era.* Private edition distributed by the University of Chicago, 1933.

Speeches of Hon. Schuyler Colfax and General J. O'Neill, Delivered at the Great Fenian Pic Nic, Chicago, August 15, 1866. Undated pamphlet.

Stacey, C. P. *Canada and the British Army, 1846–1871.* London, 1936.

Stampp, K. M. *The Era of Reconstruction, 1865–1877.* New York, 1965.

Stebbins, H. A. *Political History of New York State, 1865–1869.* Columbia University Studies, LX, no. 1. New York, 1913.

Stone, C. *Dana and the Sun.* New York, 1938.

Strauss, E. *Irish Nationalism and British Democracy.* London, 1931.

Tansill, C. C. *America and the Fight for Irish Freedom, 1866–1922.* New York, 1957.

Thomas, B. P. and H. M. Hyman. *Stanton: The Life and Times of Lincoln's Secretary of War.* New York, 1962.

Tsiang, I-Mien. *The Question of Expatriation in America prior to 1907.* Johns Hopkins University Studies in Historical and Political Science, LX, no. 3. Baltimore, 1942.

Tucker, Glenn. *Poltroons and Patriots: A Popular Account of the War of 1812.* 2 vols. New York, 1954.

Van Deusen, G. *Horace Greeley: Nineteenth Century Crusader.* New York, 1964.

——. *William Henry Seward.* New York, 1967.

Waite, P. B. *The Life and Times of Confederation, 1864–1867.* Toronto, 1962.

Warner, D. F. *The Idea of Continental Union Agitation for the Annexation of Canada to the United States, 1849–1893.* Lexington, Ky., 1960.

Watkin, E. W. *Canada and the States: Recollections, 1851–1886.* London, 1887.

Weinberg, A. K. *Manifest Destiny*. Baltimore, 1935.

Whelan, J. G. "William H. Seward—Expansionist." Unpublished Ph.D. dissertation, University of Rochester, 1959.

Winks, R. W. *Canada and the United States: Civil War Years*. Baltimore, 1960.

Wittke, Carl. *The Irish in America*. Baton Rouge, La., 1956.

Wolseley, G. *The Story of a Soldier's Life*. 2 vols. London, 1903.

Articles

Bourinot, J. G. "Canada and the United States: An Historical Retrospect," *Papers of the American Historical Association*, V (July, 1891), part 3, 89–147.

Cox, LaWanda and John H. "Andrew Johnson and His Ghost Writers," *Mississippi Valley Historical Review*, XLVIII (December, 1961), 460–479.

Davis, H. A. "The Fenian Raid on New Brunswick," *Canadian Historical Review*, XXXVI (December, 1955), 316–334.

Flournoy, R. W., Jr. "Naturalization and Expatriation," *Yale Law Journal*, XXXI (1921–1922), 702–719, 848–868.

King, C. L. "The Fenian Movement," *University of Colorado Studies*, VI (April, 1909), 187–213.

Martin, Chester. "British Policy in Canadian Confederation," *Canadian Historical Review*, XIII (March, 1932), 3–19.

McMicken, G. "The Abortive Fenian Raid on Manitoba," *Historical and Scientific Society of Manitoba, Transaction No. 32* (Season 1887–1888). Winnipeg, 1888.

Morrow, R. L. "The Negotiation of the Anglo-American Treaty of 1870," *American Historical Review*, XXXIX (July, 1934), 663–681.

Pritchett, J. P. "The Origins of the So-called Fenian Raid on Manitoba in 1871," *Canadian Historical Review*, X (March, 1929), 23–42.

Smith, J. P. "American Republican Leadership and the Movement for the Annexation of Canada in the Eighteen-Sixties," *Report of the Annual meeting of the Canadian Historical Association* (May, 1935), 58–67.

Stacy, C. P. "Britain's Withdrawal from North America, 1864–71," *Canadian Historical Review*, XXXVI (September, 1955), 185–198.

———. "A Fenian Interlude," *Canadian Historical Review*, XV (June, 1935), 133–154.

———. "The Fenian Troubles and Canadian Military Development, 1865–1871," *Report of the Annual Meeting of the Canadian Historical Association* (May, 1935), 26–35.

———. "Fenianism and the Rise of National Feeling in Canada at the time of Confederation," *Canadian Historical Review*, XII (September, 1931), 238–261.

———. "The Garrison at Fort Wellington," *Canadian Historical Review*, XIV (June, 1933), 161–176.

———. "The Myth of the Unguarded Frontier, 1815–1871," *American Historical Review*, LVI (October, 1950), 1–18.

Tremaudan, A. H. de. "Louis Riel and the Fenian Raid of 1871," *Canadian Historical Review*, IV (June, 1923), 32–144.

Trotter, R. G. "Canada as a Factor in Anglo-American Relations in the 1860's," *Canadian Historical Review*, XVI (March, 1935), 20–27.

Index

Aberdeen, Lord, 13

Adams, Charles Francis, 47, 49, 70, 74-81, 84, 88-91, 93-95, 97-100, 102-104, 114, 122, 123, 125, 126-128, 170, 174, 180, 185, 192, 194-196, 220, 228-236, 238-247, 249-261, 263, 267-269, 276; approves appointment of Sir Frederick Bruce, 49; diplomatic problems created by Fenianism, 70 ff.; policy toward Fenians, 76 ff., 89 ff.; denounced by American rally, 88; seeks liberation of Americans arrested in Ireland, 92 ff.; secures right of consuls to visit all American prisoners, 102-103; assured of lenient treatment of Fenian prisoners, 173; presents request for settlement of Civil War claims, 195; suspects Seward's motives with respect to Britain, 213; refuses support to Fenian claims for protection, 231 ff., 244 ff.; ignores Seward's instructions regarding Fenian prisoners, 233; secures commutation of death sentence against Fenians, 236; attacked in Congress, 253; requests to be relieved, 253

Alabama, 41, 60, 63, 131, 160, 185, 186, 187, 199, 210, 228, 253, 259, 260, 262, 264, 265, 278, 279, 287, 289, 293, 294, 298, 302, 303, 312, 326

Alaska, 228

Albany Journal, 56

American Society of United Irishmen, 9

American support of Irish nationalists, 70

Ancona, S. E., 153, 162

Andrew, John A., 53

Anglophobia, 79, 113, 181, 270, 293, 324, 325

Annexation, threat of, 65, 66

Archibald, Edward M., 34, 43, 51, 67, 71, 77, 108, 115, 117, 118, 157, 158, 172, 294, 298

Arthur, Prince, 297

Arthur, Chester A., 323

Ashburton commission, 49

Bancroft, George, 17, 18, 19

Banks, General Nathaniel P., 178, 180, 181, 182, 183, 184, 185, 193, 194, 198, 225, 236, 239, 261, 270, 273, 274

Bismarck, Otto von, 177

Boston *Pilot*, 317

Brett, Sgt., 241, 243, 247

Bridewell, Richmond, 81

Bright, John, 185, 216, 312

Brotherhood, the Fenian, 70, 81, 109, 110, 142, 216, 241, 269, 272, 280, 282, 292, 293, 294, 296, 313, 317, 320, 325, 326

Bruce, Sir Frederick, 49-52, 57-61, 63-70, 77, 98, 99, 106-115, 126-137, 139-141, 143, 147-150, 153, 154, 156-158, 160-169, 171-173, 176, 178, 186-188, 194, 196, 205-210, 225-227, 233, 234, 237, 238, 242; appointed ambassador to United States, 49; cultivates Seward, 50; assessment of Fenian power, 52; organizes more efficient intelligence system re Fenian activities, 57; policy toward American government, 57 ff., 210 ff.; welcomes completion of

Fenians (*cont.*)

Canada approved by, 43; removal of American restriction on export and purchase of arms allows arming of, 48; sympathy of Johnson for, 56; Canadian reaction to, 62, 65 ff., 116 ff.; fears of Anglo-Irish concerning, 82 ff.; influx into Ireland of, 84; effect of, upon Johnson administration, 101 ff.; divided allegiance of, exposed in American press, 110, 114; Johnson opposes activities of, 129; Campobello raid and consequences of, 133 ff.; Niagara raid, 142 ff.; influence of, on American election, 1866, 178-179; obtain release of confiscated munitions, 200-201; and influence on Anglo-American relations, 215 ff.; pressure transferred to Ireland, 216 ff.; raid Chester Castle, 221; raise insurrection in County Kerry, 222; use trial of members in Britain to foment Anglo-American strife, 239 ff.; responsibility for death of Sergeant Brett, and consequences of, 241; trial of members Warren and Nagle, 244 ff.; influence waning in America, 292 ff.; attempt raid on Canada, 1870, 306; American action against, 307 ff.; prisoners released by Grant administration, 314; Canadian resentment against American release of, 315; prisoners in Canada released, 316; lose power in United States, 318 ff.

Fish, Hamilton, 284, 290, 291, 295, 296, 298-304, 307, 308, 311, 314, 315

Forster, W. E., 275

Franklin, Benjamin, 4

Freedmen's Bureau bill, 128

Galt, Alexander, 107, 108

Gilbert, Humphrey, 2, 3

Gladstone, W. E., 62, 86, 96, 119-122, 124, 125, 216, 279, 280, 283, 296, 297, 316, 318

Godkin, E. L., 48

Godley, Dennis, 66

Grant, U. S., 127, 286, 291, 298, 308, 311, 313, 314

Grant administration, 280, 289, 290, 295, 302, 303, 307, 310, 313, 315

Granville, Earl, 285, 296-299, 302, 312-314

Greeley, Horace, 45, 54, 55, 216

Grey, Earl, 20, 22

Grey, Sir George, 85

Habeas corpus, suspension of, 86, 88, 90, 104, 116, 119, 126, 224, 244, 248; by Canada, 155

Habeas Corpus Suspension Act, 220, 237

Haggerty, James, 290-292

Hammond, Edmund, 171, 291, 298, 300, 305, 314

Harcourt, Vernon, 258, 262

Henry, H. H., 144

Hibernian Society of Philadelphia for the Relief of Emigrants from Ireland, 6

Higham, John, 115

H.M.S. *Simoon*, 136

H.M.S. *Tamar*, 136

Hoffman, John, 208

Home Rule, 318, 319, 321, 324

Hughes, Charles Evans, 325

Irish-Americans, 63, 111, 216, 226, 231, 232, 234, 236, 243, 248, 252, 262; dichotomy of Irish-American allegiance, 9; threat to Federalists, 10; in Union army, 42; arrest of, 87

Irish Disestablishment Act, 280, 318

Irish Land Act, 318

Irish Land Bill, 280

Irish Land Purchase Bill, 318

Irish People, 73, 76, 78, 81, 84

Irish Race Convention, 324

Irish Republican Union, 45

Irish Revolutionary Brotherhood, 24, 71

Jefferson, Thomas, 11

Jeffersonian, The, 45

Johnson, Andrew, 43, 53, 54, 56, 58-60, 88, 101, 126, 128, 129, 146, 149-151, 153, 154, 161, 179, 185, 186, 189,